# Ballots and Brawls

TURNING POINT
ELECTIONS

**General Editors: Gerald Baier and R. Kenneth Carty**

Since Confederation, Canadians have gone to the polls over forty times in general elections. Sometimes the ruling party was re-elected, other times the government changed hands, but, more often than not, the country would carry on as if little had happened. However, some elections were different. They stirred up underlying divisions, generated debates, gave rise to influential personalities, and energized and reshaped the electorate – ultimately changing the direction the country would follow. Those elections were "turning points." The volumes in this series tell the stories of these turning point elections, focusing on the players, the issues at stake, the campaigns, and the often surprising outcomes that would fundamentally reshape Canadian politics and society. For a list of titles in the series, see the UBC Press website, ubcpress.ca/turning-point-elections.

# Ballots and Brawls

## The 1867 Canadian General Election

PATRICE DUTIL

UBCPress · Vancouver

© UBC Press 2025

All rights reserved. No part of this publication may be reproduced, stored in a retrieval system, or transmitted, in any form or by any means, without prior written permission of the publisher, or, in Canada, in the case of photocopying or other reprographic copying, a licence from Access Copyright, www.accesscopyright.ca.

Printed in Canada on FSC-certified ancient-forest-free paper (100% post-consumer recycled) that is processed chlorine- and acid-free.

UBC Press is a Benetech Global Certified Accessible™ publisher. The epub version of this book meets stringent accessibility standards, ensuring it is available to people with diverse needs.

**Library and Archives Canada Cataloguing in Publication**

Title: Ballots and brawls : the 1867 Canadian general election / Patrice Dutil.

Names: Dutil, Patrice A., author

Series: Turning point elections.

Description: Series statement: Turning point elections | Includes bibliographical references and index.

Identifiers: Canadiana (print) 20240483944 | Canadiana (ebook) 20240484010 | ISBN 9780774871396 (softcover) | ISBN 9780774871419 (EPUB) | ISBN 9780774871402 (PDF)

Subjects: LCSH: Canada. Parliament—Elections, 1867. | LCSH: Elections—Canada. | LCSH: Canada—Politics and government—1867-

Classification: LCC JL193 .D88 2025 | DDC 324.971—dc23

 Canada Council for the Arts  Conseil des arts du Canada

 Canadä

 BRITISH COLUMBIA ARTS COUNCIL

 BRITISH COLUMBIA

UBC Press gratefully acknowledges the financial support for our publishing program of the Government of Canada, the Canada Council for the Arts, and the British Columbia Arts Council.

*UBC Press is situated on the traditional, ancestral, and unceded territory of the xʷməθkʷəy̓əm (Musqueam) people. This land has always been a place of learning for the xʷməθkʷəy̓əm, who have passed on their culture, history, and traditions for millennia, from one generation to the next.*

UBC Press
The University of British Columbia
www.ubcpress.ca

# Contents

Foreword: Turning Point Elections and the Case
of the 1867 Election / vii
*Gerald Baier and R. Kenneth Carty*

Preface / xii

Introduction / 3

1　The Battlefield, the Wheels, the Flies, and the
Flywheels / 26

2　The Third Liberal Showdown in New Brunswick / 76

3　A Proper Scottish *Square Go* in Ontario / 101

4　Quebec's Contest of Nationalisms / 132

5　The Clash of Imperialisms in Nova Scotia / 165

6　The Outcome / 183

Conclusion / 201

vi   *Contents*

Appendix 1: Key Players / 224

Appendix 2: Timeline of Events / 235

Appendix 3: Data Tables / 240

Notes / 242

Suggestions for Further Reading / 272

Index / 277

# Foreword
## Turning Point Elections
## and the Case of the 1867 Election

*Gerald Baier and R. Kenneth Carty*

FREE, COMPETITIVE ELECTIONS are the lifeblood of modern democracies. Nowhere has this been more apparent than in Canada, a country cobbled together by bargaining politicians who then continually remade it over a century and a half by their electoral ambitions, victories, and losses. In a continually changing country, the political parties that emerged to manage this electoral competition also found themselves continually changing as they attempted to reflect and shape the country they sought to govern. The stories of these politicians, these parties, and these elections are a critical part of the twists and turns that have produced Canada.

Canadians have now gone to the polls in forty-four national general elections. The rules, participants, personalities, and issues have varied over time, but the central quest has always been the same – to win the right to govern a complex and dynamic country. About twice as often as not, the electorate has stuck with whom they know and favoured incumbents with the governing mantle. Only about a third of the time have the government's opponents, promising something new or different, been elevated to power. But viii *Foreword*

whatever the outcome over all forty-four elections, the contest for the top prize has ultimately been between the Liberal and Conservative Parties. While other challengers have come and gone, and some have even endured, the persistence of the Liberal/Conservative dichotomy has defined the effective bounds of Canada's democratic politics.

More than one hundred years ago, a visiting French observer, André Siegfried, argued that Canadian elections were essentially meaningless because the two core parties were little more than unprincipled reflections of one another, preoccupied only with their continued existence. To the extent this was true, it reflected Canadian politicians' determination to build "big-tent" political parties able to appeal to the wide range of discordant regions and interests, religious and language groups, and parochial claims that dominated the country's political life and public conversations. If the Liberal Party dominated national electoral politics over the twentieth century, to become labelled as the country's "natural governing party," it was because its tent was larger and rooted in an overwhelming mastery of Quebec constituencies. And so a long list of Liberal leaders – Wilfrid Laurier, Mackenzie King, Louis St-Laurent, Pierre Trudeau, Jean Chrétien – kept leading their party back to office election after election. In a country being continually transformed on almost every conceivable dimension, electoral outcomes were remarkably stoic in comparison.

Occasionally, though, conditions allowed for rather abrupt disruptions of this seeming political tranquility. There were exceptions to the familiar story of incumbents cruising to victory. In part, those occasions reflected the workings of a first-past-the-post electoral system that was capable of generating both stability and volatility. The difference between hanging on to power or being roundly booted from grace could be a change of just a few percentage points in a party's support, or a strong showing by one or more third parties bleeding off a portion of the vote of one of the big-tent

*Foreword* ix

parties. So some elections were different, thrusting new and exciting personalities to the fore, generating principled debates on fundamental issues, electrifying and engaging the electorate, and reshaping the parties and the dynamics of party competition, all with lasting consequences for the direction the country would follow. These elections stand out as turning points.

The stories of the turning point elections are more than simply accounts of compelling figures, dramatic campaigns, and new political alignments. They also reveal how the pressures of demographic, socio-economic, and regional change were challenging the status quo; how the elections broke the political moulds of previous contests; and how the turn played out in the politics, policies, and governments of succeeding decades. In each of the turning point elections, we see how the evolving political landscape allowed politicians to crystallize, and often personify, the issues of a distinctive agenda and create a campaign that mobilized and reshaped the complex coalitions of supporters that constituted the nation's political parties. These turning points constituted the starting point for a new and different cycle in the contest between the two great big-tent parties that have dominated the struggle for power and office and defined the nature and evolution of Canadian democracy.

**LATE SEPTEMBER AND INTO** the early fall of 1867 marked the beginning. A new government had been installed in a new country, and its prime minister, John A. Macdonald, knew that a general election was needed to elect a parliament and legitimate this new political experiment. And so, this "turning point" inaugurates the story of Canadian general elections. But Patrice Dutil tells us that, despite its foundational nature, the election of 1867 was neither a truly national election nor a real new beginning. It was little more than a set of provincial, often local, contests that echoed old disputes, rehearsed familiar divides, and reflected old practices in the four very different provinces that constituted the new country.

Confederation itself was everywhere at issue, but hardly in the same way. In New Brunswick it was being fought over for the third time, while in Nova Scotia opponents argued it had never been tested at the polls. In the Canadas, political giants fought over who would control and shape this new creation, although it seemed to arouse the least interest in Quebec, of all places, where a third of the seats went uncontested. The nineteenth-century electoral process was rough, often violent, always expensive, and very public – only in New Brunswick was there a secret ballot for the property-owing males entitled to vote. And when it was over, the party results were not obvious, but a government emerged. Macdonald's Liberal/Conservative supporters won a substantial majority of the seats in the new House of Commons, doing so with just over a third of the vote and, as would happen many times in future elections, with a little help from the first-past-the-post electoral system.

Modern elections are often lamented as leader focused, where personality drowns out policy. Dutil's account reveals that this is hardly a new phenomenon, for the electoral battles in 1867 were everywhere centred on the time's dominant regional political chieftains. Leaders personified the ideals and the instincts of their immediate communities, and sought support to advance and implement their interests: Macdonald and Brown, Cartier, Dorion and McGee, Tilley and Anglin, Howe and Tupper – names that continue to resonate in our political memories, emblazoned on schools and public buildings that commemorate their outsized contributions to institutionalizing a democratic electoral politics for a Canadian political community.

The 1867 election decided the electoral fate of those storied personalities, but it also constituted a referendum on the fate of the confederation scheme. The big short-term winner was Macdonald, affirming his vision for a continent-wide country, and reinforcing his commanding position over its new government. In the longer term, Macdonald's remarkable success in establishing a big-tent party, capable of recognizing and embracing the conflicting claims of the country's regions and interests to win competitive elections, set the mould for generations of successful Canadian politicians and parties to come.

# Preface

**I LEAPT AT THE CHANCE** to write this book for two reasons. The first was that I love to study elections and have already written two books on the topic with my esteemed colleague David MacKenzie: *Canada, 1911: The Decisive Election That Shaped the Country* and *Embattled Nation: Canada's Wartime Election of 1917*. I'm attracted by the puzzle they represent, particularly how personalities and policy ideas interact with the voting public in light of its experience. As a political historian, I'm always curious about how political leaders shape their "pitch" by adjusting their instincts and ideas to what they think might be favourable. I'm equally interested in what government leaders have proposed and in what aspirants to power have in mind. I'm endlessly fascinated by what motivates people to vote in the first place, and then to vote in a certain way. I'm captivated by the interplay of deeply seeded attitudes forged by social, cultural, and economic experiences and the events that take place during an election. How could I turn down an opportunity to examine a contest that was completely ignored by historians? I was eager to dive in, even as the dark clouds of the pandemic hovered over our heads.

For me, it was also an opportunity to return to the study of Sir John A. Macdonald. I've already devoted three books to this figure

Parliament Hill in Ottawa, Victoria Day, 1867
Library and Archives Canada, 3362202

(*Macdonald at 200: New Perspectives and Legacies*; *Prime Ministerial Power in Canada: Its Origins under Macdonald, Laurier and Borden*; and *Sir John A. Macdonald and the Apocalyptic Year 1885*) and was readily disposed to spending more time in trying to seize his particular political genius. The idea of contributing insights on elections as well as on a critical phase of Canada's first prime minister was simply irresistible.

The general election of 1867 belongs to an early category of contests when communications technologies were sparse. There was no complete and reliable railroad that could be used to campaign. The telegraph made its start in Canada in 1846 but was monopolized by the Montreal Telegraph Company, owned by the financier Hugh Allan, and it was mostly reserved for commercial needs for urgent, pithy messages, not as a mass medium. What did exist were letters and newspapers. There was another complicating factor: politicians were unsure of how their views would be received

xiv  *Preface*

in cultures different from their own. The hope was that this would change, but in 1867 voters saw themselves first as either a New Brunswicker, an Ontarian, a Quebecer, or a Nova Scotian. A "Canadian" might be something to dream about.

In light of this reality, this volume in the Turning Point Elections series uses a different writing strategy from the rest of the books in the collection and focuses more on local campaigns and their key contests. Following a chapter that examines the preamble to Confederation – roughly from the birth of the idea in 1859 to July 1, 1867 – the second chapter begins a survey of duels and brawls across the provinces. It starts with New Brunswick's experience from the moment the idea of Confederation was hatched. That province mostly saw a struggle among Liberals as the party bifurcated. One faction followed Leonard Tilley while the other followed Albert J. Smith and Timothy Warren Anglin. Anglin was by far the most visible, however, and left a more significant imprint on the race through his newspaper, the Saint John–based *Morning Freeman*.

The third chapter analyzes Ontario and the titanic struggle between two sons of Scotland, John A. Macdonald and George Brown, each of whom carried a particular vision of the kind of pragmatism their native country was famous for. The fourth chapter surveys the race in Quebec, dominated as it was by competing visions of how the people and the province could be part of the new nationality of Canada. George-Étienne Cartier championed the radical new vision, but the *Rouges,* of course, played an important role, and the leadership brought to bear by Antoine-Aimé Dorion is scrutinized. The most resonant voice of opposition in Quebec, however, was not Dorion, but young Médéric Lanctôt, and his particularly innovative campaign is presented. The fifth chapter examines the particular fight between two visions of British imperialism in Canada. The Anti-Confederation Party (sometimes also known as the Nova Scotia Party), led by Joseph Howe, envisioned a rather romantic future for Nova Scotia as an integral and important part of Great

Britain. Charles Tupper, who certainly took no second place to Howe in his Anglophilia, was thoroughly convinced that the spirit of British imperialism was more likely to succeed if his province became an integral part of the new country of Canada, and he played the key leadership role in rallying the unionists. In Chapter 6, the results of all those collected ballots are detailed on both national and provincial scales.

Even though it was foundational, the election of 1867 also deserves to be remembered as one of the great contests of Canada's political history. It was a key event that at once created a new entity and set it on a course of development until the fractious election of 1917. This was an election about the Canada project, about the economy, and not least about belonging (to country, to church, to Catholicism, to the state, to language): "The soil we stand on is our own," declared the Halifax-based *Sun and Advertiser,* which opposed Confederation.[1] The election was also about leadership, at the national level but also at the local level. Ideas were at play, significant personalities were in conflict, and the fate of a country was set.

CRAFTING THANKS IS OFTEN on my mind as I progress through the work of writing, but I always finalize this part of the book as the editor tells me she's ready to send the electronic file to the printer. It's a moment of grace.

My first thanks go to Gerald Baier and Ken Carty for inviting me to examine an election that had completely escaped notice. I much appreciate their confidence and their many suggestions for improvements to my account of the event. Equal thanks go to Randy Schmidt, editor at UBC Press. This is our fourth book together and I hope it won't be our last. Randy is the first gatekeeper but he's much more than that. He is a reliable sounding board, a perfect cockswain, a steady and patient presence in my literary life. Behind him is the UBC Press production team: the finest team of professionals to descend on a work written in isolation and prod it through

xvi  *Preface*

the process of transforming it into a book that will be both attractive and a source of ideas for multitudes today and generations to come. I am grateful to Katrina Petrik, the production editor, and to Francis Chow for his careful copyediting.

I also need to thank Grant Webster, a young man I first met as an undergraduate at Ryerson University who went on to graduate work and then launched a career in the public service. He once again contributed a ton of research that proved invaluable to me and I am grateful for the energy and the hours he contributed to this project.

Mr. Webster's work was funded by Toronto Metropolitan University. I am grateful to the Faculty of Arts and to the Department of Politics and Public Administration for its faithful and invaluable support. In terms of the university, I must acknowledge the exceptional help provided by the Library, particularly in speedily finding things that I considered inaccessible. In so many ways, the generous staff there continues to punch way above its weight class.

This book was written in memory of the happy troubadours and court jesters of the "Tuesday Evening" dining club I belonged to for almost twenty-five years. Their thoughts and interpretations of Canada over decades echoed in my mind as I wrote this book. Like the cast of 1867, this group of savvy journalists, historians, and businessmen included nationalists, regionalists, ultramontanes, imperialists, capitalists, and socialists, as well as some Irish, a few Scots, and me, the token French Canadian. It started in May 1995 when writers and editors Nick Steed, Doug Marshall, and John Pepall first assembled a group of Toronto oddballs for a dinner of candid discussions at a time when the mood of the country was particularly sour (the Quebec referendum had been announced, the economy was still tanking, and Ontario's politics were angst-ridden). The project caught on and I was invited to join it that fall. It met each month (except in the summer) and plunged into vivacious discussions, barely cooked meats, and barrels of wine. We met for years at the Royal Military Institute, then the Albany Club, followed by the Queen and Beaver Pub and various other restaurants around town. "Pepall's group" (I liked to call it the Oddfellows Dinner, but John was the consistent convener) last met on March 5, 2019, at the Albany Club, a victim of retirements, moves, and, inevitably, too many grave illnesses and funerals. Though people came and went, the regulars of the group were (in alphabetical order): Murray Campbell, Michael Decter, Patrice Dutil, Drew Fagan, Bill Fleury, John Gray, Richard Gwyn, Roger Hall, Paul Knox, Colin Mackenzie, Douglas Marshall, Gerald Owen, John Pepall, Nick Steed, David Lewis Stein, and Ian Urquhart. I have learned immensely from each and every one of them over the years and I am deeply grateful. I benefited from their thoughts, insights, and jokes about the Canadian condition as we migrated from one government to the other and from crisis to crisis. I always considered myself immensely lucky to be among them, and I will never forget the joy that animated this witty assemblage. This book is testimony to their wisdom and generosity.

I'd be wrong not to acknowledge the contribution of the anonymous peers who read the first draft of this book. They returned the manuscript with sharp retorts, but with every goad came an encouraging remark that I was on to something special, worthy of thought ... and publication. The book was made immensely better for their help. Peer review is always a tricky thing, but once again I've been fortunate with the roulette wheel, and I am grateful. Finally, a word of thanks to Roger Hall and Barbara Messamore, who helped me in deciphering Agnes Macdonald's impossible scrawl, saving me from misinterpretations. I'm grateful to Maha, my companion for the last forty-three years, who lovingly strained her patience once again to listen to my nineteenth-century stories.

It goes without saying that none of the above are guilty of my errors!

# Ballots and Brawls

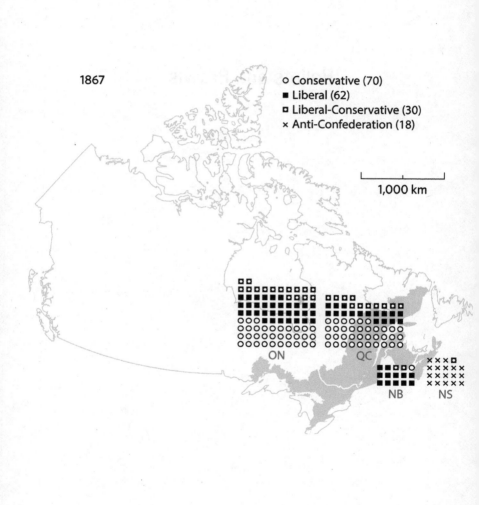

# Introduction

The nation of the United States is a MIRACLE. That of
Canada is a MYSTERY.

– Henry Olivier Lacroix, *The Present and
Future of Canada*, 1867[1]

CONFEDERATION WAS NOT simply an affair of lawyers, businessmen, journalists, and priests; it also had its bard. In anticipation of
the first general election in Canada, Henry Olivier Lacroix, treasurer
of the Montreal-based Institut Canadien, published a remarkable
thirty-two-page pamphlet, *Opuscule sur le présent et l'avenir du
Canada*. It was immediately translated as *The Present and Future of
Canada* – a rare feat indeed, perhaps the only work translated
spontaneously that summer. By day, Lacroix was an employee of
the Customs Office; by night he was increasingly known as a *spirite*
who claimed to speak to men and women of the past. Inspired
either by his job or by his spiritualism, he was moved to a rhapsodic
optimism about his new country, even though he thought the whole
idea of Canada defied gravity.

4   *Ballots and Brawls*

For him, writing two years after the end of the American Civil War, which had claimed the lives of over half a million soldiers as well as that of a president, the *nation* of the United States was a miracle of survival (the capitalized letters in the text were his idea). In the same time frame, Canada – a new composite of disparate ethnicities, geographies, and political cultures born of circumstances that only the most acute observers of constitutional politics could explain – was an unknown that awaited its first test of democracy. His Canada was a mystery – the product of three hundred years of unofficial and unrecognized existence. Until 1867, it was a country "in infancy," its existence always in doubt, shrouded in a macabre "silence of death."[2] "The world was ignorant almost of its existence," he wrote, "should the crowning work not exist?"[3]

Lacroix, forty-one, was born in the United States, the son of Quebec migrants in search of a better life. As a teenager and young adult, he criss-crossed the Western Hemisphere before settling in Montreal. Contrary to his parents, he saw a promise of fraternity and general prosperity in Canada. "Hope! Believe!" he urged in conclusion, ready with a twist of Charles Darwin's thinking (*The Origin of Species* had appeared in 1859): "With these two motors, humanity, from the bottom of the *humanimal* [sic] scale, has attained its present progress. This is a lesson of history, summed up in a few words, which cannot be contradicted, and which embraces all the periods of universal life."[4] For him, the past promised a great destiny for British North America's "new" Canadians.

Lacroix's Institut Canadien (IC), a learned and nationalist organization that hosted debates and maintained a library for its hundreds of members, was gravely divided on the Confederation issue. Lacroix personally had no doubts that he loved the new country, and he did not hesitate to present his remarks to the members of the IC.[5] His text explored the various challenges of the new land and called for fresh attitudes. He welcomed direct taxes – perhaps the only man in the country to think this way – as a way to compensate for the

Introduction 5

unpredictability of revenues flowing from custom duties. Most politicians were instead calling for reduced import taxes in order to compete internationally for trade and commerce. His best hope was not taxes, however: it was that a new spirit of fraternity, with the help of providence and good faith, would allow this "miracle" to actually sink roots.

## A Tight Race

A hundred and fifty years after the mystical Lacroix, the 1867 election challenges twenty-first-century readers because the results showed that Canada was in doubt. In this hotly contested battle for ballots, the victorious Liberal-Conservative/Conservative/ *Bleu* coalition led by Sir John A. Macdonald certainly earned more votes than any other formation. The competing coalition, led by an unfathomable combination of George Brown Liberals in Ontario, *Patriotes,* and anti-Confederationists rallied to Antoine-Aimé Dorion's *Rouges* in Quebec, and New Brunswick nationalists tied to the Timothy Anglin Liberals in that province, barely received a fifth of the vote. In New Brunswick, the Liberals received far more votes than the Conservatives, but, more importantly, four in ten voters pronounced themselves *against* both the Liberals and the Conservatives. In Ontario, over 60 percent of voters did not support the chosen candidates of the Macdonald coalition. The Quebec figures are much harder to analyze, but it is clear that a third voted against the Macdonald coalition *and* against Confederation. Nova Scotia was not so equivocal: the final count gave Joseph Howe and his Liberal/Conservative Anti-Confederation coalition over 57 percent of the vote, and another 25 percent of voters voiced their protest by voting for independent candidates. The federalists took only 18 percent of the vote. This election was no rubber stamp for the new Macdonald government.

Hard politics shaped Canada's first, and most bewildering, campaign: nationally, a staggering proportion of the electorate (over

42 percent) did not vote for either the Liberals or the Conservatives. Beyond the 8 percent of the entirety of electors across the country who voted for Joseph Howe's secessionist party, over one-third supported men who carried no reported label. Considering that it was the elite of the new country that voted – those few men with enough money to qualify for the right to vote – the result is all the more suggestive of the fragile new country's political culture. The great campaign of 1867 remains unique in the annals of Canadian political history.

Voter intentions notwithstanding, Macdonald's party was able to secure 100 of the 181 seats in the House of Commons, while the Liberals became the official opposition with 62 seats and Howe's defiant Nova Scotia delegation took all the Nova Scotia seats save one (it went to Charles Tupper, the former premier who led the Conservatives in the province).

The general Canadian attitude at the time defied easy interpretation and added to the mystery. Historians today can no more rely on public opinion polls to get a sense of what people felt was important than the politicians of the day. One Ontario newspaper conceded that it had trouble discerning issues. "The new and complicated constitution has to be carried into effect and doubtless great issues will be soon presented before the people by the dissensions in Parliament," it wrote, "but at the present the electors seem at sea, with no one able to tell them where they are."[6] And yet, the issues that animated the kitchen tables and tavern bars are still current. Unresolved then, they remain lively in our political conversations today: the balance of power between Ottawa and the provinces, the place of a regional identity in the face of quasi-rejection of the nation-state as a model,[7] the rapport with the United States, the relevance and practices of democracy, the nature of the promised "prosperity," and even the influence of international elite were debated.

The 1867 election had the strains of a tax revolt – people resented having taxes sent to Ottawa. The Ottawa *News* put it this way: "The truth is that the union is in danger from extravagance and corruption. Already a fear permeates every class of society that the complicated machinery of the new Government is going to press down the people with fearful burden of taxation."[8] The politics of that contest also bore important traces of the always vital issue of "belonging," as debates were marked by transnational issues such as imperialism (the notion that Canada's identity was bound to the United Kingdom), Fenianism (an extension of Irish nationalism in North America, dedicated to undermining British influence), ultramontanism (a hyper-Catholicism that placed allegiance to that religion above all other considerations), French radicalism (an ideology dedicated to intellectual freedom and opposed to any form of conservatism), and Americanism (the notion that the United States held out more promise than the Canadian project).

## A Forgotten Race

There's more to the enigma. It says something that even though photography was fairly common in 1867, there are precious few photographs of what happened in Canada on July 1, and there are no photos of the 1867 election on record. Here was a newborn country about to undertake its first democratic test, but only a small minority of people seemed to really care. Perhaps some like Lacroix were so excited that they forgot to hire photographers, but for every one of those, there were many who hated the Confederation project so much that they would have been positively hostile to the very idea of capturing the memory. The election campaign that followed – it started four weeks after Dominion Day because it took Canada East more time to compile the list of eligible voters[9] – suffered the same fate. Perhaps partly as a result of this neglect, or perhaps because it involved only the United Province of Canada (today Quebec and Ontario), New Brunswick, and Nova Scotia, few writers have been tempted to write about it. It's almost as though historians were happy to move on to other topics after placing a final period on

8    *Ballots and Brawls*

their treatments of how Confederation actually came about. In other words, July 1 and the subsequent election were seen as the negligible end of a story, not the beginning of a new one.

The indifference was acutely felt as Canada celebrated major anniversaries of the first election. Few of the people who fought the battle of 1867 in favour of Confederation were remembered 50, 75, 100, 150 years later, and their individual bicentennials were all but ignored by Canada's politicians. In their day, however, the wheels that drove Confederation – the names of Macdonald, Brown, Cartier, Galt, Macdonald, McGee, Tilley, Tupper, and others – were on everyone's lips.

Another reason for the neglect might be that there are no touch-stones of Confederation Canada left today. The committee rooms, banquet halls, hotels, and restaurants where men argued, laughed, drank, negotiated, and fought the first election in Canada have almost all disappeared. Province House in Halifax and the East Block on Parliament Hill in Ottawa – the building that housed the offices of most cabinet members, the prime minister, and the Governor General – practically stand alone as tangible reminders of what people and politicians saw on July 1, 1867, and during the first Canadian general election, which took place that August and September. (Province House in Charlottetown, of course, still stands, but Prince Edward Island did not join Confederation until six years after the first election.)

The *Queen Victoria*, the legendary ship that carried the Canadian delegation to Prince Edward Island for the fateful Charlottetown Conference in September 1864, was ripped apart by a Caribbean hurricane in 1866. The Hotel St-Louis on Haldimand Street in Quebec City, where the terms of Confederation were hammered out a few weeks later, was gravely damaged in a fire in 1947 and eventually closed. The old *parlement* of Quebec on Côte-de-la-Montagne, where the likes of Antoine-Aimé Dorion, George Brown, Alexander T. Galt, Thomas D'Arcy McGee, and John A. Macdonald jousted,

Old Quebec Parliament, circa 1880.
Fonds J.E. Livernois Ltée, Archives nationales à Québec, 322751

was demolished in 1894. The Legislative Assembly building in Fredericton, where Confederation was angrily debated, burned down in 1882. The Parliament building on Front Street in Toronto, which witnessed the first Ontario debates, was abandoned in the mid-1880s and demolished in 1903. The Centre Block in Ottawa, which welcomed the winners of the first election, was reduced to cinders in 1916.

## The Question of Identity

Buildings may disappear, but the legacy of that first election is undeniably still with us. The issue of "belonging," for instance, still recognizable today, mattered immensely in each of the provinces. Many intellectuals were concerned that being a Nova Scotian, a Quebecer, or a New Brunswicker was incompatible with belonging to "Canada" as a "great nation,"[10] the idea espoused by the likes of

10  *Ballots and Brawls*

John A. Macdonald, Thomas D'Arcy McGee, Étienne-Paschal Taché (the Quebec MP who first wondered aloud about the idea in 1857), or the shadowy Henry Lacroix. It was less of an issue in Ontario, but even there the notion of being recognized as a distinct part of a new country was very much alive. How could justice be attained if Ottawa controlled so many of the strings of power, such as the courts, the Senate, Lieutenant-Governors, the key revenues of the Customs Office, and all key appointments?

Beyond political labels lay the fundamental question of national unity. "The question to be decided," wrote the editorialist for the Conservative *Ottawa Times*, "is that of the Union and the Government as against disunion and the opposition."[11] That paper leaned strongly in favour of Macdonald's Liberal-Conservative coalition, a uniquely Canadian mix of political impulses. It saw through the protests of the Joseph Howes, Timothy Anglins, and Médéric Lanctôts because it did "not believe in the sincerity of the men who have raised the standard of faction in some of the Provinces." There was a larger stake here for that writer: a Canada that spread itself from coast to coast. A win by the provincialists would "indefinitely postpone" the "completion of the scheme to its ultimate purpose; and that such a result would undoubtedly imperil, if it did not destroy, the new Constitution."[12] In 1867, a win for Confederation was essential to the expansion of Canada.

But there was also the issue of distinguishing British colonies from the United States. "Every loyal and patriotic man in the Dominion has now a most important duty to perform," wrote the *St. Catharines Constitutional*, "for the approaching election will decide whether this country is to be ruled by the statesmen who have labored long and earnestly in the cause of the Union, or by those who are openly or covertly hostile to our new constitution and in favor of annexation to the United States."[13] The stakes were high, as the new government would have the duty of putting the new constitution into "practical effect."[14]

Province Hall, Fredericton, circa 1870
Provincial Archives of New Brunswick, P5-396

Canada was not founded because there was a widespread public clamour for it. A strong element of Nova Scotians was positively repulsed by the terms negotiated to join the Canada project. Many francophones across the country were alarmed at the likely consequences of submerging their ability to maintain the institutions that protected the core of their identity – law, religion, and education –

## Ballots and Brawls

in a country that would henceforth be governed by a majority of English-speaking Protestants. Protestants, in turn, were afraid of being dragged into a distorted country shaped by a demanding Catholic minority. The promises of those who aspired to a better day by doing away with such identities were hardly credible.

It's not impossible to visualize. Even today, it would be difficult to imagine populations across North American agreeing to yield sovereignty to a central authority the way those three provinces did a century and a half ago. Like all state-building practices in the nineteenth century, the founding of Canada was engineered by a handful of men who were motivated by a wide range of interests. They wanted a political stability that featured the traits of Westminster democracy, some measure of economic predictability, access to credit in order to build the infrastructures (harbours, bridges, roads, and especially railways) that were likely to bring a level of prosperity and a degree of security – the sort of defence of sovereignty that might discourage American adventurers. Many of Confederation's champions, however, had greater ambitions than simply creating a new level of government. They aspired to conceiving no less than a new "nationality," a mindset that would transcend what they considered lowly local concerns that too often impeded general progress. Lacroix told his readers:

> The national awakening shows [it is] still a task to be accomplished, and what is done heartily and with wisdom, will render the rest easy before long. Between the idea and its accomplishment there must be time; there are roads to be made through woods, meadows, hills, mountains; sometimes there are tunnels to be pierced before the end is reached.

For him, the thousands of problems that awaited the new country would be solved by people of good faith, people who demanded betterment in every aspect of life.[15]

*Introduction* 13

Political parties were viewed with some suspicion. Egerton Ryerson, the highly influential superintendent of education in Canada West (now Ontario), made a strong argument against them in *The New Canadian Dominion: Dangers and Duties of the People in Regard to their Government*, a thirty-five-page pamphlet published in the summer of 1867. Ryerson, who "rejoiced" in "our new birth as a nation," deplored the divisiveness of political parties and hoped that civic education would be promoted instead in order to ensure the country's prosperity: "It devolves on the electors of Canada, in the spirit we now cultivate, and in the choice we now make of our first legislators, to stamp upon our country its future character, and determine for our children their future destinies."[16]

But Ryerson's voice was ignored, dismissed as naive. Party labels mattered, even if they were sometimes fudged. "Liberal" was commonly used in Ontario and New Brunswick, and to some degree in Quebec. It was a term claimed to signal an ideological inheritance from the "Reformers" who had challenged British dominance in the affairs of Nova Scotia and of Upper and Lower Canada. It also echoed the British party of the same name that had supported Sir Robert Peel's ("the Peelites") renunciation of trade protectionism. Over the years, dominant politicians such as Lord John Russell, Lord Palmerston, and William Gladstone distinguished themselves as "Liberals" in Parliament, and the habit gradually rubbed off on the Canadians. In Upper and Lower Canada, the Liberal moniker made its appearance in the 1850s and was in common use by the 1860s. Joseph Howe in Nova Scotia liked to call himself a "Liberal" on occasion, as did Leonard Tilley in New Brunswick (that is, until he became a Conservative!).[17]

The Liberals liked to continue thinking of themselves as rebels. In Ontario, they drew inspiration from the actions and thought of William Lyon Mackenzie. They seemed comfortable with being "opposed" to government – far more, it seemed, than to form government themselves. They liked to promote "freedom" and "rights,"

14   *Ballots and Brawls*

and especially "free trade" and smaller, money-conscious government. Some went further than others in all these areas. In Ontario, a small group of rebels called themselves "Clear Grits," though by the time of the 1867 election that nickname had disappeared.

In Quebec, "liberalism" was too extreme a label. The "opposition" had its roots in the *Parti patriote* that had arisen in opposition to the British presence on Canadian soil. In the aftermath of the 1837–38 rebellions, the men who recognized themselves in opposition to trade protectionism and the inherent arbitrariness of monarchical government called themselves *Rouges*.

The Conservatives were far more confident in their beliefs, which were strongly anchored in old Toryism that had roots in British and Canadian soil. Conservatives enjoyed authority and relished exercising it. They liked the attitude of the Tory Party in the United Kingdom that had been prompted into existence by another of Robert Peel's actions: the Reform Bill of 1832, which had extended electoral rights to the middle class. If "Conservative" was nothing more than a nickname in British politics, it was easily adopted in Canada. In Quebec, the more conservative members grouped under a "*Bleu*" banner. Their program favoured economic growth, protection of trade if necessary, an appreciation for British traditions, an intense fidelity to the Roman Catholic Church, infrastructure building, and a sense that principles of subsidiarity should be favoured.

Both the "Liberals" and "Conservatives" were hothouses of diverging opinions, and their leaders never had the luxury of being confident that they had the unanimous support of the members. There were extremists as well as moderates on all sides. The "coalition" of Liberals and Conservatives that formed the government in the Province of Canada in 1854 gave birth to a new label, prompting Macdonald to label himself a "Liberal-Conservative" to the end of his days.

*Introduction* 15

For the most part, in most areas, the issue in 1867 was far more likely to dissolve into a battle between Canada-friendly parties or local-preference parties. Thus, in Nova Scotia, the Confederationists,[18] led by forty-six-year-old Charles Tupper (a good friend of Sir John A. Macdonald), were opposed by the provincialists (the "Nova Scotia Party," or "antis"), led by Joseph Howe. In New Brunswick, it was a contest between Leonard Tilley, forty-nine, the ardent defender of Confederation, and an uneven pair: Albert J. Smith, the Liberal premier of New Brunswick for seven months in 1865–66, and the Liberal journalist Timothy Warren Anglin, forty-five, who just hated the idea of Confederation. In Quebec, there was a slightly clearer situation. On the Confederation side, the leader was the recognizably beardless George-Étienne Cartier, fifty-three, who represented the Macdonald government. His adversary was the Liberal Party (or the Reform Party as it was sometimes known, or simply the *Rouges*) led by Antoine-Aimé Dorion. Dorion, forty-nine, was not particularly clear in terms of his allegiances. Once, he had been in favour of joining the United States. Now, he instinctively hoped for an independent Quebec, but he did it with little conviction. He did not trust its possibility or even its desirability, given its intensely conservative and fundamentally Catholic orientation. His penchant was to support the status quo for the moment: to live with the current system, but perhaps with the idea of creating in Canada a federal system, where French Canadians could have their own jurisdiction in Quebec and Ontarians would have the same in Toronto.

Dorion was far less enthusiastic regarding Canadian confederation in the summer of 1867, but seemed resigned to it. At the same time, there were other *Rouges* who rejected that compromise completely. Chief among them was Médéric Lanctôt, just twenty-nine years old. He was so utterly convinced of his cause that he personally ran against Cartier in the riding of Montreal-Est.

16  *Ballots and Brawls*

The contest in Ontario was personified by Macdonald himself, now fifty-two, and the leader of the Reform Party in Canada West, George Brown, forty-nine. Another force in Ontario was William McDougall, forty-five, once an ally of Brown's and an arch critic of federalism, who now bought Macdonald's vision and even joined his cabinet. His constant campaigning in the new province – and his sharp targeting of his former friends – made him a singularly influential and hated figure in the campaign.

### A Harsh Political Culture

Oh, and there were brawls of all sorts. Something unusual happened in Prescott in Eastern Ontario. It was, according to a young law student, "the most disgraceful, scandalous, may we add sacrilegious, riots, which ever desecrated the house of God." The young author, a certain John Gray, accused Father E.P. Roche of St. Mark's Parish of getting involved in the election campaign. Worse, Roche had used "Five Point epithets," called infants "brats," and treated women as "dirty sluts" and "filthy swine." Father Roche had been the pastor since 1845 and was known to deliver "very high falutin and windy" sermons, but now seemed unchained. Prescott tended to vote for the Reform Party, and Roche was determined it would not happen again. Walter Shanly, a noted and accomplished civil engineer and railway specialist, was the Conservative candidate federally and Macneil Clarke, the mayor of Prescott, ran in the provincial riding of Grenville South. Both were born in Ireland.

On September 1, Father Roche "threatened his hearers with an electioneer harangue" while arguing in favour of Shanly and Clarke, and most of the parishioners walked out. After Mass a week later, on September 8, he launched another "violent harangue" against the Liberals and claimed that "the interests of the Catholics of this section were more secure in the hands of Macneil Clarke" than in those of his opponent John McCarthy, who was also a Catholic. Apparently, Father Roche threatened to withhold the sacraments

*Introduction* 17

from those who did not follow his wishes. There might have been a thousand people at St. Mark's that morning, and again they stampeded out of the building.[19]

The language in Prescott seemed emblematic of the campaign, prompting a *New York Times* journalist to observe that while "Canadian politics have always been very stormy," new heights of rhetoric were being scaled and that the country's newspapers were just "too passionate in their politics."[20] Alexander Mackenzie actually called the journalism of his friend George Brown "Globe terrorism."[21] "Backwoodsman" from the village of Saint-Élie, near Sherbrooke, Quebec, said that the progress made in Canada had distinguished it from countries such as Spain and Mexico. That said, he called for a "higher tone of political morality," stating that too often good manners were forgotten in times of election. Politicians too often were "deceitful, rude, boisterous or ill-mannered." He concluded that Canadians had to "respect themselves" and that passions should be cooled so that "the science of politics should be better understood and appreciated by us, for it is really a noble science."[22]

British North America was not the place where existentialist questions were debated in coffeehouses and *salons de thé,* the way Camillo Benso (the Count of Cavour) and Giuseppe Mazzini famously used them to create the networks necessary to achieve Italian unity just a few years earlier (Giuseppe Garibaldi's guns helped also, no doubt). In Canada, it was the newspapers that provided the venue for debate. A count carried out in 1864 revealed that there were about 23 daily newspapers across British North America, as well as 27 tri-weeklies, 16 semi-weeklies, 226 weeklies, and 27 monthlies.[23] Timothy Anglin, Leonard Tilley, Joseph Howe, Charles Tupper, George Brown, John A. Macdonald, Médéric Lanctôt, Antoine-Aimé Dorion, and George-Étienne Cartier all had newspapers express their views on the issues and about their adversaries. Anglin, Brown, and Lanctôt were active, professional editors. In this regard, the practice of politics of 1867 is very different from what it is today, but the critical role of communications was no different.

The *New York Times* journalist was also struck by the fact that "the different factions seem to be more violent than ever," noting that colourful (not to say purely invented) epithets such as "annexationists" and "disloyalists," as well as "corruptionists" and "knaves," were routinely hurled (he could have included "unmanly" and "turncoats"). He recounted that "leaders fall foul of each other in a style that might teach something even to the extremists of this country." In light of the raw new habits being developed, he also hoped that the new Canada would not become "another Mexico" after its independence.[24]

## The Act of Voting

There was no privacy of politics in 1867, and ballots were contentious acts. On polling days, voters verbally expressed their choice in front of an audience. Except in New Brunswick, which had been inspired by Australia in adopting the secret ballot in 1855,[25] voting in 1867 was in the open – everyone knew how everyone else voted. (The secret ballot was widely adopted in 1874, two years after it was introduced in Great Britain; the practice started in 1884 in parts of the United States.)

Elections were loosely arranged affairs, a practice that left room for a good deal of abuse. Polling took place on different days in Quebec, Ontario, and New Brunswick, depending on the riding. The votes were typically held over a two- or three-day period. On the first day, candidacies (or "nominations," as they were called then – and anyone could declare himself a candidate) would be announced. If one candidacy went unchallenged, that person would be acclaimed. In some cases, voting would begin immediately. Most of the time, voting would begin the next day, and the tally would be revealed at the end of the first day of voting. Voting would resume the next day (giving each campaign a measure of how many voters they had to rally to the polling station), and a victor would be declared. Sometimes, the winner would be revealed a day later. To complicate matters, the same man could stand for election in both the provincial and federal legislatures in Ontario and Quebec. A candidate could run in any number of ridings if he so chose (and many did).

It was rumoured that the Macdonald government angled to make sure that winnable ridings were scheduled early so as to build momentum, but the evidence is unconvincing and its impact remains certainly debatable. Nova Scotia deliberately scheduled its vote (exceptionally, held on one day only) on the last possible day so as to have the last word. The voters there knew full well that Macdonald's coalition was to form the first elected government when they voiced their choices.

Voting was an act of citizenship, to be sure, but it was also an act of courage. In Canada, particularly, the conduct of pre-1867 elections had been fraught with violence, manipulation, and corruption of the worst sort.[26] One had to stand on conviction, or at least on a suitable bribe or promise of drink (little wonder that the prohibitionist movement grew strong in those years). The *Christian Guardian,* the Methodist publication founded by Egerton Ryerson in 1829, was not alone in its concern. "The body of the people should unite," it urged, "with entire unanimity to vote against any candidate who employs or even encourages, any kind of bribery or intimidation in order to gain his cause."[27] "Does anyone doubt that such a state of things is common?" asked the *Sarnia Observer.* Critics of the Conservative Party, in particular, consistently levelled the accusation that railway money steered votes away from Liberal candidates. The practice was no doubt widespread, but it is impossible to measure its impact. No records were kept and the results are simply too puzzling to allow any observer to conclude that any particular riding was "bought." It is evident that candidates on both sides did their very best to secure enough money to buy votes. In

20   *Ballots and Brawls*

Ottawa, for instance, Edward McGillivray, a leading businessman and former mayor, pulled out of the race against Joseph Merrill Currier, a wealthy lumberman and publisher of the *Ottawa Daily Citizen* (as well as the MP for Ottawa in the Province of Canada), because he could not compete with Currier's purse. "If what he says is true," the *Quebec Gazette* commented, "then the Metropolis of the Dominion is one of the most ingeniously corrupt constituencies on the face of the earth, and needs to be looked after in any future context." McGillivray reported that the bribery was not confined to a few cases but that "men by the score" had pledged to vote for Currier, "demanding that they should be paid for carrying them." He felt that he "could not be a party to such utter demoralization of the community." Without an ability to buy voters, his defeat was certain. The election was fraudulent and he would have no part in carrying out such an "open flagrant crime."[28] Did it make a difference? Currier, as the incumbent, had a tight hold on the seat, and many allegations of bribery were undoubtedly valid, but they went unproven.

Currier's people made their own accusations. The *Daily Citizen* charged that in the election of Dr. Grant in the riding of Russell, "the most flagrant bribery and corruption of the electors were resorted to; an unscrupulous and lavish expenditure of money – obtained somehow – was made, and voters were purchased wholesale and openly."[29] Bribery was seen as a disease of electors, not of the government. "The principle of a democratic government for enlightened people is faultless, but nothing tends so thoroughly to destroy the benefits arising therefrom as bribery in the elections," wrote the *Sarnia Observer.* Any candidate who won by bribing voters could not claim to represent anything other than "his own purse." The paper went further, calling bribery "high treason" and "a crime against honesty and morality."[30] Some suspected that American money (rumoured at around $50,000) was behind the Brown "Liberal Republican" party. "Will the lovers of British institutions

*Introduction* 21

and British freedom, permit those vile factionalists, in the West, and their Rouge and annexationist allies in the east, to triumph even with the aid of 'material assistance' from their Yankee sympathizers?" asked the *Ottawa Times*. "Up loyal men, and at them! Down with the traitorous Coalition!"[31]

Ontario was not the only place where votes were bought. In Quebec, such purchases were made in cash and drink. Brian Young has advanced the idea that the Tories spent an average of $10 per vote, and perhaps up to $100 per vote, to support the campaigns of Thomas D'Arcy McGee and George-Étienne Cartier.[32] In Nova Scotia, Archbishop Connolly estimated that in some ridings, votes were bought for twenty pounds.[33] Timothy Anglin, the New Brunswick anti-Confederation leader, later conceded that everybody was trying to buy people off during these elections.[34]

Not everyone was entitled to vote. One had to be a male of at least twenty-one years, and had to own property of some sort – $150 in Nova Scotia, $200 in rural Quebec, $300 in urban Quebec, $200 in Ontario, and 100 pounds in New Brunswick. If a voter in New Brunswick had no property but did have an annual income of at least 400 pounds, he could vote. In Nova Scotia, such a voter had to show a minimum income of $300. A voter who met the property requirements in more than one riding could vote in another also. Anyone working for government or who was in receipt of any assistance from the state (which was exceptionally rare) was not allowed to vote. Indigenous men were specifically disallowed the franchise in Ontario, unless they lived off-reserve and received no money from the government.[35] (Regrettably, this is the only mention of the Indigenous realities in this book, because they were never invoked in the debates.) It meant that roughly 15 percent of the entire population was actually entitled to express a view on polling day.[36] By twenty-first-century standards, it was a completely undemocratic election, but few made that point in 1867 (or since) because no states had ever been created as the result of a democratic vote. The two countries that were created roughly simultaneously with Canada, Germany and Italy, were the products of wars and decisions made by local duchies. The United States was created because elected representatives made that choice, and the 1864 presidential election saw Abraham Lincoln re-elected by 15 percent of the electorate also, as in Canada. If anyone had a problem with the process, it was mostly because they disagreed that elections should take place at all. They opposed Confederation, in large part because they saw the constitutional arrangement as illegitimate in the first place.

And there was undoubtedly a share of dirty politics. The historian Marcel Bellavance argues that the *Bleus* won at least two seats in 1867 by literally kidnaping the opposing candidate on election day, and points particularly to the riding of Montmorency, which ultimately acclaimed the Conservative Joseph Cauchon.[37] Violence against voters was deployed in more than a few ridings as teams squared off in intimidating each other's voters. It also meant that threats were likely. The local scenes were not much different from the famous one depicted a hundred years earlier by the English painter William Hogarth. His *The Polling* (1758) memorably depicted a tumultuous scene of intimidation and inducements where even the sick and the dead were processed in their civic duties. Except for all the wigs, it could well have been a Canadian vignette in 1867, complete with a red (Liberal) and blue (Tory) flag. The *Cleveland Herald* noted the violence, reporting that "affairs in the new 'Dominion' open badly." Reporting on the state of affairs in Montreal, it argued that the event did "not speak well for the future welfare or the new nation that is to be." It emphasized that that there was no harmony between the provinces or even among the peoples of each province, and the future of Canada did not seem promising. The "old differences between French and English, Roman Catholics and Orangemen have been prominent and bitter."[38]

*The Humours of an Election III: The Polling,*
1754–55, by William Hogarth (1697–1764)
© Sir John Soane's Museum, London

There was also some vote suppression. Elections in each riding were placed under the direction of a returning officer appointed by the government, and there were instances of abuses of power. In Montreal, for example, polls were supposed to be arranged in alphabetical order, but that rule was not always respected and the process soon degenerated into a confusing free-for-all that discouraged voters. In other ridings, polling stations were placed at the most inconvenient locations so as to give particular electors a hard time.[39] In Verchères, the returning officer had electors pledge their allegiance twice in order to slow the voting procedures, hoping that Liberal supporters would leave.[40] In New Brunswick, Catholics (including Acadians) had long been repelled by the demand that they pronounce an oath of allegiance to the monarch in order to vote.[41] That said, Catholic Church leaders left no doubt that the eligible members of their flock had an obligation to vote and to avoid violence. Father Patrick Dowd, an Irishman who had studied at the Séminaire de Saint-Sulpice in Paris before taking up his post at St. Patrick's Church in Montreal in 1848, remarked during Mass that the city had been peaceful after the infamous riots of 1849 and that the disturbances around polling stations as elections began were unacceptable. "Is that happy state of things to be disturbed by a lawless set of misguided men, in peaceable citizens to be deprived of their right to vote by brute force?" he reportedly asked. The popular priest answered himself in his usual colourful language worth citing at length:

> No, no, that cannot be; I know that there are not many of them here, but I called upon everyone of you who are present to become Apostles of Peace, and tell those misguided and foolish men that the peace of the city is to be maintained at all hazards. If the civil force is not sufficient, the military force will be called out to the last man, and, if needed, I will myself shoulder a musket, and shoot down those who dare to intimidate and keep back from the polls peaceable citizens. I am no party man; nor could I be; I never followed any man or party. I only know you as your pastor, and, as such, if it was required of me, I'm willing to spill the last drop of my blood in your defence. In the name of God, let not the peace of this fair city be disturbed; let each man vote for whom he can conscientiously record his voice, in keeping with the teaching of our venerable bishop. But do not attempt to prevent others from exercising their rights in the same way. I care not who is elected, if the peace of the city is only preserved, and every man is allowed to vote as he chooses. Then I should be satisfied, and God's blessing of rest upon you.[42]

Clearly, there was a sense of duty to answer the call of democracy and, to a certain degree, to legitimize the new state. The *Advertiser and Eastern Townships Sentinel* in Quebec observed that "the duty of every man is to do nothing that will precipitate the County, at a busy season of the year, into a contest out of which no great good to the country can be gained." It encouraged men to vote their "hearts" in selecting the best representative. "There should be no hanging back," it continued with nationalist flourish, "for the man who has not the moral courage to vote either one way or the other, has not the interest of the country at heart."[43]

The electoral campaign was launched on August 7, when the writs were issued. The results had to be returned on September 24, making for a six-week campaign. (The ridings of Gaspé, Bonaventure, Chicoutimi, and Saguenay received exemptions because they were so vast; they had to return their writs on October 24 and they voted for the newly formed government.)

Although Macdonald made efforts in this direction, there were no real national campaigns organized in 1867, certainly not in the sense that they would be understood in the twenty-first century. Communications efforts were made through newspaper networks as roads and railways were not sufficiently developed for a leader (or his representatives) to be able to cross provincial borders. Canada's electoral history was thus born in a spirit of harangue and dispute – hardly a basis on which to predict a grand democratic and united future.

# 1

## The Battlefield, the Wheels, the Flies, and the Flywheels

IT HAS LONG BEEN explained that Confederation – and the 1867 election that sprang from it – was the solution to a political and economic malaise that struck a good portion of the elite in the United Province of Canada, New Brunswick, and Nova Scotia. It did not have to happen that way. Most politicians, most of the time, would have done nothing (like those in Prince Edward Island and Newfoundland) and, as the historian Ged Martin convincingly demonstrated, there were many good arguments against Confederation.[1] But in 1864, many in the political class particularly felt pressure to act, and they were hardly alone. A good portion of the capitalists in the various colonies felt hamstrung by political instability – eleven governments in the Province of Canada since 1848, for instance – which had paused the growth of investment, particularly in the building of infrastructures that were needed for access to both resources and markets. Certainly, an important portion of decision-makers of all sorts in Great Britain also felt that something had to change.

## The Battlefield:
## British North American Society and Economics

In 1864, the vast British territory north of the United States was sparsely populated. Above the forty-ninth parallel in the west (which had been established in 1846), the lands were mostly inhabited by dots of nomadic Indigenous and Métis communities. The population thickened as the border tumbled down the shores of the Great Lakes and then climbed towards the forty-fifth parallel, which marked the boundary between the Province of Canada and New York State, Vermont, and New Hampshire and then bumped wildly north to shape the territories of Maine, Quebec, and New Brunswick.

The territory had been more or less settled for a generation, but massive immigration from the United Kingdom and the outbreak of civil war in the United States reshuffled geopolitical diplomatic cards. In one of the great blunders of diplomatic history, Great Britain cheered the breakaway Confederates of the South in order to show that it sided with its own cotton manufacturers, who depended on low prices for their raw material, and to undermine the growing behemoth on the American continent that threatened its colonies to the north. It proved to be terribly short-sighted. Within two years, the Confederacy showed it did not have the economic infrastructure to fight the Union. The standing army that existed after four years of war, and the expansionist musings of William Seward, the American secretary of state under Abraham Lincoln and his successor, William Johnson, were a grave concern.[2]

The overtures towards Confederation in the spring of 1864 came during a febrile period in North American history and around the world. General Ulysses Grant, now at the head of the Union Army, had triumphed in the Battle of the Wilderness (May 5–7, 1864) and launched the Overland Campaign that would ultimately defeat the Confederate Army. The numbers of war dead were expected to climb dramatically, and the first graves were dug that month at Arlington National Cemetery, formerly the home of Robert E. Lee, the general leading the Confederate Army. That spring, the United States was also at war with many of the Indigenous communities in the Northwestern territories, such as the Cheyenne and the Arapaho. Elsewhere, the Taiping Rebellion in China was nearing its bloody end, but new conflicts erupted in northern Europe, as Prussia pressed for more territory from Denmark. In South America, Brazil declared war on Uruguay, and Paraguay was soon also involved in the expanding conflict. The Dutch finally took Sumatra, and a coalition of Western forces bombarded the Japanese city of Shimonoseki. In other words, political maps were being redrawn everywhere, at great cost to human lives. Optimists for peace and healing in light of all these conflicts welcomed the founding of the Red Cross in Geneva that year.

Relatively speaking, the British colonies in North America were small. The United States had a population of roughly 31.5 million people in the mid-1860s. According the census taken in 1861, the population in the United Province of Canada was almost exactly ten times smaller: 3,295,706 people. Canada West, that section now known as Ontario, had a population of about 2,195,700 inhabitants, of which 36,568 were French Canadians. Canada East, now known as Quebec, was almost half as large: just over 1,100,000 people, of which about 800,000 were French speaking.

Canada was expanding at a rate of 4.3 percent a year, followed by the colony of New Brunswick, at 2.6 percent.[3] In 1864, Nova Scotia hosted a population of around 350,000 people; New Brunswick was home to around 270,000; and Prince Edward Island had 80,000. The population that inhabited British North America was remarkably homogeneous. The *Year-Book and Almanac of British North America for 1867* indicated that 79 percent of the people living in Canada had been born in the country, with at least two-thirds being of British stock, drawn from all quarters of the United Kingdom, including Ireland. There was remarkably little net population growth in the Maritimes, as many immigrants passed through to get to the United Province of Canada. Of the 18,958 people who arrived in Eastern British North America in 1865, for instance, about 16,000 appeared to have settled in Canada West, and the remainder in Canada East.

One social reality divided populations in every colony (beyond language, of course): Christian denominations. In the 1860s, Protestants constituted 55 percent of the population, self-identifying mostly as Anglicans (about 28 percent of the Protestant segment), Presbyterians (about 26 percent), Wesleyans and Methodists (about 24 percent), Baptists (10 percent), and Lutherans and Congregationalists (constituting less than 3 percent each).[4] The other 45 percent of the general population was Roman Catholic.

At this time in Canada's history, location largely dictated what kinds of jobs were available. In Ontario and Quebec, most people made their living in agricultural pursuits. Out of 837,718 recorded labourers, approximately 41 percent (342,649) of jobs were on the farm. In 1860 alone, a total of 28,213,760 bushels of wheat, 39,506,359 bushels of potatoes, and 45,634,806 bushels of oats were produced. In 1866, the top agricultural export was flour, with a value of $5.2 million. The second most valuable export was raw barley and rye, with a value of $4.6 million, and the third was raw wheat, with a value of $3.1 million. The best news about agriculture was revealed in July 1867 when wines from Clair House Vineyard in Cooksville, Ontario (now Mississauga) won some recognition at a French exhibition as notably "*solide*," considering their long trip across the Atlantic in various temperatures. The *Toronto Leader* gushed: "They resemble more the great French table wines than any other foreign wines they have examined."[5] Those who toasted Confederation could do so with a fine local drink indeed.

30   *Ballots and Brawls*

Great Britain and the United States bought the majority of exports from Canada's mines – mainly copper ore and iron. In the year ending in June 1866, the value of metal exports was almost $350,000. Foodstuffs and other items were exported to many countries. Canada was also investigating trading options with countries and colonies in the tropics, including British Guiana, Jamaica, Barbados, Trinidad, Antigua, Santo Domingo, Cuba, Puerto Rico, and Brazil.

The beginnings of manufacturing were evident in Toronto and Montreal. The shipbuilding industry was growing, with Nova Scotia, New Brunswick, and Prince Edward Island producing a total of 572 new vessels in 1865, up from 399 new vessels in 1860. In an explanatory note, the 1867 edition of the *Year-Book and Almanac of British North America* noted Canada's trade advantage in having access to "an abundance and excellence of timber," which made ship construction in the Maritimes much cheaper than in Europe and at least 40 percent cheaper than in the United States. These early years showed promise for Canada's infrastructure. In 1867, 471 electric telegraph stations dotted British North America. The Grand Trunk Railway, which included the Montreal and Champlain and the Buffalo and Lake Huron Railways, was 1,377 miles long, and its road and equipment alone were valued at $81 million. The economy in Canada was improving. At the end of the fiscal year 1865, the total value of all Canadian imports was $44,620,469. A year later, it was $53,802,310. The duty collected in the 1865 amounted to $5,633,378, and it was $7,330,725 in 1866. The total value of exports from Canada in 1865 was $42,481,157, and had grown to $56,328,380 in 1866.[6]

There was little trade between the regions, and the trend was declining. The economy was also hamstrung by a low degree of interprovincial mobility, and the lack of communication between Canada and the Maritimes worked against business and economic integration. That said, each provincial economy was growing fast during the period 1850–64, though there is evidence that Quebec's was a little more static.[7] In Nova Scotia and New Brunswick, forestry was an important industry, and labourers and lumbermen accounted for 211,243 of all recorded workers. In 1864–65, the quantity of lumber exported was worth close to $13 million. Fisheries provided jobs to approximately 30,000 people. Mining activity was evident in a few districts. Charles Tupper saw coal as the salvation of Nova Scotia and of Canada because it could find markets in other parts of British North America and bring wealth. Along with its ability to be shipped by rail and sea, coal could "make Nova Scotia the great emporium for manufactures in British America."[8]

## The Impasse in the United Province of Canada

What animated the Confederation debates in 1864 in the United Province of Canada was not economic activity, however. It was the politics that seemed to threaten whatever shoots of prosperity might spring. There was a serious parliamentary impairment. The election of 1863 had given the Reform/Liberal Party sixty-six seats, eight more than in 1861. Reform was popular in Canada West, taking forty-one seats out of fifty, but much less so in Canada East, where only twenty-five of the sixty-two ridings gave it seats. Macdonald's coalition of Conservatives, moderate reformers from Canada West, and *Bleus* (the moniker of *conservateur* did not suit them, or their aspirations) in Quebec, meanwhile, was flagging. In 1861, it had taken seventy seats, but in 1863 could only boast of sixty-two MPs. What kept them in power was the support of two moderate reformers in Canada West and twenty-five *Bleu* MPs from Canada East. What impaired execution, however, was the rule that bills occasionally had to win the support of a majority of seats in both Canada East and Canada West. In such conditions, earning the confidence of the legislature was extremely difficult. A new system was desperately needed.

One obvious solution was to split Canada West from Canada East and return to the state of things as they stood before 1840. The second obvious solution was a sort of federal governance where Canada East and Canada West would both have their provincial government, but a supranational legislature would also be created. That notion appealed to some, particularly in Canada East, because it would allow a French Canadian majority in a province like Quebec to conduct its affairs in a manner that would win support. The discussion remained vaguely theoretical, as the powers that a "national government" might enjoy remained abstract.

The third idea of a broader union – one that would encompass far more than the "Canada" of the time – was not new; in fact, ideas about a continental federalism were almost as old as the British conquest itself.[9] Jonathan Sewell, the chief justice of Lower Canada, had proposed such an idea to the Duke of Kent in 1814. Lord Durham included a discussion on the subject in his 1839 report. The legislature of Nova Scotia passed a resolution in 1854 to the effect that a union or confederation of the British provinces "would promote their advancement and prosperity, increase their strength and influence, and elevate their position." Even Joseph Howe had proposed that a "union of a federal character" be explored to bring more stability and predictability to the British colonies in North America.[10]

Opinion in Quebec was divided. The idea of Confederation had never been far from consideration, simply because the United States provided a vivid example of how a federal state – a republic, no less – could at once contain two levels of government. The American experiment was creaky and disputatious in the 1830s and 1840s, but sufficiently dynamic for a segment of politicians to pronounce themselves in support of annexation in the late 1840s. People like Louis-Joseph Papineau, the eminent leader of the *Patriote* movement in the 1830s, liked the idea of creating such a republic (at age eighty-one, he was very much alive in 1867 but played no role in the election).[11] In the summer and fall of 1857, Joseph-Charles Taché, certainly one of the most accomplished men of his generation (a medical doctor, a learned man, as well as an engaging politician), published a series of thirty-three articles in the *Courrier du Canada* arguing that the politics of the United Province of Canada were shaped by a governance structure that did not work and that a federal structure would be more suitable.[12] (It was later issued as *Des provinces de l'Amérique du nord et d'une union fédérale*.) It had an immediate impact on George-Étienne Cartier and simultaneously fired George Brown's imagination.

Federalism lent itself more than any other regime to protecting local cultures while allowing the colonies to develop common markets that could guarantee some sort of prosperity and providing a bulwark against the American republic. Slowly, the idea won adherents. As his government with John A. Macdonald sought new legitimacy in August 1858 (following the infamous double-shuffle), Cartier committed to examining the possibility of a federal union of British North American colonies, and to consult both the maritime communities and the government in London. On October 25, 1859, a committee of the *Rouges* in Lower Canada submitted a report supporting a federal system of government to replace the legislative union, and the party organ, *Le Pays,* published it four days later so that the idea could spread more broadly. Surprisingly, even the hardline young independentist *wunderkind* Médéric Lanctôt was tentatively supportive, because the union of the Upper and Lower Canadas had been ruinous to public finance in terms of debt and unfair in terms of the redistribution of customs revenues.[13] Alexander Galt, the influential Conservative member of Parliament for Sherbrooke who seemed to carry the views of the English-speaking business class in Quebec, wholeheartedly supported the position. George Brown saw in the proposal the possibility of realizing the "representation by population" agreement he had long sought, and also proposed a resolution at the Reform convention in Toronto that supported a federation project. The fact that Brown

## 34   Ballots and Brawls

warmed to the idea raised suspicions, but the *Rouges* tried to see him in the best light possible, setting aside his long record of anti-Catholicism and often Francophobic rhetoric.

Lanctôt may have had to swallow hard – he had written just months earlier in the *Courrier de Saint-Hyacinthe* that Brown, notwithstanding his many talents, "had done more than any other to slow the progress of genuinely liberal ideas." Brown, in his mind, was probably no worse than Allan MacNab, a "Compact Tory" who seemed to be vehemently opposed to any progressive measures, even as joint premier of the Province of Canada. "Those who took MacNab will swallow Brown, without added spice," Lanctôt wrote.[14] The enthusiasm was not long-lived. When the notion was presented to the legislative assembly on February 28, 1860, twenty-eight MPs from Upper Canada voted in favour and twenty-five against. In Lower Canada, all the votes went against the notion, except for those of Antoine-Aimé Dorion and Denis-Émery Papineau, two *Rouge* members, as well as the more moderate anglophone Quebec MPs Thomas D'Arcy McGee and Lewis Drummond.

On the Pacific coast, British Columbia leaders were not particularly vocal about the idea. The vast expanse of land between the Rockies and Canada West was empty, to the eyes of white pioneers, save for the few Indigenous settlements and the larger community at the intersection of the Assiniboine and Red Rivers (what is known today as Winnipeg). Merging with a distant community thousands of miles to the east simply made little sense.

The idea of a grand federal state re-emerged four years later. On May 30, 1864, the year-old Liberal government of Sandfield Macdonald and Antoine-Aimé Dorion collapsed. The prospect of a government led by John A. Macdonald and Étienne-Paschal Taché seemed shaky at best, especially when it was revealed on June 14 that in 1859 the Macdonald-Cartier government had agreed to loan the Grand Trunk Railway $100,000 without a clear appropriation from Parliament. The government was likely to lose a vote of confidence and was poised to ask that the legislature – which had been elected just a year earlier, in 1863 – be dissolved. George Brown, the leader of the Reformers, instead suggested something unthinkable: he offered to support the government on the condition that it explore the possibility of a broader union with the Maritime colonies. On June 22, Macdonald (in English) and Cartier (in French) read out the accord struck with the Liberals, agreeing to explore a "federal union of all the provinces of British North America." Canadian politics moved onto a new battlefield.

Weeks later, Macdonald was told that a meeting of the leaders in the Maritime colonies was being organized to discuss some sort of union, and he asked permission for a delegation from the Canadas to be invited. There was an important issue that had to be discussed among all the British colonies: railway access to the ports on the Atlantic coast and progress on the idea of building a semicontinental railway that would link southern Ontario and Halifax. As Toronto financier D.L. Macpherson told Macdonald in June 1864, that railroad was of critical importance: "Without it there can be no federation. It is the keystone, the very foundation stone."[15]

## New Brunswick's Wheels

With the benefit of hindsight, it is clear that the 1867 election campaign had really gotten underway forty months before the first votes were cast. The notion of a broad federation of British North American colonies could be disseminated only if political wheelers lent themselves to the task. In New Brunswick, the idea of joining forces with other colonies was energized by Arthur Hamilton-Gordon, the young Lieutenant-Governor. To many, he was nothing but a privileged young bachelor who seemed to resent New Brunswick's often petty politics, but his enthusiasm carried a significant level of authority because he had worked with the elite of British government, and people suspected that his advice carried weight in the metropole.

Arthur Hamilton-Gordon, early 1860s
National Portrait Gallery, AX9573

Hamilton-Gordon, like his predecessors in the British colonies of North America, was quite comfortable with demanding accountability from the governing party in his colony. Born in late 1829, he was barely thirty-two years old when he arrived in Fredericton. The scion of the prominent Aberdeen family, he had attended Cambridge University and thought of becoming a pastor, but grew to admire his father, George Hamilton-Gordon, the 4th Earl of Aberdeen, a leading politician of his day. After Cambridge, his first posting was in 1852 as assistant private secretary to the prime minister, who happened to be his father. Aberdeen, who was in office until 1855, had long been a force in shaping British foreign policy, and had a keen interest in North American affairs. That rubbed off on young Arthur. After serving as MP for a few years, he was sent to New Brunswick in 1861 by Lord Palmerston's government, and people knew that Palmerston had a very high regard for the Hamilton-Gordon family. As a Scot, Arthur felt at home among the elite of British North America.

As the leading military figure in the colony, young Arthur Hamilton-Gordon grew concerned about defence as the war south of the border took an important, final turn. He also fell in love with the idea of an intercolonial railway that could link New Brunswick's centres with Halifax and Quebec City. He attended key railway conferences, such as the one in Quebec in 1861 and in London the following year, and was often impatient with the slow response from the Canadians. New Brunswickers grumbled that his unbridled enthusiasm on this issue was frittering away the colony's bargaining position.

The combination of military events in the United States, the intercolonial railway impasse, and the pettiness of New Brunswick affairs peaked in his mind in 1863, and he called for a meeting of the government leaders in New Brunswick, Nova Scotia, and Prince Edward Island. Going beyond mundane issues, he called for a discussion of better ways of collaborating, including a discussion of the concept of "Maritime Union." To those who would listen, he revealed that he was increasingly convinced that while Maritime Union could be a useful option for New Brunswick, a larger union with the Canadian colony could be well worth considering also.[16]

This was a tonic to Leonard Tilley, the prime minister of New Brunswick. Born in Gagetown in 1818, Tilley was the son of a storekeeper and religiously devout Loyalist who grew up to be a druggist. He became prosperous and moved in political circles on the strength

Leonard Tilley, 1869
Library and Archives Canada, 3496704

of his influence in the temperance movement. In 1854, he was elected to the New Brunswick Legislative Assembly as a "reformer" devoted to the idea of responsible government. In 1861, he was named to head the government of the colony. Tilley could be impulsive, but he was a stubborn man who could not resist a challenge and had the ability to rally people around him. He was clever and ambitious but not addicted to power; he was a shrewd and strategic player willing to play second violin in order to get what he wanted. Tilley warmed to the idea of a broad union of British colonies, but latched on to the practical and more immediate possibility of a Maritime Union. In the summer of 1864, he was keen to new ideas.

John A. Macdonald was confident that Tilley was "in every relation of life ... a good man in the very best meaning of the word." Tilley's biographer noted that his "strength was in his ability to negotiate and to find compromise and to offer alternatives. He always looked for the practical and the workable solution," even though he had a "foxy appearance" and was "awfully politic."[17]

## The Ontario Wheels

Though his reputation has been gravely tarnished in the twenty-first century, the best-known political player in Canada West was John A. Macdonald, once felicitously described by journalist and historian Joseph Schull as "that cork on the sea of politics, who had somehow bobbed to the top." Macdonald, born in Glasgow, Scotland, in 1815, came to Canada as a five-year-old and settled with his family in the Kingston area. He was always a promising boy, alert and congenial, and easily followed his uncle in apprenticing in law. He quickly distinguished himself as an alert young barrister, willing to talk to anyone, never repugnant to either the progressives or the conservatives he encountered.[18] With the years, as he made contacts in the business sector, he deepened his interest in politics. He ran for Kingston's municipal council in 1843 and won. The next year, he ran for a seat in the legislature of the province of United Canada and won again. He married a cousin, Isabella Clark, that year, and settled down to learn the craft of legislative and parliamentary tactics, dedicating himself to knowing almost everybody who worked for the government. In 1847, he entered cabinet as receiver general, and in 1854 was named attorney general. Over the next ten years, he would serve in that portfolio almost continuously, and was premier or co-premier three times.

Macdonald's personality made him a natural politician. He could be stubborn, but his strong will was always tempered by a sympathy for human beings that gave him the ability to compromise. He was always eager to learn, willing to try new ideas. He was witty and

John A. Macdonald, 1868
Norman Collection, Library and Archives Canada, C-006513

loyal, optimistic and assertive at the same time. A tireless worker, Macdonald inspired loyalty. His political calculus was more sophisticated than most. He was easily convinced that the path to success in the Canadas was paved by a coalition of progressives and conservatives and by an alliance of Protestants and Catholics. Like many Upper Canadians, he saw a grand opportunity in the vast territories that stood to the west. He liked the business class, where he had many friends, and was convinced that prosperity for the country could be achieved only if merchants and manufacturers made profits.

George Brown, 1880s
Photographer Hunter & Co., Library and Archives Canada, C-009553

Macdonald's chief rival was George Brown, another dominant figure in Canada West politics. Born in 1818, in Alloa, about forty kilometres north of Macdonald's Glasgow, Brown came to Canada as an adult, by way of New York City. At the same time that Macdonald volunteered with the local militia in Kingston to fight the rebels of 1837, Brown migrated with his father, Peter Brown, to New York City and contributed significantly in establishing a shop on Broadway Street. Five years later, Peter Brown launched a newspaper, the *British Chronicle,* which, perhaps not surprisingly given its title, won many readers in Upper Canada. The readers were so enthusiastic that the elder Brown pulled up stakes and established himself in Toronto. The first issue of the Toronto-based *British Chronicle* appeared in July 1843.

The Browns had a combative Scots Presbyterian streak and were comfortable in the Free Kirk movement in Ontario. They were easily provoked by the ideas of privilege, mixing a dose of American free thinking with an attachment to things British. In 1844, they launched the *Globe,* a newspaper dedicated to the reformist ideals that had animated revolts in the past, and the Browns were caught in the swirls of its politics. George Brown won his first election to the Legislative Assembly in 1851 at the age of thirty-one, defeating a fellow reformist on a platform demanding free trade, representation by population, and improvements to the transportation infrastructure of the province. Brown was hardly a radical in temperament, the way the impetuous faction "Clear Grits" wanted to be, but he was driven and could easily manage collaborations. Confident and intelligent, he had charm and he loved his work as a journalist and propagandist. He was direct and outspoken, and willingly worked long hours. The work of being in politics was something that did not agree with him, however, even during the few spells when he was in government. Brown was an idealist who treasured consistency, two characteristics that don't usually sit well in politics. All the same, with him as a guide, most Grits and Clear Grits usually voted together, and his forceful campaign for "Rep-by-pop" – the idea that Ontario (Canada West) needed more seats in the legislature in proportion to its size – and his occasional anti-Catholic utterances won most of them over.

### The Quebec Wheels

Quebec's champion for Confederation was George-Étienne Cartier, without doubt the political rainmaker in Canada East. Born in September 1814, Cartier was only a few months older than Macdonald. As a young man, he gravitated towards the rebellious

George-Étienne Cartier, 1871
Photographer Topley Studio, Library and Archives Canada, PA-026375

circles of Lower Canada. He followed Louis-Joseph Papineau passionately and joined the Société des fils de la liberté, a militia that saw battle with the English army at Saint-Denis in November 1837, the only victory for the *Patriotes*. Cartier escaped capture by taking refuge in the United States, but returned a few months later to resume his law practice in Montreal. He remained a proud *Patriote*, joining the Saint-Jean-Baptiste Society, and soon became a follower of Louis-Hippolyte La Fontaine's more moderate politics. A man with a huge appetite for life and work, he devoured books as a student and young lawyer. He was independent of spirit, easily made friends with people of all classes, from workers to archbishops, and was generally liberal in his views. He was a remarkable networker, careful to make notes on the strengths and weaknesses of the people he encountered. Not least, he proved to be a very able lawyer and, like Macdonald, became a favourite of the business class. He was as realistic in business as he was in politics, and he was ambitious. A man of wide culture and intelligence, he had friends and networks everywhere – in business, in the Catholic Church, and, not least, among men and women of letters.

Cartier ran for a seat in the legislative assembly in 1848 and won. He was appointed to cabinet in 1854, and three years later joined Macdonald as co-premier until 1862, without doubt the most productive government in the history of the United Province of Canada. The two men formed a strong bond based on common convictions. Both were promoters of capital, moderate in their views, open to new ideas, and slightly suspicious of democracy's potential excesses, but especially open to the possibilities of a strong country north of the United States. Cartier complemented Macdonald perfectly, and the reverse was equally true. His strong majority on the Quebec side of the legislative assembly gave Macdonald all the support he needed. Macdonald complemented Cartier in turn, giving him the administrative skills and ability to defend the government passably well in Canada West.

The other important wheel in Quebec was arguably Antoine-Aimé Dorion. Born in 1818 to a political family (his father was a *Patriote* member of the Legislative Assembly while Dorion studied at the Nicolet Seminary), Dorion elected to become a lawyer and was admitted to the bar in 1842. He was an intelligent, disciplined thinker and a man of impeccable integrity. He was governed by a strong sense of duty, and was not afraid to undertake radical changes of direction if necessary. Ideas such as broadening democratic participation, free trade, and educational reform mattered to him immensely, and he was concerned that liberal ideas needed direction in Canada East. To that end, he was instrumental in founding

Antoine-Aimé Dorion, 1868
Photographer Topley Studio, Library and Archives Canada, PA-025253

*Le Pays* in 1851. He was elected to the parliament of the United Province of Canada in 1854 as a member of the Liberal Party. Never impulsive, he was not known as a great orator, certainly not in the league of a Cartier. He was a determined advocate, but had trouble forging alliances. Like Brown, he was in politics for the promotion of ideas; actually governing did not seem to appeal to him personally. He believed in freedom and self-reliance and was at his best in standing up to injustices. Though he was co-premier with Sandfield Macdonald in 1863–64, he did not join the coalition government proposed by Brown in 1864, even though he had shown himself in the past to be willing to consider federalism as a solution.

Dorion was not sure of what to make of Macdonald's idea of attending the Charlottetown conference in September 1864, was slow to respond, and then declined. He certainly did not share his counterpart George Brown's penchant for the idea. Among his backbenchers, and among the more ardent *Rouges* outside parliament, were a different mindset altogether. In Quebec, the reaction was very different, and very divided.

### Nova Scotia's Wheel

Cartier and Macdonald were always eager to shake hands with Dr. Charles Tupper of Nova Scotia, for good reason. Born in 1821 into a strongly Baptist family in Amherst, Tupper was educated in Wolfville, fifty miles south if one crossed the Bay of Fundy. From there, the impressively intelligent young man was sent to study medicine at one of the most prestigious medical schools in the world: the University of Edinburgh. He graduated in 1843 but he loved the place and stayed for three more years (and retained a lifelong attachment to Great Britain). He returned home to start a practice in 1846, but found medicine to be limiting. He was ambitious, for himself and for his province, and found it hard to see his patients often reduced to misery for reasons beyond their control. He decided to take a turn at politics in 1855 and ran as a Conservative in Cumberland County against the most dominant figure in Nova Scotia politics, Joseph Howe. Tupper surprised even his biggest supporters by beating Howe, but he was destined to sit on the opposition benches as the Conservatives generally performed poorly.

Tupper could not abide losing; it was against his energy and his temperament. A friend described him as "of medium height, straight, muscular and wiry, and with intense nervous energy, which gave him quickness of movement and ceaseless mental activity."[19] P.B. Waite described him as irascible and humourless but born with a political hide that was "impervious to the shafts of an opponent," who could respond with remarkable "parliamentary blather and ...

Charles Tupper, February 1874
Photographer Topley Studio, Library and Archives Canada, PA-025385

exaggeration." He also described him as "always at full tilt": intense in battle and resolved to win every and any debate, and a "parliamentary bully boy" who took no prisoners. Tupper had a fine mind, at ease with scientific concepts and always in command of his facts, using the English language with flourish, and he had an admirable ability to manage affairs.[20] Those abilities were joined with a medical temper that was sensitive to human needs (he always carried his medical bag). Over the next few years, his indomitable energy and soft-hearted charm won over adherents. In the legislature, he harried the Liberal government with his scathing arguments and command of statistics and numbers. At the same time, he made a bid to secure more support from the province's Catholics.

48   *Ballots and Brawls*

They responded and gradually moved their support to the Conservative Party.

Tupper was named provincial secretary in 1857 and developed a taste for the politics of development. Arguing for mining and manufacturing development as well as for the railroads that would interconnect them with markets, he called for increased competition in the business sector. He joined discussions on railroads of all sorts, and launched a line that would connect Halifax to Pictou, another that would tie the capital to Annapolis, and above all, one that would cross his own Cumberland County and eventually connect to the imagined intercolonial railway that would link it to Quebec. He was passionate about railways to the point of travelling to London in order to make his points.

The Conservatives lost power in 1859, but Tupper was personally re-elected. As the idea of a grand federation took root in Canada that year, he voiced his support. In a speech to honour the opening of the Mechanics' Institute in Saint John, New Brunswick, he argued that Maritimers did not wish to be "a source of weakness" for the British Empire, but were instead favourable to "building up on this side of the Atlantic a powerful confederation" that could join central Canada.[21] He pointed to divided colonies, "divided by petty jealousies," that were constantly "legislating against each other, with five hostile tariffs, five different currencies and our postal communications under the control of five different departments." His solution was that the colonies of British North America, "drawn together by a common interest and with a common system of jurisprudence," come together in a "unity of action which is essential to progress."[22] In that same speech, he described the ambition of integrating Rupert's Land as well as British Columbia to create "a great and powerful organisation, with British institutions, British sympathies and British feelings, bound indissolubly to the Throne of England by a community of interests."[23] While in opposition, Tupper moved a good part of his practice to Halifax, was named the provincial capital's chief medical officer, and even served a term as president of the Medical Society of Nova Scotia.

The Conservatives were returned to government in 1863 and Tupper was named premier in 1864, just in time to express his enthusiasm for the idea of a Maritime Union, a project well supported by the Lieutenant-Governor, Sir Richard Graves MacDonnell, who, like his counterpart in New Brunswick, was convinced that government in Nova Scotia was petty and ill equipped to lead the colony into the future.[24]

## The Wheels Set in Motion, 1864

There was also a lot of hope in some quarters of Canada as the delegation of parliamentarians made its way to Charlottetown in August 1864. Their purpose was to join a hastily arranged meeting of Maritime premiers and their guests. The capital of Prince Edward Island was not ready – there was a shortage of rooms as tourists had flocked from all parts of the island to see the visiting circus, leaving the Canadians frantically searching for hotel rooms.

Charlottetown in September 1864 promised nothing, and no one in the Maritimes expected a breakthrough. The host of the meeting was John Hamilton Gray, fifty-three, the prime minister of the colony, a Conservative and a powerful speaker. At his side was William Henry Pope, a younger (thirty-nine) but equally energetic Conservative. Known on the island for their dynamic spirits, the pair were careful not to create an ambiance of expectation, and were equally careful to ask three members of the Liberal opposition to also represent the island.

In fact, there was no clear agenda, nor was there a blueprint of what New Brunswick Lieutenant-Governor Hamilton-Gordon had in mind. All the same, the colonies recognized that they faced common problems. One imperative was to find a way to build a railway that would ship products from the hinterland to Halifax (whose almost year-round port gave access to Europe and the southern parts of the United States that were more difficult to reach by rail) and vice versa. That idea was an old one, but it could not be afforded by the Maritimers alone. They had appealed to the Canadians time and again for many years already, hoping that an investment by the government there, or perhaps moneys contributed by capitalists abroad or in Montreal and Toronto, could make the plan a reality. Any such plan would require endorsement by government and, most likely, some sort of financial guarantee, if not an outright subsidy.

It was meant to be an informal meeting. The government did not even arrange for someone to formally greet the visiting delegations. A hundred years later, the painter Rex Woods captured the scene in a compelling work depicting William Henry Pope rowing to meet the Canadians aboard the *Queen Victoria*. The five-man delegation from Nova Scotia, which included the Conservative prime minister, Charles Tupper, as well as Adams Archibald, the leader of the Liberal opposition, arrived first and without fanfare. New Brunswick's delegation of five, headed by Leonard Tilley, the Liberal prime minister, and Conservative leaders like Edward B. Chandler and John Hamilton Gray (not to be confused with the premier of Prince Edward Island), wasn't feted either, even though it was escorted by Lieutenant-Governor Hamilton-Gordon. (Newfoundland's premier and attorney general, Hugh W. Hoyles, approached Charles Tupper about possibly attending, and Tupper did extend an invitation, but in the end Hoyles did not attend.)[25]

The regional newspapers decided not to bother much about it. They would rely on the dispatches coming out of the local *Charlottetown Islander* and the weekly *Examiner*. The sole exception was a reporter sent by the *Saint John Telegraph*. If anyone had a party in mind, it was the bipartisan group of interlopers from the United Province of Canada that arrived the next day. Loaded with armfuls of champagne, and accompanied by no less than twenty-three reporters, they arrived in Prince Edward Island as the Maritimers started their talks, but stayed aboard the *Queen Victoria* as there was no room available in town.[26]

The Canadian delegation, slightly larger than all the Maritimers put together, was headed by John A. Macdonald, the deputy premier of Canada, as Sir Étienne-Paschal Taché, the nearly seventy-year-old premier, was too ill to travel. It was a delegation that represented a powerful coalition of Liberals and Conservatives who eagerly sought a solution to the breakdown of politics that had, to their minds, undermined the prospects of the economy. The delegation included two other key people. One was Alexander Galt, widely respected as the best economist of his generation (though economics was hardly a profession in those days), and Thomas D'Arcy McGee, a key opinion leader of the Irish Catholic community across British North America. Both had become champions of the idea of a pan-continental union of the British colonies. None of the *Rouge* politicians accepted the invitation to join the party.

The talks proceeded surprisingly quickly. There were, understandably, major concerns about how much local autonomy would be lost in a union scheme. It was Cartier who gave reassurances, emphasizing that Quebec's legislative intentions could be confidently followed. He argued that in a federal scheme, each colony would retain a significant share of constitutional powers as well as representation in Ottawa. The provinces would be granted the powers necessary on the matters they cared the most about. Besides, the federal union would create a senate of sixty seats, with twenty each dedicated to Quebec and Ontario, and another twenty to represent the Maritimes provinces. Galt, for his part, emphasized the economic benefit of scaling up government, dismissing fears that maritime colonial coffers would be drained. Canada would assume a great deal of the Maritimers' debt, in fact, enabling them to borrow more on their own good credit. There were other benefits, but most importantly Ottawa would be responsible for the lion's share of funding for the Intercolonial Railway, which Maritimers perceived as the panacea to any fear of economic stagnation.

The Canadians knew what they were doing, and Charlottetown was buzzing with Maritimers from New Brunswick and Nova Scotia who were strongly inclined to support union. The Islanders, however, were a lot more divided. Gray was not entirely convinced, but under the Islanders' noses the idea of a broader union caught fire. As discussions progressed, the project of a union of four provinces was hatched. Obstacles were systematically overcome in the collective imagination, and the shoots of a consensus emerged that a union of sorts would bring advantages to each colony. Out of the blue, the delegates agreed to discuss the idea of a merger, and further resolved to meet again in a few weeks in Quebec City to nail down some basic principles, particularly on the governance arrangements of the new entity.

## Cementing Ideas in Quebec City

The conference broke up after a night of revelry, champagne, and lobster on September 8, and more talks were arranged in Halifax, Saint John, and Fredericton in the days that followed, partly to deepen the commitment to build a new government architecture and partly as an exercise in public relations. To celebrate the rapid progress, Tupper hosted a sparkling dinner at the Halifax Hotel on Hollis Street on the evening of Thursday, September 12. The post-Charlottetown talks fuelled optimism that a breakthrough had been achieved, and Macdonald was asked to speak to the issue of union. "It absorbs every idea as far as I am concerned," he said gravely at the outset. "This meeting in Halifax will be ever remembered in the history of British America." Not hesitating to personalize the matter, he continued: "For twenty long years I have been dragging myself through the dreary waste of colonial politics."

I thought then there was no end, nothing worthy of ambition, but, now I see something which is well worthy of all I have suffered in the cause of my little country. This question has now assumed a position that demands and commands the attention of all the Colonies of British America. There may be obstructions, local difficulties may arise, disputes may occur, local jealousies may intervene, but it matters not – the wheel is now revolving, and we are only the fly on the wheel, we cannot delay it – the union of the colonies of British America, under one sovereign, is a fixed fact.

Macdonald was not merely embroidering on Aesop's fable *The Fly on the Axle,* where a fly sitting on the axle of a moving chariot brags about how its efforts had raised the dust behind the cart. Putting a more sophisticated mechanical spin on the story, he also alluded to a basic engineering metaphor that demonstrated real insight. The short fortnight in Charlottetown and Halifax had provoked a turn of the wheel, but success depended on the steady energy supplied by a *flywheel* that could only be activated by a shared commitment to finalize negotiations. Macdonald made a solemn announcement that evening and the audience liked what it heard. He described the Charlottetown commitment as a modest leap, in a way, as the colonies were already loosely aligned by a "common allegiance" to a unifying sovereign. He was practical in emphasizing the need for a common defence that "will enable us to be a nation and to protect ourselves as we should." Comparisons with the United States were sensitive, but Macdonald was alert to the issue. He knew that Canadians had volunteered to fight with the Union forces by the tens of thousands, but was also aware, although he did not support it, of the strong pro-British sentiment in Nova Scotia that inevitably was infected by favour for the South. After a side note saluting the "gallant defence" of the South, he insisted that the United States was not a failure. "On the contrary I consider it a marvelous

54 *Ballots and Brawls*

exhibition of human wisdom," he said, but vowed to avoid its mistakes. Macdonald called for a "strong central government" that would hold the rights of sovereignty except in matters specifically awarded to the provinces. He emphasized that the new country would be composed of "British Americans," not Canadians or New Brunswickers or Nova Scotians. He envisaged nothing less than a new nation.

Macdonald also spoke about the importance of the Intercolonial Railway. "It cannot be denied," he conceded, "that the Railway, as a commercial enterprise, would be of comparatively little commercial advantage to the people of Canada." But here defence needs again reared their heads: "We wish to feel greater security – to know that we can have assistance readily in the hour of danger." His view was not that London wanted to abandon Canada. "There may be a few *doctrinaires* who argue for it, but it is not the feeling of the people of England," he reassured his listeners. London's view was that Canada should put itself "in an attitude of defence." "It is a mistake," he declared: "Canada is ready to do her part. She is organizing a militia, she is expending an enormous amount of money for the purpose of doing her best for self-protection." Macdonald was speaking to men who were very aware that the Gladstone government was concerned about the place of Canada in British defence and eager to "shift the sense of responsibility."[27] His remarks were not merely coincidental. At the end of August 1864, London had sent Lieutenant Colonel William Jervois, the government's expert on British North American defence, to inspect British North America's defences and engage with the colonies on the topic. His eventual report (1865) concluded that the territory could never be adequately protected, leading many to conclude that the United Kingdom could gradually withdraw its military presence from the North American continent.

The evening ended with flourish. "Everything, gentlemen, is to be gained by Union, and everything to be lost by disunion.

Everybody admits that Union must take place sometime," Macdonald concluded. "I say now is the time. Here we are now in a state of peace and prosperity, now we can sit down without any danger threatening us, and consider and frame a scheme advantageous to each of these colonies."[28] The Canadian delegation then divided. A portion departed for New Brunswick, first going to Saint John and then to Fredericton, while others, including Macdonald, returned to Quebec City to think through the matter of creating a new federalism.

The Quebec Conference started only a few weeks later, on October 10, with thirty-three men present from all five colonies as Newfoundland decided to send a two-man delegation to act strictly as observers.[29] As at Charlottetown, only four were French Canadian (12 percent of delegates), even though the French-speaking population would constitute roughly a third of the population of the new country: Étienne-Paschal Taché, George-Étienne Cartier, Jean-Charles Chapais, and Hector Langevin (there was no Acadian or Franco-Ontarian representation and it never occurred to anyone to invite representatives of the Indigenous community). All the same, the idea of Confederation continued to make its way, strengthening with every day. Macdonald, ably aided by his friend Hewitt Bernard, the chief clerk in the office of the attorney general, masterminded the agenda and the discussions. Tilley and Galt were key to creating a consensus, as was Tupper. George Brown proved eloquent on many occasions.

Macdonald delivered a long speech the next day. He essentially proposed (seconded by Tilley) a series of resolutions that were summed up by a concept: shared government. The motions were supported unanimously. With the rain falling incessantly outside, the mood soured, particularly over the matter of Senate appointments. The question of the separation of powers in a federal system was a key concern. The provinces wanted control over key issues like education and the right to determine the language in Parliament and in the courts. They also wanted to the power to raise their own taxes.

The charms of Macdonald, Tilley, Tupper, and Cartier worked their magic, and even George Brown proved convincing. It was decided that a new country, Canada, would be created and that a federal system would be adopted. Ottawa, soon to be accoutred with a brand-new Parliament Hill and the building infrastructure necessary to house a proper administration, would be the national capital. Government in Ottawa would follow the Westminster model. Victoria would remain the Queen, and the structures of the new government would be patterned after the United Kingdom. Tacked on to that model, however, would be a concept borrowed from the Americans and from New Zealand: two levels of government, each with a clear list of exclusive jurisdictions and with clear powers of taxation, would be recognized in a new act of the British Parliament.[30] The provincial governments would yield a significant degree of sovereignty but would have exclusive control over matters that directly concerned their population: property and civil rights, education and local administration. Ottawa would assume the debts of the provinces, assume the maintenance of a good part of the transportation infrastructure, and control trade and commerce, banking, and key areas of the law, such as criminal and copyright law. Ottawa would also assume responsibility for relations with Indigenous peoples as well as management of the country's external relations.

Foreign affairs was also an important concern. As the delegates debated mostly domestic topics, two dozen escaped Confederate soldiers travelled north and created a base in Canada. On October 19, they raided St. Albans, Vermont, about fifteen kilometres from the US-Canada border, robbing a bank and killing a man. The criminals were arrested a few days later, but were soon released because Canada, as a neutral country, could not extradite them to the United States. For many people, the St. Albans raid showed how weak Canada was in its response. It was subject to British diplomatic rules and appeared feckless by tacitly helping soldiers from the Deep South, which went against the wishes of the majority.[31]

The centralist argument was propounded by Macdonald, who warned that while Ottawa would be the new national capital, it would need to be strong to ensure that the country could prioritize growth and consistency of governance nationwide. Importantly, the rights of Catholics and Protestants to their schools would not change. The provinces would have jurisdiction over matters of "private or local nature" that had not been specifically given to the national Parliament. The work was also apparently executed by Macdonald. The process was efficient and methodical, and within two weeks, seventy-two resolutions had been agreed to, with no less than fifty drafted by Macdonald himself. "As it is, I have no help," he told James R. Gowan, an Ontario judge. "Not one man of the conference (except Galt in financial matters) has the slightest idea of constitution making. Whatever is good or ill in the Constitution is mine."[32]

The Parliament in Ottawa, like the one in London, would feature two houses. In the first, the number of members would be determined by a count of the population, with the assurance that Quebec's numbers would not be diminished. Ontario would start with 82 seats, while 65 would come from Quebec, 19 from Nova Scotia, and 15 from New Brunswick. Newfoundland was promised 8 seats if it joined, and Prince Edward Island would have 5 seats. The Upper House, "the Legislative Council," would be appointed by the government and have 72 members, 24 from Quebec, 24 from Ontario, 10 each from New Brunswick and Nova Scotia, and 4 from Prince Edward Island. Issues like currency, trade, and criminal law would go to Ottawa, while key issues like education and municipal management would remain provincial. Agriculture and immigration would be split between the two levels of government. Ottawa would have the right to reserve and even revoke provincial legislation, and would also nominate the Queen's representatives in the provincial capital.

## 58 Ballots and Brawls

One resolution showed a general agreement that other colonies, such as Newfoundland, British Columbia, and even the North-West Territories, could eventually join Canada. Each province would similarly have a bicameral system, though Ontario ultimately decided to adopt a unicameral system.

Thus it was that in less than sixty days, the colonies of New Brunswick, Nova Scotia, and the United Province of Canada agreed in principle to a merger. Many Maritimers were still unsure: many wanted explicit – constitutional – guarantees on a host of issues, not least regarding the building of the Intercolonial Railway. Macdonald refused, and Tilley was deeply unhappy: "No delegate from this Province will consent to Union unless we have this guarantee ... all will be lost without this," he predicted a few months later.[33]

### The Indispensable Flywheels

The delegates parted company on October 24 with a general feeling of satisfaction. Macdonald and Cartier felt that much had been accomplished, as did Tupper and Tilley. Immeasurable amounts of energy had been expended by the turning wheels of the Confederation idea. Its success would now depend on the flywheels of politics: those men who had reserves of energy necessary to keep the momentum going when things seemed lost.

The general reaction to the seventy-two resolutions was slow in coming as people deepened their understanding of the implications of each. Events to discuss the Quebec Conference were held in Montreal, Ottawa, Toronto, and Niagara-on-the-Lake. As winter slowly draped the colonies, events organized abroad shocked the population and new threats to the *entente* emerged.

The historian C.P. Stacey observed that the fall of 1864 was hardly a time of elation but rather one of the "darkest moments" of the period, again drawing attention to the tensions that tore Catholics and Protestants apart. On Guy Fawkes Day (November 5), a band of armed hoodlums marched down the streets of Toronto, throwing a real scare into the Catholic population.[34] Concerns about the ongoing civil war in the United States also dampened optimism. In January 1865, George Brown pessimistically listed the obstacles facing the Confederation project:

> The civil war ... in the neighbouring republic; the possibility of war between Great Britain and the United States; the threatened repeal of the Reciprocity Treaty; the threatened abolition of the American bonding system for goods in transit to and from these provinces; the unsettled position of the Hudson's Bay Company; and the changed feeling of England as to the relation of great colonies to the parent state; – all combine at this moment to arrest earnest attention to the gravity of the situation and unite us all in one vigorous effort to meet the emergency like men.[35]

The malaise was real. The Civil War, which was clearly in its last months as the Union Army marched decisively south, continued to alarm. The *New York Herald*'s pleas for the full annexation of Canada caught the attention of many. On February 11, 1865, it published a thirteen-column article demanding that the army move north to prevent attacks like the one on St. Albans. In Nova Scotia, discomfort was expressed when the Halifax *Morning Chronicle* started publishing a series of articles in January 1865 denouncing the idea of Confederation. Named the *Botheration Letters,* they were written by Joseph Howe, who had to use a pseudonym as he sat on the British Empire's Fisheries Commission and knew that his views went against the wishes of London.

The business class was also tense. A few months later, as Brown predicted, the US government formally ended the reciprocity agreement it had struck with Great Britain in 1854, leaving Canada in the lurch as there was no indication that the Americans were keen on renewing negotiations. "I was a good deal in the United States during 1866," remembered Richard Cartwright, a Conservative from Kingston at the time, "and I found their temper exceedingly bitter" towards Great Britain.[36] Canada had done well under the old arrangements. Americans had been willing to pay good prices for Canadian harvests and farm animals such as cattle, horses, and sheep. Manufactured products were mostly subjected to some sort of tariff (tariffs were the main source of revenue for governments in those days), and local industrialists felt some protection. Canada had imposed some tariffs on soap, starch and clothing, and some textiles in 1858, and iron in 1859.[37] For Brown, this became personal. Macdonald organized a delegation to Washington, DC, in an attempt to rekindle interest in a reciprocal trade deal, but did not include Brown. The *Globe*'s editor thus resigned from the government in December 1865, an important turning point in his career.[38]

Business proponents organized in response to the US policy. They created the Manufacturers Association for Upper Canada in Toronto and the Tariff Reform and Industrial Association in Montreal, both of which were formalized in 1866. The Industrial and Manufacturers Association of Nova Scotia was created in 1866, but was never particularly vigorous. The colonial governments all imposed a new tariff to protect agricultural products, although duties on most goods were reduced from 20 to 15 percent.[39] Those policies were attractive to many Maritimers so as to protect their own agricultural sector and reduce the cost of living. On this all the British colonies in North America appeared to be united. They wanted low tariff walls and trade agreements that would specify conditions and give them the ability to strike a balance between revenue generation through tariffs and protection of domestic industry.

Tariff protection lent support to the idea of Confederation. The other pillar of support came from the British government. Its message was that the colonies in North America had the assets and abilities to look after themselves, and that the time had come to cut the umbilical cord to London. It was not a popular message, particularly in the Maritimes, which were concerned that the military might of the Union Army could be directed towards British territory. Despite Macdonald's reassurances, there was a fear that cutting the link to London would allow the colonies to drift into the cultural and political morass of the United States. The threat from south of the border was not imminent but it was real, and the conviction that the US cultural magnet could have a corrosive effect on British Loyalists over time continued to win hearts and minds. Only a solid political entity that could legitimately lay claim to territory could enable a resistance. The core conviction of Loyalist ideology – that American republicanism had to be fled – could be realized only by the creation of a strong national government.[40]

In Quebec, of course, opinions were divided. *La Minerve*, the *Bleu* newspaper based in Montreal, argued that if Confederation would safeguard French Canada's special interests, its religion, and its mores, it was worth giving it a chance.[41] Church leaders probably thought the same thing, but kept relatively quiet on the subject. On the other hand, there was palpable opposition to the Quebec Conference idea, and the first anti-Confederation meeting took place at the Institut Canadien-français de Montréal on February 1, 1865.[42] The Legislative Council spoke on the issue three weeks later, on February 20, 1865, and declared itself massively in favour of Confederation. The debate in the Legislative Assembly consumed many more hours. Macdonald, of course, spoke enthusiastically in favour of the resolution, conceding that giving powers to a provincial level of government was not his favourite option, but that the deal hammered out in Quebec City was still a valuable and practical one. Thomas D'Arcy McGee also spoke eloquently and emphasized the American appetite for territory: "They coveted Florida, and seized it; they coveted Louisiana, and they purchased it; they coveted Texas, and stole it; and then they picked a quarrel with Mexico which ended by their getting California." McGee then considered the position of British North America:

62   *Ballots and Brawls*

The acquisition of Canada was the first ambition of the American Confederacy, and never ceased to be so, when her troops were a handful and her navy scarce a squadron. Is it likely to be stopped now, when she counts her guns afloat by the thousand and her troops by hundreds of thousands? ... Only vigorous and timely preparation would protect British North America from the horrors of a war such as the world has never seen.[43]

George-Étienne Cartier gave a most eloquent defence of the concept of the "new nationality" that seemed at once ambitious and naive:

Objection had been taken to the scheme now under consideration, because of the words "new nationality." Now, when we were united together, if union were attained, we would form a political nationality with which neither the national origin, nor the religion of any individual, would interfere. It was lamented by some that we had this diversity of races, and hopes were expressed that this distinctive feature would cease. The idea of unity of races was utopian – it was impossible. Distinctions of this kind would always exist. Dissimilarity, in fact, appeared to be the order of the physical world and of the moral world, as well as of the political world. But with regard to the objection based on this fact, to the effect that a great nation could not be formed because Lower Canada was in great part French and Catholic, and Upper Canada was British and Protestant, and the Lower Provinces were mixed, it was futile and worthless in the extreme.[44]

Cartier was not naive. By "nationality" he did not mean "nation." He did not hope to create an identifying amalgam of the various peoples who lived across British North America, but did aspire to a new understanding of comradeship among them, and a desire

The Battlefield, the Wheels, the Flies, and the Flywheels 63

to build something new. It was not an idea of a nation based on bloodlines or blood ties, but one based on common aspirations.

On March 11, the Legislative Assembly proceeded to a vote. Ninety-one MPs voted in favour of the Quebec resolutions, 33 against. In Canada East, 37 MPs favoured it, 25 were against. Among French Canadian legislators, the vote was 26 in favour, 22 against. All the *Rouges* voted *contra*, but even Cartier had some trouble with his troops: four *Bleus* voted against it, as did 11 *"violets,"* stubborn MPs with independent streaks. Most of those opposed represented Montreal ridings or were situated along the American border. The fear in Quebec was palpable: what Macdonald and Cartier were proposing was a legislative union that guaranteed a path to assimilation – Confederation was only a disguise.[45] The vote was won, but it was clear that Macdonald and Cartier still had to win hearts and minds as well. The legislature passed the motion. A few weeks later, two days after the surrender of General Robert E. Lee at Appomattox Court House, Macdonald wrote to Brown, worried that the United States would turn its sights on Canada as it was "flushed with success."[46]

The vote in Canada, taken five months after the Quebec Conference, proved to be the only beacon of hope. Prince Edward Island announced that it would not pursue the idea of Confederation, and Newfoundland declared that it was not interested either. Far more daring, Leonard Tilley had called for an election on the issue, and on March 6, 1865, his Liberals were officially announced as having been defeated in New Brunswick (more about this in Chapter 2).

The loss in New Brunswick completely froze Nova Scotia's enthusiasm also. Tupper introduced a motion in the Nova Scotia House of Assembly on March 22 renewing support for a strictly Maritime union. Then on April 10, he declared that he would not introduce a motion in favour of Confederation for fear of meeting the same fate as Tilley. The idea of a union, of a country that could span in short order the entire continent, the idea that seemed so promising at the end of October 1864, appeared to have been defeated within five months.

Even Antoine-Aimé Dorion was prompted to declare that the Quebec City accord had been "killed." But the Canadians were not so easily conquered. Shaken by the loss of momentum, Macdonald told Tupper that "there is nothing left for us but the bold game":[47] the government would need to broaden its support among those who were likely to agree with it. That meant London and, surprisingly to some, Catholics. On March 24, the Canadian government petitioned the British government for a meeting with four members of the cabinet to discuss "the means whereby [Confederation] can be most speedily effected and the "existing critical state of affairs by which Canada is most seriously affected"; the cost-sharing agreements that would fund the defence of Canada "in the event of war with the United States"; the re-establishment of a reciprocity treaty with the Americans; the settling of the North-West Territory; and the claims made by the Hudson's Bay Company.[48] A delegation was formed to go to London. The conviction was that the British government had the tools necessary to convince the Maritime colonies, and that while time was of the essence, time could also heal "misunderstandings."

The Canadians made their case. On June 24, London sent a message to all the governments in the Maritimes. It ordered the colonies to do everything necessary "so that all British North American colonies should agree to unite in one government." Premier Albert J. Smith himself was in London in July and personally told Edward Cardwell, the colonial secretary, that the British government was "not in a position to know what was for the benefit of New Brunswick, or what suited the province."[49] He issued a harsh rebuke (drafted in part by Timothy Anglin) rejecting the notion that London could be so involved in North American matters.

The talks in London in the wake of the Maritime chill and the assassination of President Abraham Lincoln were productive and in some ways encouraging, but hardly provided a guarantee that the future of Confederation was secure. All the same, there were encouraging signs for the business class. In July 1865, the Detroit Boards of Trade Convention was held and six hundred delegates attended, including over fifty from British North America. There was a lot of talk about annexation, but it was Joseph Howe, always the free-trader, who changed minds with a remarkable speech that was strongly applauded. Instead of annexation, a pro-reciprocity resolution was adopted.[50]

Over the next year, the legislatures in New Brunswick and Nova Scotia contemplated what had been agreed to at Quebec. New Brunswick's politics were quickly shaken by a rejection of Confederation, but the response in Nova Scotia was quieter. Confederation was touted as the elixir that could cure many ills. It was an agreement designed to incentivize communities to live together under a set of rules that were specific but negotiable. Macdonald later called it matrimony – not an inaccurate description. The project was a radical departure in governance and had the potential to change economies and the sense of belonging for each citizen. It had many opponents and far more numerous skeptics. In Canada East (Quebec), many francophone Catholics were weary. Creating a national government in which English-speaking Protestants would govern spending and legislate on vast areas of jurisdiction without any awareness of the French Catholic root was unthinkable. A plea titled "*Représentation de la minorité parlementaire du Bas-Canada à Lord Carnarvon, secrétaire des colonies, au sujet de la Confédération projetée des provinces de l'Amérique britannique*" was sent to London, arguing that voters had not been consulted, but to no avail. In the Maritimes, the idea of a Maritime union similar to what had been tried in the United Province of Canada slowly – and only slowly – made its way.

## Ballots and Brawls

The people of Prince Edward Island were not interested in linking their fortunes with either of the more populous Nova Scotia or New Brunswick. In Newfoundland, the idea was hardly worth even discussing.

The next step was to pursue consultations with London to hammer out the Quebec entente into a constitutional document.

### The End of the Beginning:
### The London Conference of December 1866

On November 7, 1866, Macdonald, along with Cartier, Galt, Langevin and his assistant Hewitt Bernard, and a few others boarded a ship in New York City that would return them to London, where the Nova Scotia and New Brunswick delegations had been waiting for months. The first meeting took place on December 4, 1866, at the Westminster Palace Hotel, the same place that had been used in the spring of 1865. Macdonald was nominated as chairman of the conference by Charles Tupper, who was seconded by Tilley. The men agreed that the task at hand was to codify the Quebec Resolutions, which had been hammered out two years earlier. Key issues were resolved one by one. Tilley finally succeeded on a key demand: the commitment to build the Intercolonial Railway was constitutionalized in section 145 of the *British North America Act.* (It was repealed in 1893 when the project was completed.) Macdonald was easily the most authoritative mind of all the negotiators, and it was he who took the lead in negotiating final arrangements with the Gladstone government. He spent time in mid-December with Lord Carnarvon, the secretary responsible for the colonies, at Highclere Castle, Carnarvon's home. On Christmas Day, Macdonald confirmed in a letter to Carnarvon that the Canadians and Maritimers had unanimously agreed to a set of resolutions.[51]

In London, Galt realized that British businessmen had turned against the idea that the British government owed anything more to Canada. "I cannot shut my eyes to the fact that they want to get rid of us," he told his wife. "They have a servile fear of the United States and would rather give us up than defend us, or incur the risk of war with that country." He confided that he was in doubt as to whether Confederation could hold because the lure of annexation to the American economic engine was so strong. He also indicated that Macdonald was "rapidly feeling" as he was. The fear of a repeat of the War of 1812 was genuine.[52]

That said, London wasn't all drudgery and work. Macdonald went to Paris for two days, accompanied by Langevin, Cartier, and William McDougall. The purpose of their junket was serious: to investigate the validity of the Hudson's Bay Company's claim that it had legal right to Rupert's Land. After poring over ancient maps, consulting a few documents in the Archives nationales, and speaking to a few officials, they quickly concluded that the company "were usurpers, trespassers, as far as this interior tract of country is concerned."[53] They returned convinced that the acquisition of Rupert's Land was nothing more than a matter of cash and process. Rarely has a trip to Paris had such consequences. Dodging the broken streets and sidewalks of the French capital, torn up by the Baron de Haussmann's radical redesign of the city (not least because of the grand exhibition that was to take place in the summer of 1867), the men shed any doubt that their Canada could reach the shores of the Pacific.

Perhaps more relaxed, and perhaps increasingly aware that the challenges of governing a country with an appetite for territory might be a lonely, demanding affair, Macdonald cast eyes on the young sister of his dependable assistant, Hewitt. Her name was Agnes, and her family roots on her mother's side were deeply Scottish. Macdonald had first met her in Quebec City in 1860, as Agnes (and her mother) were dependent on Hewitt and followed him as the capital changed. He had seen her again many times, in Ottawa and in Toronto, but something about seeing her in London scrambled his mind. She was thirty-one years old and responded

68 *Ballots and Brawls*

to Macdonald's interest. Within days, Macdonald proposed, Agnes accepted, and they were married on February 16, 1867, at St. George's Church in Hanover Square, with much of the Canadian delegation in attendance.

Macdonald's frantic activity since 1864 made him look like his hair was on fire. It actually ignited during his stay in London, just after he proposed to Agnes and before New Year's Day, after an exhausting day of negotiations with the British. To relax a little before sleep, he had grabbed some newspapers to read. He fell asleep, of course, only to be awakened by the smell of his bed, pillows, and curtains burning. Startled and in a panic, he threw everything to the floor, showering every feather he could find onto the fire. He woke Cartier in the next room, Galt in the other, and together they found the buckets needed to douse the flames. "I would have been burnt to death, as it was my escape was miraculous," Macdonald told his sister. In fact, he suffered serious burns to his back, scalp, forehead, and hands. A doctor visited him for three days to bandage his injuries, prescribing rest for a week and prohibiting him from reading in bed.

Well, that would never work.[54] The pressure on all delegates to make a success of London and emerge with an agreement was intense. The window was closing, and the threat of opposition was always lurking. George Brown wrote to his friend Luther Holton on January 17, 1867, that while Macdonald could hold off to get better terms from London or from the potential provinces, he was not likely to let the opportunity pass. Most people, Brown thought, "consider it now or never." "Cartier perfectly understands his position, and the sooner confederation comes the better," he told Holton. "Of course, you in Lower Canada have a difficult card to play; but those who settle this question, it appears to me, are playing your game for you." Ontario was still strongly pro-Confederation, in Brown's view, and Cartier seemed to have such control over Quebec that his views were likely to carry the province.[55] From Nova Scotia, Joseph Howe

The London Conference,
December 1866 to March 1867, at the Westminster Palace Hotel
Library and Archives Canada, Acc. 1961-39-1

and Premier William Annand issued an impassioned brief to the Earl of Carnarvon (and to both Houses of Parliament), pleading for the proposed bill to be dramatically altered.[56]

While the London Conference crunched resolutions and pondered constitutional formulations, the United States and Russia finally closed the deal on the former's purchase of Alaska for $7.2 million. Strengthened by the deal, Secretary of State William Seward turned to Sir Frederick Bruce, the British minister in Washington, to see whether London would be ready to cede land to compensate the United States for the losses caused by attacks of the Confederate Navy, notably by one of its most destructive ships, the *Alabama*. In the middle of winter, Seward's first thought was apparently of the Bahamas, but then he raised the possibility of taking British Columbia, especially now that the deal for Alaska was being sealed. Alarmed, the BC legislature passed a motion declaring its interest in joining Canada. The idea grabbed the public's attention in the spring of 1867 and generated much commentary in the press.

Given the context and the willingness shown by British North Americans to come together, British parliamentarians were enthusiastic supporters of the Quebec Resolutions and John Stuart Mill, Earl Russell (the expert on the British constitution among the Lords), and Prime Minister Gladstone had supported the British North America Act. It was given royal assent on March 29, the day before the Alaska purchase was signed by President Andrew Johnson. Queen Victoria declared that Canada would see its first day on July 1. Joseph Howe, who had travelled to London to lobby against Confederation, had no choice but to accept the verdict. Still, he could not hide his disappointment that Parliament had not invited the dissenters to appear before it. Nova Scotia had been treated by Westminster with "lazy contempt," and Howe was in the mood to mete out punishment to "the rascals who have sold the country" and who had prompted Britain to relinquish her place in North America.[57]

### The First Dominion Day, July 1, 1867

By some estimates, up to twenty thousand people made their way to Parliament Hill that morning – an entirely suspect figure as it was substantially more than Ottawa's entire population.[58] Lord Monck was sworn in as Canada's Governor General. He in turn announced that Cartier, Galt, Tupper, Tilley, McDougall, and William Howland were henceforth to be known as Companions of the Order of the Bath, the fourth most senior of the British orders of chivalry. Monck then declared that John A. Macdonald would henceforth be known as a Knight Commander of the Order of the Bath. "John A." became "Sir John A." around noon on July 1.

Macdonald pretended it was a surprise (he had actually learned of it only that morning, and promptly informed Agnes that she would henceforth be known as "Lady Macdonald"). Though it will never be known for sure how cold the chill that descended on cabinet really was, people immediately noted the distinction between the seven men. Cartier and Galt were hurt – Tupper, among many others, remembered Cartier as "deeply offended"[59] – and angry. Cartier actually refused the honour, though the men stayed on their best behaviour that day (Monck realized his error and both Cartier and Galt were given knighthoods later that summer in recognition of their tireless efforts to bring about Confederation). Tilley probably deserved it more given his efforts since 1864 but, modest to a fault, was happy to be remembered by the Governor General's first gift, and continued to serve loyally for another twenty-six years. He was made Knight of the Order of St. Michael and St. George in 1879.

But decorations didn't seem to matter: the ceremony carried on and the new government inspected its troops. Macdonald's men then retreated to the East Block and were sworn in to their respective offices. Four men were sworn in as Lieutenant-Governors of the new provinces of Ontario, Quebec, New Brunswick, and Nova Scotia. It was now time to start governing, to "set the coach in motion," as Lord Monck put it. Canada was on holiday, and as fireworks were set off that evening, some started thinking about democracy: the new government needed the legitimacy of the people, and elections were coming up.

Macdonald's first cabinet ensured that every province was well represented. The prime minister also saw to it that some minorities could be seen around the table. Edward Kenny, for instance, had a double duty: he represented Nova Scotia and Irish Catholics across Canada (as a one-time mayor of Halifax, he could also be seen as representing municipalities). Galt represented Anglo-Protestant Quebecers and the business community. No thought was given to representing Acadians, and the French minority in Ontario was still much too small to warrant consideration. The most important feature of Macdonald's cabinet was its hybrid nature: seven of the

72  *Ballots and Brawls*

ministers were Macdonald Conservatives while six were Reformers/ Liberals (who went by either name). It was a cabinet of rivals, but unified around the cause of legitimizing the Confederation project.

It was also a large cabinet, probably larger than many might have expected, but Macdonald felt justified in following the British practice: at the time, Lord Derby (Edward Smith-Stanley), the British prime minister, counted seventeen men around the famous cabinet table at 10 Downing Street. Macdonald's cabinet consisted of the following:

- Agriculture: Senator Jean-Charles Chapais, 55, Merchant, Quebec, Catholic
- Customs: S. Leonard Tilley, 48, Pharmacist, New Brunswick, Protestant, Liberal
- Finance: Alexander Tilloch Galt, 50, Quebec, Protestant
- Inland Revenue: William Pearce Howland, 56, Businessman, Ontario, Protestant, Liberal
- Justice and Attorney General: Sir John A. Macdonald, 52, Lawyer, Ontario, Anglican
- Marine and Fisheries: Senator Peter Mitchell, 42, Lawyer, New Brunswick, Methodist, Liberal
- Militia and Defence: Sir George Étienne Cartier, 58, Lawyer, Quebec, Catholic
- Postmaster General: Senator Alexander Campbell, 50, Lawyer, Ontario, Protestant
- President of the Privy Council: Fergusson Blair, 52, Lawyer, Ontario, Methodist, Liberal
- Public Works: William McDougall, 45, Lawyer, Ontario, Protestant, Liberal
- Receiver General: Senator Edward Kenny, 67, Businessman/ Banker, Nova Scotia, Catholic
- Secretary of State of Canada: Hector Louis Langevin, 40, Editor/ Lawyer, Quebec, Catholic

- Secretary of State for Provinces: Adams G. Archibald, 53, Lawyer, Nova Scotia, Protestant, Liberal

With an average age of just over fifty-one, it was also a cabinet of experienced men. Edward Kenny, sixty-seven, was the eldest by far; Hector Langevin was the youngest at age forty. Four of the thirteen were Catholic (far less representative than it could have been). Four – almost a quarter – were senators, one from each province. Though Ontario constituted half the population of Canada, only five of the thirteen ministers came from that province, including the prime minister. Macdonald recruited three Liberal Party members from that province – Brown's former colleagues who had supported his quest for Confederation: McDougall, Howland, and Blair. McDougall was a Toronto lawyer, a pillar of the Clear Grit movement that had long demanded universal male suffrage, representation by population, inexpensive government, free trade with the United States, and the abolition of clergy reserves. He held the distinction of probably being the only Canadian to have heard Abraham Lincoln deliver his Gettysburg Address in person in 1863.

Howland, born in the United States, had served as minister of finance, receiver general, and postmaster general in the United Province of Canada.[60] Macdonald was fond of him, privately describing him as an "upright, honourable and kind-hearted [a] man as one could ever meet."[61] The third Liberal was Adam Fergusson Blair, like Macdonald a Scot born in 1815 and a lawyer from Canada West with deep political experience. Alexander Campbell, the former dean of the Faculty of Law at Queen's University, a thorough Conservative and very close friend of Macdonald, rounded out the Ontario component of cabinet.[62]

The presence of the three "traitors" outraged the Liberals. The idea that the coalition that had been created to give Confederation some momentum from 1864 to 1867 would continue after July 1 was considered nothing short of high treason.

Quebec was represented by Cartier, Langevin, Jean-Charles Chapais (a very successful farmer and merchant and former mayor of St-Denis-de-La-Bouteillerie),[63] and Galt, the director of the British American Land Company and of the St. Lawrence and Atlantic Railway. All of them were *Bleus,* distinguished in business as well as political management. The two New Brunswick representatives were also accomplished administrators. Tilley had long been a leading businessman and railway promoter in addition to defending Confederation. He, in turn, convinced Macdonald to include Peter Mitchell, the New Brunswick premier, in cabinet. Since 1864, Mitchell had been a chief proponent of Confederation. Trained as a lawyer, he was a prosperous lumberman and shipbuilder from Miramichi. He had a reputation as an able administrator; that was enough for Macdonald, who named him to the Senate.[64] Nova Scotia brought a lot less administrative talent to the table. It was represented by Adams Archibald and Senator Edward Kenny.

The real surprise was the absence of two of Macdonald's best political friends: Charles Tupper of Cumberland County, Nova Scotia, and Thomas D'Arcy McGee from Montreal, who had served in cabinet since 1863. The situation had stressed Macdonald to the limit and had been resolved by Tupper, who pleaded with McGee: "The union of the provinces is going to end in a fiasco unless we give way. We are the only two men who can avert that calamity." McGee agreed, and Macdonald was speechless for once. "What are you going to do, Tupper?" he asked. Tupper responded that he was content to simply run for a seat, as was McGee.[65] Tupper would eventually find his place in cabinet. McGee, who would have represented the Irish Catholic vote (and, arguably, the vote of men who enjoyed alcohol immensely), had to wait.

The new Canada that was unveiled in Ottawa was the product of the wheels that had set the project in motion and the flies who had encouraged it along the way or had tried to stop its progression.

The Battlefield, the Wheels, the Flies, and the Flywheels   75

It overcame many obstacles because the framers of the new constitutional deal somehow found the flywheels necessary to maintain the project's energy even as the wheels were sometimes stuck in the mud. The first election under what the *Montreal Herald* called "our present mongrel constitution, which is neither that of Great Britain nor that of the United States; but a contradictory mixture of both sorts" would take place within three months after the creation of a new Canada.[66]

Macdonald was confident of a win. Opinion was in his favour, he thought. The *Globe* could not agree. The Liberal organ was optimistic of a victory, calculating that Reformers might reach 80 to 85 seats, with at least 65 in Ontario and 20 in Quebec. New Brunswick's Liberal *Morning Freeman* figured that all the Reformers would need were 11 seats in New Brunswick and 16 seats in Nova Scotia to form a government in Ottawa. The Conservative *La Minerve*, for its part, bullishly predicted that the Macdonald coalition would get 123 seats to the opposition's 58, a crushing majority of 65 seats.[67]

# 2

# The Third Liberal Showdown
# in New Brunswick

**DOMINION DAY IN** New Brunswick was a rather sober affair. In the old capital of Fredericton, now a new provincial capital with a population of about six thousand, the government had arranged precious little in terms of celebrations. Barracks Square filled up quickly, with bunting outlining its perimeter. A sign proclaimed: "To-day Union makes a Dominion of a Province, Enlarges our Country, Dignifies our Manhood, Expands our Sympathy, Links us with thirty-five hundred thousand fellow subjects in our own land, and fifty millions human beings north of Panama. God save the Queen." All sorts of people filled the streets in anticipation of seeing the Calithumpians, the local theatre troupe, put on a show, but nothing materialized. It was a day off, so many people decided to take excursions to the countryside that morning, and soon the trains were running at capacity for various return trips.

Saint John, with a population of about forty thousand, was roughly comparable to Quebec City and Toronto (fifty thousand) in 1867. The first national holiday was greeted there with some anticipation. In the early dawn, the economic and intellectual capital of the province offered a gun salute by the men of Fleming and Humbert's Foundry. The local *Empress* announced that it would depart at 8 a.m. for a goodwill trip across the Bay of Fundy to visit Annapolis Royal and Digby in the neighbouring province of Nova Scotia. At 11 a.m., the 15th Regiment put one of its drills on display. By the time the military was done, the partying was over. The afternoon was quiet, stores remained closed, and, in the mocking words of one reporter, "people in their holiday attire walked listlessly about the streets looking in vain for some means of amusement, and admiring the foresight of the Government which was so kind as to give them a holiday without providing any means whatever of enjoying it."[1] The mood was altogether different in the eastern part of town, where much of the Irish had settled into poverty. There, fights broke out and flags were flown at half-mast.

A Dr. Livingstone made the news in Saint John and across the province when he flew his Union Jack at half-mast. It was not clear what he was communicating, but two toughs asked him to either raise the flag or remove it. Livingstone refused to do anything. The flag was cut down moments later and Livingstone demanded that the interlopers and two others be arrested. Two weeks later, the judge was not sure what to do. He declared that the law was "arbitrary" in this case, and decided against empanelling a jury. He noted that July 1 had been declared a holiday and that "her Majesty's 'loving subjects' were called on to so observe the day." He heard from two eyewitnesses and determined that none of the accused men were guilty.[2]

Timothy Anglin's *Morning Freeman* called Dominion Day "an insolent party challenge."[3] The day was botched, in his view, and he devoted more column inches to an account originally published in the *Boston Journal* of the coronation of Franz Joseph as king of the Hungarians. Anglin certainly had a way with words. He published a mock obituary notice a week before Dominion Day that announced: "Died, – at her late residence in the City of Fredericton, on the 20th day of May last, from the effects of an accident which she received in April, 1866, and which she bore with a patient resignation to the will of Providence, the Province of New Brunswick, in the 83rd year of her age."[4]

Anglin was seeking a definition for what "opposition" might mean in this contest. He had been a Liberal all his life, but had broken ranks with colleagues who had switched sides and supported Macdonald and the Canadians on the road to Confederation. He would continue that opposition, and perhaps convince himself to accept the new federal structure. It was "not easy to see what to do with Confederation," he wrote, but offered that "the forging of this link is not yet quite finished."[5] In this fight, the Conservatives had little to say, as the most vocal belligerents on both sides seemed to be Liberals or former Liberals. In New Brunswick, the election of 1867 would take on the appearance of a Liberal Party civil war.

It is important to underscore that the 1867 election in New Brunswick would be the third in thirty months. The arguments for and against Confederation had been articulated and hashed out in March 1865 and again in May 1866. Shaped by those trying experiences, the political environment was considerably different from that in the other provinces.

### The March 1865 Election

Leonard Tilley, the Liberal prime minister of New Brunswick who had attended both the Charlottetown and Quebec Conferences, was fully committed to a broad union of colonies in British North America. Perhaps it was even more meaningful: as his biographer put it, "Confederation had entered his soul."[6] Returning home from the Quebec Conference, however, Tilley was greeted with harsh criticism and immediately informed his friend Alexander Galt that he was perceiving a "strong current rising against Federation."[7] Within weeks, Albert J. Smith, Tilley's attorney general, declared his opposition to the Quebec Resolutions and triggered a movement of opposition. An Anti-Confederation Party quickly grew around him, essentially a bipartisan coalition drawn from both the

*The Third Liberal Showdown in New Brunswick*  79

Conservative and the Liberal Parties. People as varied as Timothy Anglin, the fiery Irish Catholic editor of the Saint John *Morning Freeman*, and Joseph Coram, a prominent Orangeman who had once provoked a riot in Saint John, gathered around Smith. Piqued by the audacity of his former colleagues, Tilley called an election at the end of January 1865, barely three months after returning from Quebec City. He wrote to Governor Arthur Hamilton-Gordon that he had "many prejudices to overcome" and that "chances of success would have been increased by adhering to our original design."[8]

Tilley was a bold Liberal, but was closer to Macdonald in perceiving the political and cultural necessity of maintaining links with Great Britain.[9] At the Quebec Conference, his suggestion that the constitution be read "with a view to the perpetuation of our connection with the Mother country so far as our circumstances will permit" struck the right compromise. He rallied support for the notion that the Canadian government would assume the debts of the provinces. He especially liked the idea of promoting railways, again much like Macdonald and the Canadians; in fact he was categorical on this issue: "We won't have this union unless you give us the railway."[10]

Tilley had made two key contributions to the Quebec Conference. First, he had basically killed off the idea of Maritime union. Second, he had promoted confederation with Canada. Tilley was described as "always clear, cogent and to the point" by the *Morning Telegraph* when he returned from the Quebec Conference. He had all the talents of a successful businessman. He chose his objectives well, worked hard, and communicated his plans effectively. The historian P.B. Waite, always perceptive in describing characters, saw him as "clever," with the foxlike features of being "quick, resourceful, persistent and at times, courageous."[11] A contemporary noted that he possessed "that essential knowledge for a good party leader, the knowledge of where and when, *to stop.*"[12]

80    *Ballots and Brawls*

There was a great deal of pressure on Tilley to put the issue of Confederation to a legislative vote, but, concerned about internal party strife, he leaned more towards calling for an election. He and his government had been chosen after the election of 1861, and a new mandate was inevitable. There is evidence that Lieutenant-Governor Hamilton-Gordon also put pressure on Tilley to call an election, because he had changed his mind and thought Confederation would be ruinous for the province. Tilley had to call an election by June 1865 anyway, and Hamilton-Gordon was inclined to think that Tilley needed a new mandate to pursue Confederation.

Macdonald, on the other hand, found Tilley's gambit exasperating and "unstatesmanlike."[13] He would have preferred that a resolution be simply put to the legislature – just as in the Province of Canada. Macdonald reminded Tilley years later that "it was agreed at Quebec that the Resolutions then agreed to would be submitted by the several Govts to their respective legislatures at the next Session."[14] According to his biographer, Tilley "had a totally unprepared and hostile public on his hands, and one of the main obstacles to overcome was the dislike and distrust of a grasping Canada. Long before any of the other public leaders, Tilley realized that Confederation required an extensive publicity campaign to overcome prejudices and false information. Tact, patience, time and effort were all required."[15]

Undeterred, Tilley launched an electoral campaign on January 21, 1865. Voting started on February 28 and ended almost three weeks later, on March 18. Albert J. Smith, now named the opposition leader, continued his opposition to Confederation, raging against the plan that had been dreamt up by "the oily brains of Canadian politicians"[16] and that would guarantee high taxes, including direct taxation.[17] Anglin, the Catholic editor of the *Morning Freeman,* was opposed to Confederation. Tilley felt increasingly alienated from Catholics. He consulted Bishop Sweeney of Saint John, who feared the Orange wave emanating from Canada West.

The Third Liberal Showdown in New Brunswick    81

For dissenters like Smith and Anglin, and the influential like George L. Hatheway (Tilley's former minister of public works), the Quebec accord offered little to New Brunswick except more taxation to fund projects that would mostly be pursued in Canada. They were unimpressed by promises of the Intercolonial Railway or of reliable federal subsidies. There was a twist of the political knife in their ruminations. The people of New Brunswick would "have to pay also for making a highway – a railroad – between Canada and the Pacific, a project on which old George Brown has breakfasted, dined, and supped for the last twenty years," commented the *Fredericton Headquarter*.[18] The Liberals of New Brunswick were far more interested in developing North-South relations. J.W. Cudlip, a Saint John merchant, member of the legislature, and diehard "anti," expressed the view of the commercial interests of Saint John as he emphasized the priority of connecting with the Americans. "It would then give the people who travelled and who had an eye to our resources, an inducement to come in and develop them," he argued. The economic momentum, in his view, had accelerated in that direction, and he proclaimed himself an annexationist.[19] Even the defence argument had grave weaknesses, according to the New Brunswick critics. None of the colonies had bulked up their militias because they did not have the means. Threats – outside of the United States – were non-existent. Was Ontario going to come to the defence of Quebec or New Brunswick? Should Nova Scotians rush to the defence of Ontario? Great Britain – the dominant sea power of the time, was likely to offer the best guarantee of defence anyway, especially for the Maritime provinces. It went beyond mere economic measures, of course. New Brunswick would lose its autonomy, and for many in the colony that was far too much to ask.[20]

Tilley appealed to Macdonald for more concrete assurances on the railway, an issue that for him would likely win over many friends to the cause of Confederation. He went further, demanding that the commitment be written into the constitution. "The delegates from the Lower Provinces could never have consented to the union on any other terms," he assured the premier of the United Province of Canada. "Now I can assure you that no delegate from this Province will consent to union unless we have this granted. And we will certainly fail in all our elections unless I have word ... saying that this security will be given us. All will be lost without this; as it is, great alarm and anxiety has been created."[21]

Macdonald could not yet commit, Tilley had no convincing answers, and the result was a disaster for the cause of Confederation. Both Tilley and his party were defeated in early March by a combination of Liberals, Conservatives, and Catholics that took thirty-five of the forty-one seats in the Legislative Assembly. On March 27, 1865, an anti-Confederation government was formed by Albert J. Smith. Prominent among its members were Anglin and Hatheway. The new government, bolstered by a large majority in the legislature, seemed in a strong position. None of the important men of the pro-Confederation party held seats in the new assembly, although a few would continue to ably uphold the unionist point of view in the Legislative Council.

Tilley had called the election to debate Confederation, but local issues crowded out the question. To compound problems, many voters were tired of Tilley – he'd been in power too long. His anti-alcohol views, often tinged with a slight anti-Catholicism, were alienating. Tilley himself held a post-mortem. He had lost the election in part because he had acted in haste and was unprepared for the campaign. The second factor was more obvious: "the strength of political prejudice" against his government. The third was the issue of the Intercolonial Railway and its expansion into New Brunswick. The last was "the unaccountable opposition of nearly all the Roman Catholic voters."[22]

But Tilley, unshakeable as ever, never lost faith. The new government headed by Smith was deeply divided, including Irish nationalist radicals like Anglin and people who were not unconditional opponents of Confederation. More importantly, while his government had been soundly defeated, the reality was that the voters were very deeply divided. Tilley's party had garnered 15,556 votes, only 393 fewer than Smith's party, giving him and his allies all the reason for optimism that support could return to the Confederation idea. He quickly decided he could change opinion by working the networks he knew well. His ties to temperance societies were still strong and could be useful in convincing voters to support the union. He also resolved to do his best to fix his relations with Catholics.[23]

Tilley's defeat had a chilling effect. In Nova Scotia, Tupper delayed the vote and started talking again about Maritime union instead of a Canadian confederation. In Quebec City, the Macdonald government reacted coolly to the verdict in New Brunswick. Three weeks after the defeat, Macdonald opted to appeal to the British government, perhaps hoping that it could put pressure on New Brunswickers to reconsider their anti-Confederation views. The position on national defence was weak, he conceded, but he reassured a friend from Prince Edward Island: "I do not despair of carrying out our great project sooner or later."[24]

Macdonald's delegation to Whitehall included Alexander Galt, George Brown, and George-Étienne Cartier, and had the goal of defanging the newly elected New Brunswick government's opposition to Confederation. Galt stressed that Confederation was a means of continuing the British connection when he declared that a decided expression of policy on the part of the British government would have "a most marked effect on the loyal and high-spirited people of the Maritime Provinces." For his part, Macdonald was convinced that the opposition in New Brunswick was soft. By early April, he was already hearing from authoritative voices that the press was likely to change its mind if it knew the degree to which "the British government are anxious for the union," and urged that this be done before the end of May. There was an opportunity in that it was rumoured that Hamilton-Gordon, who still much preferred that a Maritime union be pursued, was to be reassigned. Tilley told Galt that pressure had to be exerted on London "to send us a man who is heartily in favour of the Union and none else."[25] Macdonald was also admonished to persuade London to appoint a new Lieutenant-Governor who could act in a "friendly and in earnest" manner in favour of Confederation and could turn the situation around, given the fluidity of views: "That is the tendency of the public mind," Macdonald was told.[26] It was not a coincidence that in June 1865, Edward Cardwell, the colonial secretary in London, communicated to all the colonial governors in the Maritimes that they had to take measures to ensure their own defence.[27]

Smith's government quickly proved incompetent and was put to the test in a first by-election later that fall in the riding of York. Charles Fisher, a former premier who still enjoyed a sterling reputation, ran against the government to great effect. Tilley demanded that Macdonald support Fisher. "Is there any chance of the friends in Canada providing half the expenditure, not to exceed five thousand dollars for their share?" he asked. York County could be won "if we can go into the field with a fair share of the needful." Macdonald passed the note to Galt: "What about the moneys?" was his inquiry.[28] The money trail has been lost to historians, but Fisher won.

Fisher wrote jubilantly to Macdonald about his victory and its impact on public opinion throughout the province, but he politely reminded Macdonald of the day of reckoning. His expenditures had been large. "We look to you," he wrote, "to help us out of the scrape, for if every dollar is not paid it will kill us at the general election. If it is met fairly, we have a plain course open for confederation." He represented the victory as the turning point in the great Confederation struggle. It had inspired Confederationists everywhere with visions of ultimate success. "Do not allow us to want now or we are all gone together," he warned.[29]

There were lessons to be learned. Clearly, money had played a role. The politicians also noted that Roman Catholics appeared to be as strongly opposed as ever. There were about six hundred Catholic voters in York County, and Fisher had despaired of winning them over. "I find them," he wrote, "still in a solid phalanx united against confederation, and I know that no argument but one from the church will reach them."[30] Macdonald worked on that line of argument, and church leaders in the colony quietly began encouraging Catholics to vote for Confederation supporters. Macdonald may also have played a hand in encouraging London to support railway construction – surely a pro-Confederation gesture – in the colony. On November 9, 1865, construction of the Western Extension of the Intercolonial Railway began at South Bay, but it stopped soon thereafter because Premier Smith had awarded the contract unilaterally and Anglin resigned from cabinet in protest. The railway corruption had disgusted him, but so did the government's performance in the by-election.

A month later, Lord Monck wrote to congratulate Macdonald and his colleagues on Fisher's election. "I think," he declared, "that this is the most important thing that has happened since the Quebec conference." Fisher's victory had reignited hopes and galvanized the Confederationists in New Brunswick as well as in Canada. Monck added a line to his letter indicating that the thinking in London had evolved considerably. He pointed to a "spring campaign," confident that the York County by-election had been "a good omen of success."[31]

The strategy became obvious as the snows melted in the late winter of 1866. Hamilton-Gordon had taken note of Fisher's win and of Anglin's departure. A window of opportunity was opening as he followed orders from London to do anything possible to support Confederation. Time was increasingly of the essence, and momentum had to be maintained especially as the political landscape kept changing. The Smith government was falling apart as resignations accumulated and various key individuals were appointed to the courts. Tilley, meanwhile, continued campaigning through the fall of 1865 and winter of 1866, and he could be persuasive. One letter to a newspaper characterized him as "crafty" and "remarkably well versed in all the petty arts of management by which a political party may be kept well in hand."[32]

The pressure from London and from Tilley's campaign in favour of Confederation was felt when Hamilton-Gordon delivered the Speech from the Throne on March 8, 1866, and indicated that the British government wanted to see New Brunswick join the new Confederation. All indications are that it was Tilley – not the government – who wrote it. A motion of no-confidence was introduced four days later and debated for well over a month. On April 10, the Smith government announced that it was resigning.

The month of March 1866 had witnessed an upheaval in the politics of New Brunswick that transformed both it and Canada. For weeks, citizens were alarmed by rumours that well-armed Fenian veterans of the American Civil War were mustering in the small northeastern communities of Maine, preparing for an attack on New Brunswick and Nova Scotia. Hamilton-Gordon added drama by calling out the militia in New Brunswick; Sir Richard Graves MacDonnell did the same in Nova Scotia. Four days after the Smith government resigned, Fenians raided Indian Island, near the St-Croix River. The US Navy dispatched a series of ships, including the powerful gunboat USS *Winooski,* near Campobello Island. The Royal Navy sent a small flotilla itself, including the eighty-one-gun double-decked steamer HMS *Duncan.* Though the scare was over in less than ten days, it had an explosive effect on the debate regarding New Brunswick and Confederation. Tilley used the crisis to his advantage, denouncing the Smith government for its total paralysis.

The Third Liberal Showdown in New Brunswick   87

On April 16, Hamilton-Gordon provoked a coup of sorts. Using the Fenian threat as a pretext, he asked the opposition – Tilley, Mitchell, and Fisher – to assume direction of the government. He then prorogued the Legislative Assembly. Anglin, for one, was caught off-guard and in disbelief. He vigorously denied that the Fenian threat was serious and argued that it was "insulting" to argue that the colony could not defend itself against the "mad and reckless" Fenians, who were nothing but an "unorganized rabble."[33] He grew increasingly strident in its attacks on the governor. "I will skin him as I never yet skinned a recreant and deceiver,"[34] he wrote. "I hope most sincerely that when an election does occur no party will have any cause or even plausible pretext for dragging your name before the public, and discussing your conduct or your motives."[35]

Peter Mitchell, a forty-two-year-old lawyer and shipbuilder, was a man of very assertive views. He could be brusque and irreverent and had little patience for petty party politics. He opposed prohibition (legend has it that he freely distributed rum to those who would support him with their votes) and often clashed with Tilley. He assumed the prime minister's office (Tilley would be provincial secretary, though he had not been elected to the legislature). "Premier Herr von Bismarck Mitchell" took on the leadership of the Confederation Party as the legislature was dissolved on May 9 and yet another election was set for June 20. "We have a hard fight before us," Tilley wrote Macdonald, "but we must put it through."[36] It would cost money, he added, anywhere between "$40,000 to $50,000 to do the work in all the counties," and $35,000 would be needed for Saint John, Charlotte, Westmorland, York, and Kings.[37]

New Brunswick was now the site of a pitched battle on the Confederation landscape. Tilley called for a political bombardment of sorts from the Canadian government so that New Brunswick would not be left "out in the cold."[38] "We must have the arrangement carried out and without delay that he talked of when I met you at

Quebec," he told Galt. He asked for specifics to be telegraphed in cipher code. A few days later, Tilley was bolder: "Assistance must be had of a substantial character, suggesting $40K to 50K."[39] Was it only money? The testimony of John Hamilton Gray, a defeated pro-Confederation candidate, justified the emphasis upon the crucial role of the bankers in the overthrow of the government. A week after the election, Gray informed Macdonald that "the banking interests united against us. They at present have a monopoly and their directors used their influence unsparingly. They dreaded the competition of Canadian banks coming here and the consequent destruction of that monopoly – and many a businessman now in their power felt it not sage to hazard an active opposition to their influences."[40]

The election was hard-fought and New Brunswickers weren't easily bought. It was a fight between Leonard Tilley and Peter Mitchell, who ran on a platform of "Union or Disunion," and people like Albert J. Smith and Timothy Anglin, who, under the banner of the "Constitution Party," focused on the necessity of keeping New Brunswick as it had been before. Both groups believed in their chances of winning but Anglin expected a real conflict to break out. The forces needed to "look the enemy in the face, confront him boldly and never show any symptom of want of hope or want of courage," he had told a colleague a few months earlier.[41] Anglin spoke on April 5 and 6, covering practically every issue faced by the colony, and concluded that no good would happen to New Brunswick if the union option was pursued, and that he would oppose it. "At present the Provinces are distinct communities with conflicting interests," he told the legislature, "and the Quebec Scheme does not reconcile them, and the difficulties can only be overcome by sacrificing the Lower Provinces altogether."[42]

Large rallies were held in Saint John – in one case, a riot broke out, killing a man – as Anglin and Smith campaigned together.

Another riot broke out at a schoolhouse in Tracadie in Gloucester County in Northern New Brunswick when Premier Mitchell showed up to support the local pro-Confederation candidate, one Dr. Gordon. Acadians were not known to support Confederation and resented the fact that they had to swear allegiance to Queen Victoria and show that they owned property in order to vote. It is not clear how the hostilities were provoked, but one of Mitchell's people was assaulted. Mitchell ran to the scene, drew his revolver, and pointed it at the crowd assembled around the school so his protégé could escape.[43]

Tilley deftly used the Fenian threat. He focused on Charlotte, the nearest town, which had voted against Confederation in 1865, and talked up the fact that a better-equipped volunteer militia would play a stronger role.[44] The temptation to channel anti-Catholic sentiment was also evident. The Baptist *Christian Visitor* pointed out that Irish and French Roman Catholics opposed Confederation and implied that they were thus sympathetic to the Fenians. But Tilley had managed to make friends on that front: both Bishop John Sweeny in Saint John and Bishop James Rogers of Chatham (which covered the northern half of New Brunswick) declared themselves supportive of Confederation.

The first voting day was May 25, the day after the Queen Victoria's birthday, and the last was June 12. The Confederation Party led by Peter Mitchell won thirty-three seats against eight for the "Constitutionalists" led by Smith. Even Anglin lost his seat. It was a complete reversal of the election of March 1865. The Confederation Party won by a strong majority: 55,665 votes to 33,767. In Saint John, Tilley won a tight race on June 7 (1,761, compared with 1,703 for his best opponent). "The loyal Protestant and British sentiment which was been so nobly declared at the polls will raise this Province in the eyes of England," declared the supportive *Religious Intelligencer.*[45]

The alchemy of pro-Confederation guidance by the Catholic Church, the Smith government's incompetence, the defence needs highlighted by the Fenian scare, and the strong pro-Confederation messages coming out of London changed the political situation in New Brunswick. According to Richard Cartwright, the Fenian raids of 1866 "were a more serious menace than we were willing to admit then or now."[46]

The assembly was convened on June 21 and a resolution was quickly approved on June 30 that the government would enter into the final negotiations for Confederation. Tilley had proven to be a highly effective leader. Following the defeat of 1865, he had quietly but methodically recalibrated his forces and arguments and orchestrated one of the great comebacks in Canadian election history. The Canadians were happy, and confident of how the victory had been won. "He [Tilley] owes everything to us," Galt informed Macdonald.[47] His job done, Tilley set sail for London to prepare for the conference that would hammer out the terms of Confederation.

### The 1867 Election

The third election was again fought on the issue of Confederation. As in Quebec and Ontario, the elections in New Brunswick were scattered across the calendar. Unlike the other provinces, however, New Brunswick decided that its Legislative Assembly would remain as it was in 1866, and disallowed dual representation in both the provincial and federal legislatures. New Brunswick was also exceptional in adopting written ballots. Over the next year, by-elections were held to fill the seventeen provincial seats left vacant by members of the legislature who chose to take their careers to Ottawa.

Tilley was in a position of strength. He was unleashed against the anti-Confederationists including Anglin, who had hounded him for the last two years. The *Daily Evening Globe* noted that he had been a victim "in season and out of season, by daylight and by dark, in the House of Assembly and out of it, in the lobbies, in the galleries, in the hotels, at the street corners, behind process, in Canada, in England, by sleeping and by walking, – a course that was humiliating to his own manhood."[48] He had proved himself a deft operator at the London Conference, convincing participants that New Brunswick had special needs and that the special grants owed to the four provinces had to be revised. New Brunswick was initially supposed to receive an annual subsidy of $50,000 but it was raised to $63,000 until 1877. He also won the argument that the commitment to build the Intercolonial Railway should be constitutionalized. Tilley returned home from the London Conference hailed as a hero (March 29 in Saint John and April 1 in Fredericton). As his biographer put it, "he had returned from a humiliating defeat to carry his province triumphantly into the union ... Tilley's struggle for Confederation could not be matched by any of the other leaders."[49]

The June 1866 victory gave Tilley all the room he needed to take a big lead in the 1867 elections – at both the provincial and federal levels. As the summer of 1867 began, most of the best men in the province were working in Ottawa. Now a minister in Macdonald's government, Tilley returned to Fredericton as Peter Mitchell's cabinet tried to ensure a succession. Tilley was still provincial secretary, and as such was in charge of the budget for much of the summer.

"Politics in this Province are strangely muddied just now," Anglin wrote in early August 1867.[50] "Indeed, people seem to care little how the local Legislature is filled up now; and as for the local government they generally cannot be much worse." The politics of the new province did not appear to cause much excitement through most of the summer, and only began to sharpen in mid-August when Andrew Wetmore, a forty-seven-year-old Fredericton lawyer who had converted to the Confederation cause only in 1866, was named premier and minister of finance and replaced Mitchell, who was aiming for a seat in the new Canadian Senate. The reporter for the *Charlottetown Courier* noted at the end of August that it was "impossible to speak with certainty of the relative strength of parties in the province." The Tories in particular seemed to be confused as various supporters of Confederation competed for seats, thereby impairing their chances. The reporter concluded that "there is every prospect that New Brunswick will return a fair anti-ticket to the first dominion parliament."[51]

The earliest election would take place in Northumberland, where nominations would be accepted on August 29, the polls taken on September 4, and the results announced on September 7. The last one would be in Gloucester, which would accept nominations on September 14, take the polls on the September 18, and declare the winner officially on September 21. The most consequential day would be September 16, when five ridings would declare their winner.

Tilley would mastermind the election campaign in the province for the unionists. He was determined to stamp out the "antis" in New Brunswick, especially at the federal level, whether they were old Liberals like him or Conservatives.[52] He expected that, at the most, fifteen Liberals would be elected. Brown was skeptical. "He had better look to his own following," he wrote to Luther Holton in Quebec, doubtful that the New Brunswick Reformers could win much support with their anti-Confederation message. "I have a letter from one of his strong men, speaking for himself and others, entirely approving of our [pro-Confederation] course up here," he concluded confidently.[53]

### The Anglin Factor

The Liberal Party under Smith was a mess, and the task of motivating its partisans to vote fell to Timothy Anglin and his newspaper, the *Morning Freeman*. Located in a handsome building at 35 Prince William Street in Saint John, it was a four-page spread of which three entire pages were devoted to advertising of all sorts. One page was reserved for editorial, and most of it was filled with

Timothy W. Anglin, 1872
Photographer Topley Studio, Library and Archives Canada, PA-026338

commentary on the *Saint John Morning News*, the Tilley paper (which was often called "stupid"[54]), the *Morning Journal*, or the *Daily Evening Globe*, which were in turn obsessed with Anglin. The Confederationists were nicknamed the "schemers" who were endlessly trying to "humbug the people." "We write for the whole Province," Anglin claimed.[55]

It often seemed as though Anglin was at odds with most people. Born in 1822 into a firmly Catholic middle-class family in Clonakilty (County Cork), Ireland, he was of the Great Famine generation. In 1849, he settled in Saint John, a city that had absorbed approximately thirty thousand Irish migrants in the previous five years, more than doubling its population. Within weeks of his arrival, Anglin had been nicknamed "Klonkilty Bog-Trotter." Upon witnessing a riotous Orangemen's parade, he could hardly believe his eyes; he decided to create a newspaper that would address the discomforts of the rapidly growing community and, ideally, remove the rationale for violence. Thus the *Morning Freeman* was born with Anglin, a creative and imaginative force, as editor.

Anglin was the Irish Catholic counterpart to George Brown. Combative to a fault, he could never turn down an opportunity for a fight. He had opinions about everything, notably about people with power and authority and anyone or anything related to anything Tory. An able orator and a redoubtable writer, he sprang from the same stock as Thomas D'Arcy McGee. Perhaps more sensitive to the plight of the downtrodden Irish poor in Saint John than McGee could ever be, he was often prone to administering tough medicine in his criticism of the community's behaviour. He had everything in common with McGee, but could never see himself fitted with a Tory coat. An Irish nationalist, he was suspicious of McGee's promotion of a "new nationality" for Canada. Like Brown, he did not appear to like French Canadians much, but he was politically smart enough to recognize that he needed their support. He was even suspicious of the Scottish influence in the Ottawa government, noting that Anglo-Saxons appeared "almost excluded" from "all political power" while Celts (a very inclusive category that included Scots, Irish, and French) dominated public affairs. In his view, only Howland and Tilley could be considered Anglo-Saxon, and both were problematic for different reasons.[56]

He was elected to the New Brunswick legislature for Saint John in 1861. He proclaimed himself in favour of extending suffrage, the secret ballot, and other democratic reforms. He was decidedly Liberal, insisting on small and economical government and the pursuit of free trade. That said, he was suspicious of the United States and of the enthusiasm often expressed for it in America-friendly New Brunswick.

He especially did not like Leonard Tilley, who always seemed to be dedicating his life to eliminating what Anglin considered himself to be: a drinking, Catholic Irishman. He fought temperance and prejudice all through the 1850s and 1860s, making a name for himself and his newspaper. Anglin was nothing if not predictable. If Tilley was arguing for confederation, he was programmed to try to defeat it. Anglin's attacks were so unmerciful that he was accused of being motivated by personal hate, not merely politics. "Mr. Anglin never thought enough of Mr. Tilley to hate him," the *Morning Freeman* responded, but did aver that Tilley was "one of the most selfish, ambitious, unscrupulous men that ever took a prominent art in the politics of the Province."[57]

He was described condescendingly as "a clever Irishman" by James Hannay, an early historian of New Brunswick politics. It was true that Anglin had trouble convincing people that he was worthy of their confidence.[58] He lasted only a few months as a minister, unable to reconcile himself to the Smith government's attempts to build the Western Extension of the Intercolonial Railway by secretly giving a contract to the European and North American Railway and the Eastern Maine Company. Essentially, his view was that those contractors did not have the capacity to undertake, let alone complete, the project, and the government was taking an enormous risk. But it went beyond that. He was not appreciated by his colleagues. A reporter for the *Daily Evening Globe* noted that Anglin was "subjected to a course of persecution from an unscrupulous press," but far worse from Leonard Tilley.

Timothy Anglin was a key champion of anti-Confederation resolve, and he looked forward to the election. "The people of this Province suffered themselves to be duped and humbugged," he wrote angrily in early August. But he no longer had much fight in him. He accepted the situation because he would obey the voice of the majority of the people and because he felt that it was only by

96  *Ballots and Brawls*

adopting this course, by "submitting to the inevitable," that he could still make a contribution to the public good.[59]

The issue for him was now the merits of the British North America Act, not so much the politics of running against Leonard Tilley. It would not be easy. The economy was doing relatively well in 1867 New Brunswick. Tilley started proclaiming that a confederated Canada would pursue a low-tariff policy. Anglin, for his part, saw only that "greed of office was the chief characteristic of these men from first to last."[60]

The *Morning Freeman* greeted the new Canada with as much cynicism as it could muster. Anglin's column listed the number of job openings in the Senate, the New Brunswick Legislative Council, the courts, and the government administration that had been created for politicians in the new national capital as well as in the province. Such positions were "promised beforehand to the men who asserted that in working for Confederation they were actuated by the most noble and patriotic motives. Theirs is the loyalty and patriotism that pays."[61] He wondered: "What think the public of this summary of the office-making, selling, &c, of the last few weeks?"

But Anglin's larger problem was his opposition to the Church leadership's support for Confederation. A convinced reformer, he was not enthusiastic about either the Howes or the Browns of the world. When Brown toured New Brunswick in November 1865 to connect with like-minded pro-union liberals, he failed to convince Anglin.[62] Anglin, representing a Saint John riding, wanted a commercial and trade policy that would bring obvious benefits to New Brunswick, not Canada. When the Bank of Montreal opened a branch in Saint John, he saw it as designed to crush the Bank of New Brunswick.[63]

He lambasted the "mongrel" approach of the Macdonald government. "When will they commence the opening of the North West?" he asked. "The people have a right to know." He wanted clear positions on the Intercolonial Railway and on defence. "The time for humbug ... ought to be past."[64] "None of us ... have much reason to like the leading men of either of the great Canadian parties, and those of our representatives who become partisans of either will not take the course best calculated to serve the interests of those they represent."[65] Anglin himself wrote in the *Morning Freeman* on August 3 that "he was by no means in unison with Mr. Brown or Mr. Howe, and he may find it quite impossible to unite with either of them as leader of a political party." He went further: he would support the Macdonald government if it chose the northern route for the Intercolonial Railway.

Anglin could be harshly critical of McGee. He profiled him in a lengthy article as a shameless opportunist whose late association with the Macdonald-Cartier alliance had caused him an enormous loss of prestige and influence.[66] Anglin spoke for many Catholics when he argued that they "owed no allegiance to either of the two great parties in Quebec and Ontario, and in this Province they can scarcely be expected to attach themselves to the member of the Macdonald Administration," especially since Macdonald had not named one Catholic to the Senate and Tilley had refused to grant Catholics the rights they enjoyed in Lower Canada.[67] Anglin insisted that his opposition to the Church leaders' stance was done "with the most profound respect for the Bishop, and the most unqualified obedience to his authority as Bishop," but that he had a right, as a Catholic, to be "perfectly independent in matters purely political."[68]

One of the most implacable opponents of Confederation, Anglin decided to run for a seat in the House of Commons. He could hardly run in his home riding in Saint John, given the humiliating result of 1866, but an improbable opportunity arose in Gloucester, likely to be the last election in New Brunswick in that campaign, a move that immediately drew the ire of George Brown's *Globe*. Brown argued that the only requirement of the Intercolonial Railway be that it follow the most efficient route to the Atlantic. With Anglin advocating that the railway travel through the northern riding of Gloucester, Brown saw an opponent. He was bemused by what his Liberal cousin was saying.[69]

It showed the deep self-contradiction of the situation. Anglin was running against the Confederationist forces, but for the Liberal Party. He was thus opposing Leonard Tilley, who had once been a key ally in George Brown's pro-Confederation forces. The campaign was further complicated by the fact that francophones dominated the riding.

There was no natural alliance between the New Brunswick Liberals and the roughly fifty thousand Acadians who lived in the province. They lived in their own space and minimized contact as much as they could with the outside world. Focused on traditional institutions to simply survive as Catholic francophones, the Acadian community did not have a newspaper until *Le Moniteur Acadien* was born on Dominion Day 1867. Henry Lacroix, the Montreal mystic, saw the revival of Acadianism as a positive by-product of the new federalism. He portrayed the Acadians as "New Lazaruses" who were emerging from the "heavy shadows which surrounded them."[70] For his part, Anglin wished the newspaper "all success,"[71] though he admitted he was quite ignorant of the Acadian state of affairs.[72]

That said, he had powerful supporters in the Church hierarchy and, according to his biographer, there were things that did unite him to Acadians. Like them, he had been against Confederation, and notwithstanding his loss in the June 1866 election, he was a man of high profile in the province. Since very few Acadians had the right to vote, he was presented as a man who, though unable to converse in French, could represent and defend their rights in Ottawa. Anglin would run as a Liberal and thus continue his fight against Sir John A. Macdonald, alongside Brown and Howe, though he had great reservations about both of them.

With the blurring of lines between the Liberals and the Conservatives, the race in New Brunswick was tight, and it was not clear whether voters would support or turn away from Confederation. Tilley, the former Liberal, was now a Liberal-Conservative of the Macdonald sort and was indefatigable in his campaign. Albert J. Smith, arguably the leader of the anti-Confederationists/anti-Conservatives, ran an almost invisible campaign. Anglin, for his part, was hanging tough and making a case that an Irish intellectual from Saint John was the right man to represent Acadians at the other end of the province. For many, Confederation – becoming a part of a greater whole – made sense. The Acadians, almost entirely cut off from the politics of Confederation, were suspicious, as were most Catholics, but those views were rapidly changing.

Anglin's platform was the clearest statement of what the anti-Confederationists stood for. He criticized the fact that Macdonald had thirteen ministers in his government, while the United States, ten times larger, needed only seven members of cabinet. Canadians were likely to pay, Anglin wrote. "If they will be humbugged by any knave, they are fit for nothing else."[73]

Taxation was a key issue for Tilley's opponents and the eighty cents per person cash transfer promised from Ottawa was too small a subsidy. One such opponent would provoke his audiences with dialogue like this: "Father, what country do we live in?" "Son, you have no country, for Mr. Tilley has sold us all to the Canadians for eighty cents a head."[74]

"We have now had a month's experience of the working of Confederation and its practical effects," the *Morning Freeman* announced in its lead editorial on August 3, 1867, concluding that it was a failure and rattling off a list of broken promises, ranging from immigration to trade and manufacturing. "Where are the capitalists?" it called out. A month later, on September 3, Anglin said the same thing: "He must be blind or infatuated indeed who does not now perceive that Confederation will not and can not do the good, or any material portion of the good so many foolishly expected from it."[75] He pretended to wax nostalgic, remembering the "bustle and animation of the streets of St. John a few years ago," and lamenting that "our business is not better; but worse."[76]

That said, Anglin's arguments were being heard, and Tilley could hardly be assured of victory. New Brunswick had see-sawed on the issue of Confederation, first falling hard against it in the winter of 1865, then tricked into voting for it in the spring of 1866. In late August 1867, voters began casting their secret ballots, the only ones with such a choice in the new Canada.

# 3

# A Proper Scottish *Square Go* in Ontario

**CANADA STARTED WELL IN** the new province of Ontario. In Ottawa, a giant bonfire was lit on the ordnance lands across the street from Notre-Dame Cathedral Basilica and a cannonade of 101 guns fired an unforgettable salute at midnight. At dawn, church bells clanged across town and in the smaller neighbouring villages, and High Masses were sung. The weather cooperated, bringing the special gift of a beautiful, bright day.[1] In Toronto, George Brown greeted the morning sun after spending the entire night writing an article fitting for the occasion. On the morning of July 1, readers of the *Globe* – including a crowd of some two hundred waiting outside its office who were desperate to read Brown's reaction – were treated to a six-thousand-word essay on the significance of the day. "We hail the birth day of a new nationality," Brown declared. "A United British America, with its four millions of people, takes its place this day among the nations of the world." He wished it the "blessings of health, happiness, peace and prosperity."

Queen's Park in Toronto – in those days it was only a park – filled quickly. The Royal Proclamation of Confederation was read, *God Save the Queen* was sung, cheers followed, and families partied to celebrate the constitutional arrangement that promised a new beginning. In Kingston, Macdonald's hometown, a good crowd gathered around City Hall to ring in the new polity, but the further west one went, the less enthusiastic the reception. London's thirteen thousand people had heartily celebrated the Queen's birthday on May 24 but greeted Confederation with a shrug, with many eagerly looking forward to a quick train ride to Windsor three days later to see the American Independence Day fireworks in Detroit. The city council defeated a motion to spend money on the first Dominion Day. Enjoying a day off, volunteers played a game of very Scottish shinty on Cricket Field and the local military volunteers mounted a military review. A torchlight procession was improvised by the local fire brigade that night.[2]

Politics in Ontario were very different from the Maritimes or Quebec. There was no issue of whether Confederation should have happened or whether a local political culture had been supplanted by a foreign entity. The new national capital was in Ontario, and the idea of Canada as a solution to governance and economic problems had been promoted aggressively by Ontarians, regardless of whether they were Conservatives, Liberals, or Reformers of any sort.

As in Quebec and New Brunswick, nominations and elections were staggered, but the election was practically over by September 10. The battle of Ontario, unlike in other provinces, was less about contrary visions of Canada – both the Liberals and the Conservatives shared essentially the same view that the province was likely to be the biggest winner from this arrangement – than about just plain winning more seats. Sir John A. Macdonald and George Brown thus prepared for a political fist fight: a proper Scottish *square go*. Macdonald campaigned with two distinct advantages: a passion for power and an ability to find political friends, especially among Reformers who turned into political attack dogs during the 1867 campaign, including two rabid former Liberals, William McDougall and Sandfield Macdonald. Agnes Macdonald, easily the first witness to her husband's efforts, complained in her new diary that his profession now filled every corner of their home. "The atmosphere is so awfully political that sometimes I think the very flies hold parliaments on the kitchen tablecloths!" she wrote on July 5. It's easy to imagine the particular badinage in the Macdonald household in the first few days of Confederation.

Macdonald's concerns embraced all four provinces, but he had neither the time nor the transportation necessary to campaign outside Ontario. From mid-August to mid-September, he travelled relentlessly in his home province. Until then, he scrambled to get everything in order, as cabinet, the departments, and the general "machinery of government" had to be "set in motion," to again borrow Agnes Macdonald's words. Much of July saw Macdonald overseeing the selection of returning officers and the preparation of the electoral apparatus. Letters flew to all parts of the country from his desk, asking to be kept informed, encouraging men to run and to do their best in service of "the cause," pointing out his record, but also cautioning aspirants to various positions in government. Sometimes cajoling, sometimes critical, he used his pen to motivate as best he could. In a practically indecipherable letter, he congratulated a colleague for "playing a good game" in attracting Mennonites, but joked against making things public, for fear that "Quakers might take the alarm."[3] He offered assistance to Alexander Drew, a forty-year-old lawyer in Elora, who was running in Wellington North. He was confident that despite Drew's Protestantism (Macdonald teased him, recalling his connection to "the Orange body," but privately called him a "violent Orangeman"), Catholics would support him because "as a general rule they are friendly to the Government."[4]

He appealed to Alexander Vidal to run against Alexander Mackenzie in Lambton County, assuring him that he could "get the support of all moderate men" and that it would be "a pity that so fine a constituency ... should be left in the hands of such a demagogue and brawler as Mr. Alex. Mckenzie [sic]."[5] Vidal accepted. In a few

104   *Ballots and Brawls*

cases, Macdonald got involved in local contests to try to dissuade Conservatives from running against each other. "I must beg of you for the sake of the good old cause not to split the interest but to forget all personal feelings," he urged Robert Cotton in Port Credit.[6] "In election contests the question is not who will make the best member of Parliament or who has the greatest claims," he wrote a young George Taylor Denison, who wanted to run in the riding of Toronto West. (Denison, twenty-eight, was a lieutenant colonel in the active militia and had seen active service during the Fenian raid in the Niagara Peninsula the year before.) "The simple question, in a party point of view, is who has the best chance of carrying the constituency," he pleaded, asking Denison not to run.[7]

Agnes, in love, could not help but be impressed. She was bearing witness to the birth of the governance of the country. "What novelty this all is," she wrote in her diary.

> All this new constitution has been framed in my blessed old husband's brain – sometimes I look at him in vague wonderment and ponder over all I know or can connect touching his career! Thank God he has been very successful in this ... scheme of the confederation of all the British North American Provinces & all Canada is singing his praises. He is a powerful and popular man today & with all the humblest heart as most gently judging of all mankind.

She had found "something worth living for – living in – my husband's heart & love."

Macdonald, she tells us, tempered his moods by playing a game of "patience": "He says it rests his mind & changes the current of his thoughts more than anything else." "I do like to identify myself with all my husband's pursuits & occupations," she confided to her diary in a passage that revealed so much about her and her husband:

He is so busy and so much older than I that I would soon fall out of his life if I went my own ways – as I might do disregarding him. On the whole I think he likes me near him he is so equable & so good-natured that being with him is always refreshing. I tell him his good heart & amiable temper are the great secrets of his success. He is so thoroughly patient & gentle in spirit. It is quite remarkable in so hardworked, so busy & so thoughtful a man. He can throw off a weight of business in a wonderfully short space of time, oftentimes he comes in with a very moody brow, tired and oppressed, his voice weak, his step slow, & ten minutes after he is making clever jokes & laughing like any school boy, with his hands in his pockets, & his head thrown back.[8]

It was midnight when she wrote this. It was Agnes's '67 summer of love.

## Macdonald's Coalition

Macdonald, the very embodiment of Scottish Protestantism, played his "patience" with a full set of cards, including Catholic hearts and Liberal spades. He hoped to get the Catholic vote; it could make the difference in areas where they held the balance of power.

Who carried the Roman Catholics separate School bill? The government of which I was the head and by my own personal exertions. Who got them all the money grants for their educational and benevolent institutions? Who secured them their fair share of the commutations, of the Clergy Reserves? I did. What Irish Catholics ever held office above the rank of tide waiter or messenger until I did them justice. I place them in almost every Dept and if you had to look at the Gazette of appointments or over the public accounts you will find that the Catholics have a fair share, and in some departments more than their share of the public patronage.[9]

106 *Ballots and Brawls*

For Macdonald, there was a clear difference between him and Brown. Where Brown was only promising things, Macdonald delivered. But it was up to the Catholic communities in both Lower and Upper Canada to decide, he conceded. There was a danger of subjecting "themselves once more to the tender mercies of Mr. Brown. If they do this they will regret it, not once but for ever [sic]."[10] That said, Macdonald assured his correspondent that "no effort of mine shall be wanting to get you the support of the Protestants."

He put his words to work. In the first weeks of July, the Macdonalds entertained Edward Kenny and his wife. Kenny, one of the richest businessmen in Nova Scotia and a pillar of the Irish Catholic community there, had just been sworn in as receiver general. Agnes described him as a "large, staid, sensible looking Irishman – Elderly [he was sixty-seven] and with a fine looking comfortable wife." The Macdonalds also saw a lot of William McDougall, once a fiery "Clear Grit" critic of Macdonald but now an equally mercurial supporter. The couples had become friends, and Lady Agnes recorded picking beautiful flowers from the McDougall garden in Spencerville, about eighty kilometres southeast of Ottawa. The McDougalls returned the visit, as did George-Étienne Cartier, "who never talks politics out of season, so only passing allusions were made to the subject all evening," Agnes reported with relief.

But Macdonald had another group to woo: the Liberals. The biggest political fuss of the first few weeks of July 1867 was the open question of who would be retained by Macdonald to create an interim government in Ontario. The Liberals were strong in the province, but Macdonald wanted someone who might accomplish two things: first, not outrage Liberal opinion, and second, succeed in reconciling differences. Macdonald liked Sandfield Macdonald for the job. Here was a serious man who could appeal to various constituencies. Aged fifty-five, he came from a Highland Scottish family, but he had an extra asset Macdonald appreciated: he was Catholic! Born in Eastern Ontario, he had put down deep Liberal roots in the territory since 1841, when he had first run for a seat in the Legislative Assembly of the United Province of Canada. He was named co-premier of the province in 1862 and served for almost two years. He made numerous visits to Ottawa from his home base of Cornwall in July, and was described by Agnes in her diary as "loving." He was a late convert to Confederation and had become an ardent apostle who could appeal to those who still felt reluctance.

Macdonald decided to ask the Catholic Sandfield to become premier of Ontario and clearly revealed the secret to his intensely curious wife. Luther Holton was outraged – it was a "deadly blow at the brightening fortunes of the Liberal party."[11] A few days later, Agnes reported "a bombshell in the enemy's camp," noting that there was a "great howl" in the Liberal papers and convinced that George Brown would now run against the Conservatives in the election. Sandfield Macdonald did not like Brown – he "thought him extreme," Agnes reported.[12] He was perfect for the job, in other words. The first two weeks were hard on Macdonald, but he now had to set aside cabinet meetings in order to engage in the campaign. "John is tired & looking pale," noted Agnes. "Everybody is turning their attention to election matters."[13]

At six in the morning on July 10, the Macdonalds boarded a train to Prescott and stopped in Spencerville to pick up McDougall, who declared, "Well, I am going in for it, Lady Macdonald." Agnes told him she was delighted by the news. "I am heartily glad to hear it & trust & hope too it will be all right and for the best," he responded. They shared breakfast and Sir John A. stopped at the telegraph office at Campbell's Hotel in Prescott to send messages about the Sandfield Macdonald appointment. He gave numerous interviews and then joined Agnes in the private car of the train, locking the

108 *Ballots and Brawls*

doors and lying down on the sofa, where he fell asleep in two minutes. Agnes reported that the train "raced home" through an eerie "green forest."[14]

Three days later, they again left Ottawa early in the morning and returned to Prescott for a brief stop. Their private car quickly filled with visitors. "Talking! Talking!" lamented Agnes. "For ever smilingly receiving congratulations and saying the same things – flattered and caressed ad. lib." In Prescott, they took the boat, stopped in Kingston for three hours, and resumed their trip down Lake Ontario, arriving in Toronto early on the morning of July 14. "I fell asleep & dreamed I was going to Quebec, as I had done a year before – a stranger," wrote Agnes, suddenly shocked at how her life had changed in eight months.[15] Macdonald was in "great spirits and as long as I can help him by being cheery – and smiling – I am quite satisfied."[16]

### Macdonald's Strategy

Macdonald travelled through Ontario at least four more times. In late July, he undertook a tour "through the West," going as far as London, and then Simcoe, a few kilometres from the shore of Lake Erie.[17] He started a new tour in the final week of August, beginning with Kingston on August 22, reaching Toronto five days later, where he gave an important speech on August 27 in front of the Conservative-friendly *Leader*'s office, where thousands heard him.[18] Even though many local elections had already been decided (the first one was in Ottawa on August 26–27), Macdonald again roamed the shore of Lake Ontario, appeared at George Brown's demonstration in Bowmanville on September 4, and was spotted as far as Wilmot Township (west of today's Kitchener-Waterloo) on September 11.[19] He grew so busy that his correspondence ceased on August 16 and did not resume until the election was over.

On the surface, the platform of Canada's first prime minister was a simple "let's carry on." For him, the campaign was a referendum on Canada and on his personal role in executing the constitutional leap. He appealed for voters to distinguish his Liberal-Conservative coalition from the radicalism of George Brown and the people around him. He blasted Brown for his uncompromising and anti-Catholic positions on the issue of the disposition of the Clergy Reserves in Upper and Lower Canada.[20] In Toronto, he downplayed Brown's contribution to forging the Confederation pact, going as far as to declare that "when a column shall be raised to the memory of those who achieved this result [Confederation] Mr. Brown's name will not be inscribed thereto, and his children's children will regret the course that he pursued."[21] For extra effect, he often made sure to appear on the hustings with Sandfield Macdonald, who was all too happy to rail against his former Reformer colleagues.[22] In the end, Macdonald argued that he was a better man to lead the government, asserting that even "with all his faults," he had a hold on Canadians because they knew "his heart was right."[23]

In Kingston, Macdonald squared off against Dr. W.J. Stewart, a professor of anatomy at Queen's University who also dabbled in journalism. Stewart ran as an "independent" but could at once identify himself as a "Reformer" as well as a Tory. Lore has it that Macdonald even defended him at one point against a charge of slander, arguing that Stewart's little publication was so insignificant that no harm could possibly come from any of its contents. It worked and Stewart was found innocent, but he felt no gratitude. He called Macdonald a drunk and an adulterer. The only real offence the prime minister may have committed was in calling one of Stewart's supporters a donkey. (Macdonald garnered 734 votes against 142 for Stewart; the contest attracted very little interest otherwise.)[24]

Macdonald's strategy was to forge alliances with people who were not like him, and a large part of his political successes were the product of his friendship with Catholics. On July 3, he wrote a ten-page letter to Monsignor John Lynch, the Catholic bishop of Toronto. His aim was to have Lynch use his influence to convince

110  *Ballots and Brawls*

Catholics in his enormous diocese to vote Conservative at a time when society was so divided that Toronto was known as "the Belfast of Canada."[25] "I feel that personally I have a claim upon the confidence and support of the Catholics of Upper Canada," he wrote, listing a number of initiatives (including separate schools) that his government had pushed. He reminded the prelate that he had suffered constant criticism from the Liberals ("a fanatical protestant party") and from George Brown in particular, who consistently disparaged "the Catholic hierarchy from the Pope downwards" and who "insulted all that is held sacred" by the Catholic community. Macdonald suggested that Brown was laying a "trap" during the nascent campaign by recruiting a few Catholic candidates in ridings where the Liberals had no choice. In sharp contrast, Macdonald noted his cabinet's important Catholic representation, pointing to the presence of Senator Kenny and to the closeness of McGee to the cabinet – noting that McGee was going to be a candidate for the Ontario legislature in the county of Prescott (Eastern Ontario), as were many other prominent Catholics in important ridings. He asserted that Catholics would be appointed to the Senate and that they would be influential in public affairs. Finally, Macdonald noted that the leaders of the Catholic Church in Nova Scotia and Quebec had supported Conservatives and were now "requesting ... action" from Lynch.[26]

Lynch was inclined to respond favourably to the prime minister but was too much of a realist to assume that his flock shared only one political belief. He was unequivocal: "We know that amongst Catholics in Canada there are some reformers. We know also the great majority of them are conservatives and have supported Conservative Government." But his voice carried a message in 1867: "Give a fair trial to the present government, which has successfully brought about the Confederation of the Provinces, give the present Government of that confidence which they have not yet forfeited to Catholics." He continued, in a cross-Canada spirit of Confederation:

*A Proper Scottish Square Go in Ontario* 111

In the second place I would say, join the Catholics of Lower Canada, Nova Scotia and New Brunswick in the support of the present Government. It would be a misfortune to the Catholics of Ontario to sever themselves in politics from their co-religionists of the other Provinces. It would be an error for us to alienate ourselves from the party who were willing to grant to the Catholics of Upper Canada all the educational right that the minority of Lower Canada sought for themselves which fair and just measure was defeated by the very men who now seek our patronage.[27]

Macdonald, who had worked diligently to foster reconciliation between Catholics and Protestants, would have found encouragement in that remark. It was to be his reward for ensuring that separate schools for Catholics had been part of the Confederation act. It was not an idle boast: "If they have received any money grants for their Educational Institutions, or if they have received any appointment to Office above the rank of Landing Waiter, it is due to myself," he wrote. When he heard that John Horan in Kingston had written about his support for the Conservatives, Macdonald declared that "it was all that could be desired," and that efforts be made to make sure Catholic electors be made aware of Horan's position.[28] In a letter to Francis Clarke (in Prescott, that hotbed of activity!), Macdonald expressed his confidence that Horan "would exercise his influence if asked to do so by me."[29]

His efforts to win the Catholic vote extended beyond the capital. He wrote to John Farrell, the bishop of Hamilton, alerting him that George Brown had sent a "catholic emissary" to campaign in the district. "This man must be surely a fenian in disguise," Macdonald observed, asking Farrell to "induce his coreligionists" to support Thomas Street, the Conservative candidate (Street was acclaimed).[30] He did the same with the temporary administrator of the Diocese of Sandwich.[31] Macdonald could only hope that it was Catholics who were reading newspapers hostile to the Liberals,

112   *Ballots and Brawls*

especially when they repeated the *Chicago Republican's* line that Brown was a "lion-clad jackass whose bawlings have indeed been heard, but whose fire and force are all in the rear."[32] The *Ottawa Times* opined that the Reform Party "is composed of the very basest and most corrupt material."[33]

### George Brown's Fatal Hesitations

Forthright and clear in his thinking, George Brown was never comfortable in the vague world of politics, and the heavy baggage he brought to the 1867 campaign inevitably affected his march. He had promoted the idea of Confederation since the late 1850s, and his support for a coalition government in 1864 had made all the difference. His party had hardly ever governed, mostly because its leaders really could not agree on what they would do if they attained power. For one thing, they were separated by language and religion. Brown was not trusted among the *Rouges;* none of them were beside him in either Charlottetown or Quebec in 1864, and it was evident that he could not have cared less. In fact, many Liberals in Canada East seemed content to tacitly support the Liberal-Conservative coalition that had formed the government since 1864, with John A. Macdonald acting as deputy premier to Sir Étienne-Paschal Taché (until his death) and then Narcisse-Fortunat Belleau. Everyone knew that Macdonald ran everything.

All the same, Brown had supported Macdonald and the *Bleus* in forming the political coalition necessary for Confederation, and had played an especially convincing role in the Quebec Conference of October 1864 and again in London in the spring of 1865 to convince the British government of the virtues of supporting the Canadian project. The battle won, he lost the patience for politics that had kept his efforts alive, and, citing disagreements on tariff policy, he resigned from cabinet just before Christmas 1865. His passion for communicating ideas to a buying public was far stronger than any desire to convince people who were not of his ilk. Partly this was a product of how he made his living, but it was also an integral part of his personality. He wanted to focus on his editorship of the *Globe,* and to scout new agricultural land to purchase for himself and his young family (he did buy an estate near Brantford a few months later). Brown was only three years younger than Macdonald, and though he had been deeply involved in politics since his arrival in Toronto twenty years earlier, he had no taste for the constant demands for compromise that the political life made. If politics energized and rejuvenated Macdonald, it aged Brown and wore him down.

Nevertheless, as Confederation approached, Brown was confident that his reformist ideas would find a new life in an expanded Canada. He scoped alliances with anyone who did not share the ideas of Canada espoused by Macdonald and Cartier. The Reformers, after all, had shown that they could govern during the years when they had collaborated in John A. Macdonald's unity cabinet, and there were signs that Reformers would return to base camp and fight for a distinct program. "I was never so confident as at this moment that the movement was the right one," he wrote to Luther Holton in the winter of 1867. He was optimistic that Reformers could "give a new face to the whole politics of the country."[34]

Brown persisted in thinking that the party was in good hands and decided to change his life. On March 1, he stunned the political world during a speech at Tillsonburg, when he announced that he would not personally run for a seat in the new House of Commons. The news triggered as much anger as consternation, and Brown was at pains to explain his rationale to various Liberals. "As a journalist and citizen, I hope always to be found on the right side and heartily supporting my old friends," he told Holton, "but I want to be free to write of men and things without control, beyond that which my conscientious convictions and the interests of the country demand." And that included criticizing the Liberals in the new country. "To be debarred by fear of injuring the party from saying that he is unfit to sit in parliament, and that is very stupid, makes journalism a very small business," he thought. "Party leadership and the conducting of a great journal do not harmonize."[35] He did not convince many, and scared most. The Reformers needed a leader of substance – even if only to keep the various fractions of the party united. They also needed the confidence that the formidable Brown would not turn his mighty polemical guns on them. That said, he was still a Liberal: "Where work is to be done for the reformers of Canada, and for the people of Canada, I shall not shrink from it. And I am free to state what IS the course I now intend to pursue."[36]

He himself recognized the limits of his own "ardent temperament." He was unlikely to criticize his own party, and though he was confident of success in the new Ontario, he knew his appeal was limited elsewhere. Brown recognized that Joseph Howe's efforts in Nova Scotia and the Albert J. Smith/Timothy W. Anglin Reformers in New Brunswick were sending contradictory messages. Howe, a thorough and reliable Reformer in the past, was adamantly campaigning against Brown's Canadian project. Leonard Tilley, another Reformer, was working hand in hand with Macdonald. In Quebec, the Reformers were gravely divided. Luther Holton could be encouraging in reporting that "our Rouge friends are coming round all right," and that seemed to satisfy Brown.[37] No perfect alliance was likely, in his view, because the *Rouges* would take a long time to forgive the Canada West Reformers' alliance with Macdonald and Cartier to form Confederation. "Let us fall into line naturally and by degrees," he suggested. According to J.M.S. Careless, his biographer, Brown did hope that a national party could emerge from the disparate pieces of Canada West reform, the *Rouges* in Quebec, and Joseph Howe's party in Nova Scotia, but he was not going to force the issue, almost conceding that Macdonald's coalition was destined to govern. Brown allowed that "John A. Macdonald is a very astute man, and knows well how to play one colleague off against another and if he does not succeed in getting one in Upper Canada or Nova

Scotia or New Brunswick when he wants him, he is a little more stupid than he used to be when I was in government."[38]

But for the moment he would do what he could to organize the party for the upcoming election. Whereas Macdonald could count on the support of loyal party members and Conservative voters because he had developed a reputation as an able manager for a decade already, Brown had no such advantage. And where Macdonald could count on Conservative support for the idea of forming a government and for the idea of a united Canada, Brown's natural allies on the Liberal side were divided. In the three provinces outside Ontario, most of the Liberals/Reformers could give Confederation only lukewarm support at best. In fact, many were openly hostile to forming any coalition with Macdonald and to the idea of Canada.

Through the spring, local organizers prepared nominating conventions and Brown took a leading role in rebuilding the Reform Association of Upper Canada, which would give the party a shape and a program, as well as a name that harked back to when Upper Canada was fairly independent. A Toronto branch of the Reform Association also took root, sharing much of the same leadership. The core of the party leadership consisted of three Torontonians – the reluctant Brown, the finance heavyweight William McMaster (who was simultaneously establishing the Bank of Commerce), and Edward Blake – and Alexander Mackenzie, who hailed from Sarnia. Mackenzie called for an end to coalition and a return to old party divisions so as to reinvigorate democracy. In his view, widely shared, without clear alternatives, there could be no alternation of parties in power and no democracy.[39]

Brown had no trouble convincing his colleagues that the time had come for the Reformers to return to their fundamental principles and create a party with its own identity. One could not be a Reformer and at the same time serve in a government led by John A. Macdonald. Men who were serving in Macdonald's cabinet, such as William McDougall, William Howland, and Fergusson Blair

116    *Ballots and Brawls*

would have to choose. "We must be united," urged Luther Holton in a letter to George Brown in the days before the Liberal congress; "the formation of a national party must be our constant aim." It was a statement of aspiration, but it was also something of a criticism of Brown that he was not preparing a pan-Canadian effort.[40] In order to bring unity to the party, a convention was held in Toronto on June 27–28.[41]

Liberalism in mid-century was amorphous and looking for direction. It was at odds with the French Canadians, for sure. There were few contacts with Reformers in Nova Scotia, New Brunswick, or Prince Edward Island. There were divisions in Ontario. There were "Grits," who supported a liberal agenda: freedom from taxation and onerous rules coming from government, freedom to trade, freedom to think without too much encroachment from the churches or from government bureaucrats. Then there were the "Clear Grits," who were clearly radical and on the more extreme margin of mere Reformers. Driven by a rural perspective of self-reliance, their program was hostile to any evidence of privilege in any form, and hostile to the notion that their program could not be adopted unless French Canadians supported it. Clear Grits were open to the idea of abolishing the United Province of Canada so that Upper Canada could govern itself unimpeded. Doubt was even cast on the monarchy. Every government official had to be subject to election. The Clear Grits favoured the secret ballot and admired many American practices. The problem with them, however, was that no single individual personified their instincts and thoughts. Their newspaper, the *North American* (1850–58), edited by McDougall, bore testimony to that brand of thinking.

Brown could do little, and complacency set in. Travel distances were vast, and transportation was almost impossible to fund. More importantly, each reformist tradition was deeply anchored in local political cultures that clearly tested the transferability of Upper Canadian Gritism. The expression "Upper Canada" in his own organization's name was imbued with nostalgia, harking back to a past generation. Brown could thunder and clap in the pages of the *Globe*, but his message did not resonate outside western Ontario, and it was too late to create consistent messaging across the provinces.

Over six hundred people attended the convention in the hot and humid Music Hall on Church Street. There were rumours that Antoine-Aimé Dorion and Luther Holton might attend the convention in Toronto, but the meeting was called to order without them. Brown was named chair and Mackenzie vice chair. It was observed that there were few delegates even from eastern Ontario; this was a Toronto event attended by men who lived it its environs. A partisan wrote to Brown a few days before the scheduled event to say that he could not afford the "political luxury" because he had to deal with "rotten politicians who are destroying everything." He was referring to fellow Liberals who seemed to be soft on Macdonald's ideas and who were vying for the Liberal nomination. It was imperative for Brown to announce his candidacy, this Belleville correspondent urged: "There is not a man that the Coalition dread more than yourself and I know that I only speak what thousands feel when I say that there is not a person in Canada so able to handle them as yourself."[42]

McDougall, Howland, and Blair courageously attended and made the case that Liberalism could be relevant only if they remained in the Macdonald government. They would ensure that the prime minister was controlled. Their words turned Brown incandescent with rage. Nothing aroused him like the prospect of Macdonald running a government, let alone a government of Liberals. "Tell us that we are now to condescend – tell me that we are to condescend – at this day, when we stand claiming credit for one of the noblest records public men ever could display before a country – that we are not down on our knees to Mr. John A. Macdonald! Go into the same government with John A. Macdonald?"[43]

118    *Ballots and Brawls*

The barrage continued as Mackenzie took his turn to tear into McDougall in particular, vowing to fight him to the finish. By 1 a.m. on June 28, Brown had achieved his goal of party unity, but now Howland, McDougall, and Blair were no longer Liberals. Brown's rousing speech had shown that he was indispensable, and the calls for him to run for election practically deafened him. The campaign to draft him back into political life was effective, but it was the affront of three former colleagues that motivated his return to battle: if the three deserters were staying with Macdonald, he said, he would have to run against them.

"McDougall's speech I can only characterize as atrocious," wrote Holton to Brown. And yet Holton was hearing that McDougall "had made quite an impression with a good many people." "Can this be so?" he asked urgently.[44] He urged Brown to run: "You must come in. There is no escape for you."[45] In spite of himself, Brown was again in the election, and the rumour that he would run in the riding of South Ontario – which consisted of Whitby, Pickering, and Oshawa and was held by the incumbent, Thomas Gibbs, a prominent local resident and fervent Macdonald supporter – spread quickly. Gibbs was so eager for a fight that Macdonald had to remind him that the election had not been called![46] Three weeks later, Brown made it official, announcing his candidacy in the riding of South Ontario. He would be an outsider, running against a strong incumbent from a distance, and would hardly have time to visit the district. It was an absurd gamble and the best he could hope for was that it would be a close race, "the maddest enterprise he ever put his hand to."[47] Macdonald was not too worried: "Brown will get his agitators this time," conceded the prime minister, but the moderate Reformers "will be too many for him and the Conservative Return will be large."[48] The *Stratford Baron* called Brown "a good deal of a knight-errant, prone to go forth to do battle for the weak against the strong." It did not expect great things for him in South Ontario, insisting that he should imitate other leaders: "Sir John A. Macdonald never leaves his pet borough of Kingston; his namesake John Sandfield is as closely wedded to little Cornwall; and Mr. Galt carries Sherbrooke about with him in his pocket. Risking nothing, how is it possible for men like them to lose?"[49]

Brown was well aware of his limitations, not least among Catholics. "We have had no communication whatever with the Roman Catholic clergy, but they, of course, know all about the position, and have probably determined not to interfere," he confided to Holton a few days after the convention, but was confident that pragmatism would prevail: "The most pronounced of them heretofore show a moderation, common sense, and confidence in our good faith exceedingly satisfactory."[50] Brown did not give up easily. A Catholic convention of two hundred Liberals met in Toronto on July 9 to castigate Macdonald and his coalition. The prime minister was not impressed. He called it a "pseudo Catholic convention"[51] that had "ended in a fizzle."[52]

Brown thought little of Macdonald's track record on tariffs and trade, the militia, or the possibilities of the Intercolonial Railway. "Public business is in frightful chaos as the departments remain unorganized," he argued.[53] And then there was the Bank of Montreal, which never seemed far from Macdonald's partisan politics (it was the government's banker). For Brown, "these institutions are the enemies of the people and of popular rights."[54]

The Brown program offered a variety of prescriptions, but they all gave the impression that the Liberals were only running for the role of official opposition. Offering remarkably little in terms of vision and promise, Brown proposed that the Reform Party, as he called it, would fight "demoralization, gross corruption and recklessly extravagant administration of the public finances."[55] His party would be different. Where he saw Macdonald using and discarding political friends, leaving a "path strewn with dead men's bones,"[56] Brown's party would stand against political opportunism and offered something different: a moral party. "It is time that Upper Canadians were united together in resisting these monopolies and the Government which has created and supports them."[57]

Brown argued that the Macdonald party was deeply in debt to the Grand Trunk Railway and that the reverse was also true: the Grand Trunk leadership had always looked upon the Intercolonial Railway as their prize. "Reformers are committed against handing the Intercolonial Railway over to the Grand Trunk, and against expending an extravagant sum in building it. The Intercolonial Railway was never too popular with a section of the Reform Party and Reform leaders will be under especial obligation to get it built as cheaply as possible, in order to save their credit with their supporters."[58] Brown's party would avoid such favouritism. It would be "above all things an economical party."[59]

Of course, there were problems for all to see. As Agnes Macdonald put it bluntly very early in the 1867 campaign: "John manages ... his coalition government so clearly that I don't think B[rown]. will affect much tho – he is very strong west." But she knew Brown's weakness well: "The queerest thing of all – his trying for roman catholic support after vilifying them their religion and their institutions for years past."[60] The alliance with the *Rouges* in Quebec had never been anything but instrumental – lip service at best. Brown's anti-Catholicism and apparent Francophobia were not easily forgiven. There was precious little charm in Brown's personality, and only rare glimpses of empathy pierced the steely methodism that he wore as an armour. The consequences ran deep. Brown was the leader of Reformism and could probably command the most votes, but he was not leadership material outside the westernmost parts of Canada West.

Brown was optimistic. He saw signs that the party was coming together in Ontario, he told Holton, and predicted that results would be surprising in the next election. New people like Edward Blake, the impressive young Toronto lawyer, were interested in joining the party. Blake was a promising catch, Brown believed: "excellent common sense, immense industry and great pluck. Not much of a politician, but anxious to learn and as sharp as a needle."[61] Blake shouldered all the hopes Brown could muster. He was smart and able and seemed to carry a liberal message with conviction. He was rich and liked it when people knew it: he called it his "independence." He wasn't seeking office to make money because he made more money annually than all the members of cabinet combined. Not all have seen him so positively. He was described by his biographer as a "thick-set, rather flabby looking man with a broad boyish face and small oval glasses. An uneven fringe of beard extended downward from each ear along the line between chin and neck. Nothing betrayed his great ability as a lawyer or his great potential as a Parliamentarian."[62] A contemporary described his personality "as devoid of warmth as is a flake of December snow and as devoid of magnetism as is a loaf of unleavened bread."[63]

Blake travelled for part of his campaign on his yacht, the *Rivet*, but was himself less than riveting, and when he landed in Orono, he found McDougall waiting for him. The debate was a long match, with Blake speaking through the night and into the early morning, interrupted only by a midnight storm and McDougall's challenging rebuttal. The *Toronto Leader*, a Conservative paper, described Blake's debut as "a melancholy thing."[64] The Conservative attacks had no effect: Blake became a double winner, taking both the provincial riding of Bruce South (Ontario) and the federal riding of Durham West.

The *Elora Observer*, a reformist paper, explained succinctly the Brown platform. Reform stood against Macdonald's party because, in its view, its very existence threatened parliamentary democracy. Parties consisting of coalitions of diametrically different views were by definition without principles. It followed that coalitions could survive only by endless compromise and "gross corruption,"

122 *Ballots and Brawls*

which would lead to "public demoralization." Coalition parties were not likely to attract good people but more likely "scoundrels," "as ready to sell his vote as a pickpocket the last watch he has stolen." Macdonald's initial concerns with Confederation were held against him. His government could not be trusted with the construction of a railway to the east because his experience with the Grand Trunk had been only ruinous. Canada was a new country and the new parliament would give a formative shape to the constitution. Reform, in contrast, offered "distinctive principles and broad lines of differences." Reform principles would be better.[65]

The *Erie News,* another Liberal publication, insisted that the Macdonald government was unfit to manage the Intercolonial Railway, now estimated to cost over $15 million. "If we allow John A. and his followers to manage the giving out of the contracts and to manipulate the enterprise we may expect it to cost fifty millions of dollars," it told its readers. "Reflect, then, before you decide to cast your vote for supporters of men who did much to increase your taxes." It argued that having politicians, both in Ottawa and in Toronto, who were likely to be careful with money was preferable. Pointing to the expenses of the Grand Trunk and of the Parliament building being erected in Ottawa, it did not consider Conservatives to be safe hands inspired by principles of "justice and economy."[66]

There were two Ontarian threats to Confederation, in the Liberal view. The first came from those who did not want it in the first place, but their numbers were small. The real threat came from spendthrifts like Macdonald who were likely to hold the provincial level – and Ontario – in contempt. "The new constitution concedes no principle so dear to the people of Ontario as the right of self-government," wrote the *Sarnia Observer,* "yet Sir John A. Macdonald does not hesitate to pursue a course which, if persisted in, must eventually end in the destruction of the local governments, and with them the constitution itself." For the Grits, protection of provincial rights was "the only principle in it worth contending for."[67]

## Macdonald's Attack Dog: William McDougall

Sandfield Macdonald very quickly went after Brown. At Brougham on July 24, he debated Brown before seven hundred people, and clearly left no argument unspoken. Brown thought the new Ontario premier "made an ass of himself."[68] The anti-Brown campaign, however, was galvanized by William McDougall, forty-five, who was described by the *Quebec Gazette* as a man with "genuine pluck."[69] Born in York (Toronto) in 1822 and raised on a farm north of Toronto (today's Lawrence Park), McDougall attended Victoria College in Cobourg, Upper Canada, and began practising law in 1847. He was passionately interested in ideas and in journalism, and saw himself as the legatee of the rebels and patriots of 1837 – at age sixteen, he had witnessed the battle of Montgomery's Tavern, which took place one kilometre south of the family farm. The confrontation planted in his heart and mind an uncompromising defence of justice and law. He was also of rare eloquence, a gift he applied as one of the theorists of the Clear Grit movement. It was an uncompromising blend of a form of anticlericalism (advocating the abolition of Clergy Reserves); advocacy of democratic reform (voting by secret ballot), an end to arbitrariness in decision-making, more rights for landholders and farmers, and more independence from Britain; and, increasingly, a demand to have Rupert's Land integrated into the United Province of Canada. In 1847, he and a colleague started the *Canada Farmer,* a weekly paper dedicated to agriculturalists eager to improve their husbandry of the land and of their farms. The proudly nationalist publication expanded through mergers and by 1849 was known as the *Canadian Agriculturalist.* Thrilled by the cries for a more effective democracy in Europe that year and by the evolution of democracy in the United States, McDougall set about defining a more demanding sort of Liberalism – he wanted it to be known not simply as "Grit" but as "Clear Grit": uncompromising in its demands for immediate reform to the Canadian government, including even more responsible

124  *Ballots and Brawls*

government – accountable to the people in all circumstances. He wanted to go further than George Brown's nascent *Globe*. It was a matter not only of ideology but also of style.

That said, by 1855, he was willing to compromise. He sold his newspaper and joined the *Globe* as a writer, and soon trumpeted the demands for representation by population. In 1859, he supported Brown's call for a federal union to break through the political logjam of the province, but he grew restless watching Brown in action. McDougall left the *Globe* in 1860, and essentially considered himself a free agent. Sandfield Macdonald recognized his abilities and asked him to join his government in 1862 as commissioner of Crown lands. He expanded his contacts in Washington, DC, and befriended members of Abraham Lincoln's entourage – he even attended Lincoln's celebrated address at Gettysburg, Pennsylvania, in November 1863. McDougall threw himself into the task of expanding access to the north, bought land from Indigenous bands, and encouraged settlement. In 1864, he joined the bandwagon to encourage the "Great Coalition" and participated in the talks in Charlottetown and Quebec City. He had no trouble working with Sir John A. Macdonald and gladly joined the new government as minister of public works on July 1. Agnes Macdonald had recognized in McDougall a man who could be confident, empathetic, and warm-hearted.

It was not lost on anyone that McDougall – a founder of the Clear Grit movement and long among Macdonald's harshest critics, constantly complaining of profligacy, jobbery and waste, and scandalously poor administration – was now working with Brown's political nemesis. McDougall came out of the reformist convention in Toronto in an absolutely furious state, and volunteered to attack Alexander Mackenzie, who had savagely berated him at the conference. "Macdougall [sic] and [William] Howland have returned from Toronto in good spirits," insisted Macdonald a few days after the Toronto Liberal convention. "It is believed that they have made a

William McDougall, circa 1864
Photographer William Ellisson, Library and Archives Canada, C-008362

great impression upon the members of the Convention by their manly conduct there. The split in the Reform ranks seems to be permanent, and it appears to me now certain, with the joint action of the moderate Liberals and the Conservative party proper, that a majority must be obtained."[70] McDougall was of the same view. There was a concern that perhaps Howland might be challenged in his riding by Daniel O'Donoghue, a young organizer of the nascent labour movement in Ottawa. "I shall watch Mr. O'Donoghue and at the right time shall pay him off," Macdonald reassured a supporter.[71]

After a few weeks in Ottawa to look after departmental affairs, McDougall took the fight straight to Mackenzie country, Lambton

126 *Ballots and Brawls*

County in Western Ontario, far from his own riding in the Ottawa Valley. In early August, he confronted Mackenzie at a meeting in Watford. A few days later, he repeated the gambit at Plympton when Mackenzie was giving a speech at Fisher's schoolhouse. McDougall rallied his supporters to hector Mackenzie to the point that the Liberal decided to leave, but the rowdies refused to budge. They took hold of Mackenzie's horses and carriage, and attacked both Mackenzie and his assistant. Mackenzie finally made it back to his buggy, but the road was disrupted by more stops and obstacles.[72] A few days later, at a meeting in Arkona, McDougall actually called Mackenzie a traitor – charging that the Liberals wanted the new country to crumble and be swallowed whole by the United States. Mackenzie was riled up beyond recognition. "Me, disloyal?" he shouted. "Do I not wear the Queen's uniform? Have I not camped with my fellow-citizens underfoot the British flag?" He was beside himself. "Let me tell him to his face that he is mistaken Loyalty to the Queen is a noble sentiment in which all true Liberals share, but loyalty to the Queen does not require a man to bow down to her manservant, her maidservant or her ass."[73] McDougall left the hall, but tensions ran high and more brawling ensued.

It was Mackenzie who was now in pursuit. As McDougall made his way back to Ottawa to tend to government business, he stopped for a rally in Almonte (in his Lanark County riding). Mackenzie was right behind him and challenged him openly. In the neighbouring town of Middleville, on the next day, McDougall got his revenge by interfering with a Brown meeting.[74]

McDougall debated his old colleague Brown effectively on August 14 at Brougham (now a part of Pickering). A week later, a "monster meeting" took place at 8 p.m. in Whitby's Drill Shed, attended by over three thousand people. The local candidate, Thomas Gibbs, talked first for about thirty minutes but yielded to McDougall, who identified himself as a member of the Reform Party and not as a "defender of Sir John A. Macdonald ... or the apologist for

Mr. Cartier or Mr. Galt." McDougall saluted Brown for joining the coalition in 1864 but noted the opportunism of the Liberal leader and accused him of using the impasse of 1864 to launch Canada on a new course, and doing so without consulting colleagues. "Now, that may be statesmanship. That may be an evidence of great political wisdom. Some of the party agreed with the gentleman, but, in my opinion, it was an unwise course to take," McDougall argued. "It was inconsistent with all our professions, as leaders of a great party, to permit a government which we had just condemned to remain in power without being able to offer to the public any guarantee for an amendment of their policies." The Tories, he reminded his listeners, were a minority in Ontario. Brown, he argued, had walked away from his responsibilities.

It was for that reason that McDougall had sought a presence in government: "As hostages, as it were, for the due administration of the Government, and the faithful representation of the opinions of the Liberal Party in the new constitution." McDougall argued that the "overwhelming majority" of Liberals agreed with that view." Brown was presented as an opportunist. He was against ideas and particular people but was always ready to change his mind: "If they were bad men previously, they became good when he joined them." The reverse was also true; if Brown's ideas were ignored, former colleagues were now disparaged. McDougall explained that, in his view, the ambitions of 1864 had not yet been fulfilled: "It was the object ... to build up upon this continent a nation of freemen, whose power should extend from sea to sea." "Where is Newfoundland? Where is Prince Edward Island?" he asked. "The system is incomplete," he insisted. "Now see what the work of the Government still is. Neither Newfoundland is brought in, nor Prince Edward Island not British Columbia, nor do we see the Hudson's Bay Territory – an empire in itself – in the scheme. Why? There are yet two-thirds of the confederacy outside. The great object therefore remains still to be accomplished." McDougall pointed out that Brown was inconsistent

128 *Ballots and Brawls*

on tariffs, and he mocked Brown's accusation that he had been "purchased" by Macdonald. "Purchased indeed! I do not know by what standard he judges other men, whether by his own or not. I here throw back in his teeth the charge. If there is a man in this Dominion more purchasable than he, I would like to know his name." Six Liberals had joined the coalition, after all. Finally, McDougall pointed out Brown's friends, the *Rouges* in Lower Canada. "Do you read their papers – their organs?" he asked. "Do they declare that this new constitution is a blessing, a security for the country? No, it is denounced as a danger, and a curse." McDougall finished off by pounding on Reformism, given that Howe was actively campaigning against Confederation in Nova Scotia.[75]

### The Brown-Macdonald Showdown in Bowmanville

Brown campaigned hard in South Ontario and reported to his wife, Anne, that he was making "converts." He knew it was an uphill battle. Within a week of starting his campaign, he was confident that "the result was not doubtful" but that he had to work for every vote. "The people are wonderfully kind to me," he wrote, "& I have the very pick of the respectable people on my side."[76] In Bowmanville on September 4, nominations were held for the riding of South Ontario, where Brown had chosen to run against the local incumbent, Gibbs. Macdonald had been campaigning in the area, and the Reformers were anxious that both sides should be heard. The regular candidates having been nominated by noon, Macdonald was asked to speak, but he positively refused to do so. The organizers asked Brown to start around 6 p.m., when an estimated crowd of 2,200 people waited.

Brown began: "You, gentlemen, have been told here today by the conservative speeches that I am a killed candidate – a dead man. But I never in all my life before heard of a Prime Minister being frightened to face a dead man." At that point, Macdonald took a seat in the first row, right in front of Brown, who continued:

There sits the Premier, who alone can tell us of the policy of his administration, and he dare not tell it. Anything more craven than his present attitude I never, Mr. Chairman, witnessed the head of an administration who is afraid to open his lips unless Mr. Brown will speak before him. He promised to come to address you, and now I give him the opportunity. It will not be said that I did not allow Sir John A. the opportunity he sought today.[77]

He poured scorn on everything, and hurled every invective he could on Macdonald. Macdonald then took his turn and responded to Brown's accusations. An admirer reported that the prime minister was in good form, making fun of Brown for his constant pessimism and his endlessly wagging, accusatory finger. "Looking at us with his fitly waggish air," the unidentified but friendly reporter wrote of Macdonald, "he said those simple, sensible things which generally carry conviction."[78]

Money flowed in all directions. The Conservatives were being generous, it was alleged, but it was equally known that Brown was offering very large bids for votes. The *Whitby Gazette* mentioned the names of two electors who had been offered $25 each for their votes by Brown's agents. "After this, Mr. Brown should forever hold his peace about Conservative jobbery and corruption."

The polls opened on Monday, August 26. Reform supporters turned out for Brown and gave him a lead of 11 votes. The next day, however, Thomas Gibbs rallied his troops and Brown's advantage slowly eroded. By the time every voter had spoken, Gibbs had garnered 1,292 votes, 69 more than Brown. There is little doubt that Macdonald hit hard – nothing could give him more comfort than a legislature that could not boast Brown's presence. The impact in Toronto was dramatic. "The election in South Ontario created yesterday in the city a degree of excitement second only to that which was witnessed here during the Fenian invasion last year," wrote the *Ottawa Citizen*'s correspondent.[79] The Brownites had

130    *Ballots and Brawls*

prepared an extensive demonstration. A band had been secured, torches prepared, and everything made ready to escort the leader in triumph when he returned to Toronto. By 11 a.m., it was clear that Gibbs had taken the lead, getting a huge boost in the township of Tay. Hundreds started gathering at the *Globe's* office on King Street hoping to hear good news, but the good cheer quickly dissipated. By 5 p.m., Gibbs's victory was sealed.[80]

Humiliated, Brown did not take the news well. As he prepared to board his train, a stranger rudely accosted him, saying, "Mr. Brown, I am very glad you have been defeated." Brown sprang at the man with the fury of a tiger, grabbed him by the throat, and began shaking him savagely, when bystanders intervened and forced him away from his victim. Brown left amid the groans of a small crowd on the station platform, and quietly returned to Toronto. The reaction was decidedly different in front of the Conservative *Leader*. By 8 p.m., the street was completely blocked for nearly a hundred yards, and there must have been at least five thousand people present. A large platform had been erected in the middle of Leader Lane and illuminated with reflecting lamps, and a crowd began to gather. Macdonald appeared around 9 p.m. and was received with uproarious cheering, the largest and most enthusiastic political gathering ever witnessed in Toronto, according to one partisan newspaper.[81] As one correspondent wrote in the *Ottawa Citizen:* "The people of South Ontario ... have given Mr. Brown another opportunity to seek that privacy which he has, on two occasions within the last few years, expressed a preference for. He may now retire into private life and brood over his defeat."[82]

The *Quebec Gazette* predicted that the Brown defeat would have an impact elsewhere. "New Brunswick will feel it, and Nova Scotia still more; for there, public opinion may be said to be a good deal on the fence," it surmised. It considered that voters in Nova Scotia, in particular, might want to support the Conservatives led by Charles Tupper in order to bolster Confederation. "The conviction

A *Proper Scottish Square Go in Ontario* 131

has been growing among the Blue Noses that Howeism is nothing more than annexation, focused just sufficiently to redeem it from sheer disloyalty, and detecting the sham, will be prompt to repudiate all connection with its propagators, if anything turns up to initiate a stampede. We see how the South Ontario victory stirred the national heart in Toronto, and what a thunder-voiced rebuke it administered to the factionists."[83]

"The days of his dictatorship are over," crowed the *Ottawa Times*. "Whom he brands as a 'traitor' the people honor; whom he praises as a patriot – to wit, himself – they repel with scorn. His ghoul-like crunching up of the reputations of honester [sic] men than himself has at length brought forth fruit, and even if some other constituency should open a way into Parliament for him, he must enter the House crest fallen and shorn entirely of his title to the leadership of the Reform party which up till now he has usurped."[84]

McDougall was elected by acclamation in North Lanark on the same day Brown was defeated. "I am not a bit discouraged by the result of the elections, and did not feel two minutes' chagrin at my own defeat," Brown wrote a friend. But he also insisted that he would stay in public life.[85]

He had lost his election, but with his ability to wield shovels and pens, Brown could now devote himself to his farm, his cattle, and his *Globe*. Luther Holton, who declared himself "more disgusted than disappointed" by the result, urged Brown to stay in politics.[86]

# 4

# Quebec's Contest of Nationalisms

**MONTREAL, THE NEW** Canada's largest city with about 100,000 people, was a bit muted on Dominion Day. In his morning address, Mayor Henry Starnes – a man George-Étienne Cartier considered "indispensable" to the Conservative Party during a twenty-year career on city council and as a member of Parliament – underscored the country's achievement of independence. He saw Canadians "rise out of their dependent position of Colonies, and ... take their rank, among the nations of the Earth ... an event of the happiest omen to us all – to be accepted with gratitude and pride, and to be cherished and guarded with patriotic fervour and unyielding courage."[1] Starnes hosted a luncheon at his residence a few hours later, an affair that appeared a little more impromptu than it should have been, and he apologized for the informality of the event. It was understandable. The city of Montreal had created a committee to look after festivities, but it reported in mid-June that there was little point in doing anything as apathy was the standard response to any initiative.

All the same, Montreal took the day off. In the afternoon, the Montreal Lacrosse Club organized a match against the Iroquois of Kahnawake. To underline the importance of the event, both teams posed for photographer William Notman (the Kahnawake team in their informal garb; the Lacrosse Club in carefully pressed uniforms). The club had defeated the Iroquois in 1866 and offered a double payment to the Kahnawake team if it won on Dominion Day. Led by John Baptiste Rice, known simply as "Baptiste" in the news report, the Iroquois presented "the best Indians that ever played in Montreal," according to the *Montreal Herald* reporter. The Montrealers, led by Nicholas Hughes, won the first two quarters and the Kahnawake team won the last two. It is not clear whether the tie allowed the teams to take any money home.[2]

The evening had its moments too. The Séminaire de St-Sulpice on Notre-Dame Street was lit up at dusk, as was Mr. Privet's Chop House and Dion's Billiard Saloon. Businessmen brought in fireworks from Boston. They started around 8 p.m. with a hundred-gun salute, and successive volleys were fired in honour of "The Nation's Birthday," as well as for "Success to Manufacturers," "Success to Trade and Commerce," the Montreal Ocean Steamship Company (clearly one of the sponsors), and "*Vive la Confédération.*" *United We Stand* was recited and *God Save the Queen* followed. It was a very English, very business-oriented affair, but the event on Viger Square rated a mention only in the *Montreal Herald.*[3] The festive spirit was personified by Lady Don, an Australian on the North American leg of her international tour. Known for her "high talent for comedy and burlesque," she presented her show at the Théâtre Royal to an appreciative audience.[4]

There was no great anticipation on the non-business English side either. John William Dawson, the principal of McGill University, told Joseph Howe that "scarcely anyone among the English of Lower Canada desires Confederation, except perhaps as an alternative to simple dissolution of the Union."[5] That spring, he had warned the graduating class that "the great political change on which this country is about to enter" was comparable to an alumnus having "little more than a nominal connection with his University." He was more worried over educational matters, and troubled that "we stand alone in Lower Canada as an English Minority." He was particularly upset that university matters were not considered a federal matter and feared encroachment that would "lower the standard of degrees."[6]

## The George-Étienne Cartier Strategy

John A. Macdonald and the *Bleus* of the new province were in a commanding position to start the first electoral campaign. Macdonald deferred almost completely to Cartier when it came to Quebec's affairs, and Cartier wasted no time getting organized for the 1867 election.[7] Cartier was without doubt the strongest political actor. He seemed to know everything and everyone in practically every region and sector of the province, and his mastery of the political game had no rival anywhere, except perhaps for Macdonald himself. He also had money. He had the support of the wealthy Molson and Beaudry families and, as the lawyer for the Grand Trunk Railway, could source other funds. Cartier wasted not a minute getting the campaign going, and operationalized a strategy that had been at least two years in the making. For him, Quebec could be won only if Confederation was presented as banal – a rather ordinary new phase in the francophone community's progress, even while living in what could be a perpetual minority situation. The platform of the Conservative coalition was "peaceful revolution" (*la revolution pacifique*): a transformation of governance that would be smooth, stable, and not threatening to the interests of French Canadians.[8]

Cartier could even point to a manifesto of sorts when Joseph-Alfred Mousseau (who would be premier of Quebec in 1882–84) wrote *Contre-Poison: La Confédération, c'est le salut du Bas-Canada*, a vigorous pamphlet defending the new country. The seventy-two-page publication highlighted the fact that Church leaders supported the idea. It criticized Antoine-Aimé Dorion for his association with George Brown and emphasized the *New York Herald*'s pleas for the full annexation of Canada.

The *Bleus* in Quebec had a wide arsenal at hand with which to echo Mousseau's words. They could count on fairly popular newspapers such as the daily *La Minerve* in Montreal, which Cartier controlled, and *Le Journal de Québec* in the new capital. *La Minerve*'s editorialists were busy writing that the new political system should give its readers "a legitimate feeling of pride for our influence in the past and a great hope for the future." Canada, its lead article declared on July 2, was now "a power, not only in title, but in its strength, in its population, in its wealth, and in its means for the future."[9] The *Bleus* could even count on *Le Canadien*, owned by Liberal François Évanturel, who was also an MP from Quebec, for some support: "I am in favour of the principle of Confederation, and one of those who maintain that by means of that principle the rights and liberties of each of the contracting parties may be preserved," he had written. "But on the other hand, I am of opinion ... that it may be so applied as to endanger and even destroy, or nearly so, the rights and privileges of a state which is a party to this Confederation. Everything, therefore, depends on the conditions of the contract."[10] *Le Courrier de Saint-Hyacinthe* was also an ally, vigorously emphasizing the idea that the Intercolonial Railway would become the "wealth" of the regions – mostly Témiscouata and Rimouski – it would serve. It would galvanize commerce and help settlers deeper in the territories.[11] In English, conservative forces could count on the *Gazette,* which was focused on commerce in Montreal. In Quebec City, the *Quebec Chronicle* provided friendly support.

Macdonald's view on Quebec was rather soberer and more focused on its governance. All through June, the issue of who would be tapped to form the first government in the province of Quebec was a matter of speculation. Macdonald, as always relying on George-Étienne Cartier's advice, asked Sir Narcisse Belleau, the new Lieutenant-Governor of Quebec, to appoint Joseph Cauchon, fifty-one, as premier. An intellectual journalist (he founded the *Journal de Quebec* in 1842) and deeply experienced politician, Cauchon was

136    *Ballots and Brawls*

a genuine liberal-conservative. He had supported Louis-Hippolyte La Fontaine's reformist policies from the moment he entered Lower-Canadian politics in 1844 as the Member for Montmorency. As the years progressed, however, Cauchon supported more radical policies, including the abolition of the seigneurial system and of the Clergy Reserves, and making the Legislative Council elective. He was appointed to cabinet in 1855, but resigned two years later to protest (and, very likely, to personally profit from) the government's underfunding of railways, something he cared about immensely. In 1861, he was made minister of public works in the Cartier-Macdonald government, and was reappointed to the position in 1864 when the *Bleu*-Conservative coalition was returned to office. He served as mayor of Quebec City in 1865–67. The well-bearded Cauchon was among the earliest and one of the leading champions of the idea of Confederation in Quebec, and developed his ideas in various booklets: *Étude sur l'union projetée des provinces britanniques de l'Amérique du Nord* was published in 1858 as the idea barely started to take root. His *Aux électeurs du Bas-Canada* (1863) further explored the urgency of finding a better solution to Quebec's governance. The book was adapted for an English-reading audience as *The Union of the Provinces of British North America* (1865).[12]

For Macdonald, Cauchon was a natural and eminently deserving of support, but there was a problem: the issue of governing Protestant/English-language education in the new Quebec. Though he actively sought the participation of anglophones in cabinet, Cauchon adamantly refused to create a separate Protestant school system. The leading spokesmen representing that constituency rallied against him and, to the dismay of both men, Macdonald had to pick a new person. George-Étienne Cartier, always the reliable guide on things Quebec, prompted him to turn to Pierre-Joseph Chauveau, fifty-two, another deeply cultivated lawyer/writer and a colleague in various governments during the 1850s. Chauveau had an important asset that would come in handy: he had been a friend of Louis-Joseph Papineau and of the *Patriote* cause. A Catholic of deep conviction, he also possessed a real flair for educational policy as he had been, since 1855, the superintendent of the Bureau of Education for Canada East. (Cauchon was appointed to the Senate and became its first speaker.)

There was some dissent in Conservative and *Bleu* ranks. The MP for Brome in the United Province of Canada, Christopher Dunkin, was opposed to Confederation.[13] An Englishman who had immigrated to Quebec in 1837 (after causing a riot among students at Harvard University), he saw in the Confederation project nothing more than a fatal separation of British North America from London that would harm Canada's sense of identity. Henri-Elzéar Taschereau, the MP for Beauce, saw it entirely differently but was opposed to Confederation as a "mortal blow against our nationality."[14] Such opposition was harmless. Dunkin ran in Brome for both the provincial and federal seats and won both.

Macdonald's coalition in Quebec had an ace up its sleeve to compensate for the lukewarm endorsements: the Church establishment. It was an association by default more than anything else. The Catholic clergy in Quebec had been in conflict with the *Rouge* movement for over a generation and was likely to continue being allergic to it in 1867.

## The Roman Catholic Church Factor

As elsewhere in the new Canada, the Catholic Church's leaders were generally supportive of Confederation, at least at the top of the hierarchy, and had been since June 1864, when the Great Coalition was forged. Such temporal matters did not seem to stir the various bishops in Quebec, who bought the argument that the legislative process in Canada was blocked. The alternative of a legislative union with Canada West where representation by population would determine the number of seats was seen as "*notre déchéance, et l'anéantissement de nos institutions et de notre nationalité*" (our loss of

138  *Ballots and Brawls*

dignity, the annihilation of our institutions and our nationality).[15] In the winter of 1865, Cartier declared that the clergy was generally in favour of Confederation in part because it was the "enemy" of political dissent and because it "saw in Confederation the solution to difficulties that had existed for a long time."[16]

Monsignor Ignace Bourget, the archbishop of Montreal, was onside, even though he did not personally like Cartier very much because of various business issues (Cartier was the lawyer for the Sulpicians, a priestly order that was often in conflict with the Montreal archdiocese over jurisdictional issues). Bourget issued a letter on May 23, 1867, urging his *curés* to encourage the faithful to fulfill their democratic duties, but did not mention Confederation explicitly. Two months later, on July 25, he instructed his clergy to support Confederation and told the curé of Saint-Médard Parish that "we preach against all the bad papers without attacking any one in particular but the confessors who notice the reading of such and such a paper will tell their parishioners that such reading is not allowed, and would only result in a refusal of absolution."[17] Monsignor Jean Langevin of Rimouski, the older brother of Hector-Louis Langevin, informed his flock that the new constitution was the product of legitimate authority and thus from God Himself. He called Confederation "providential" given "exceptional circumstances," and warned electors to be wary of the true intentions of "annexationists."[18] Pierre-Flavien Turgeon, the archbishop of Quebec City, whose key adviser was none other than Edmond Langevin, another brother of Hector-Louis, told his priests to "obey the commandment of God in accepting the federal union in all sincerity" and "to withhold any support to any man inclined to fight or to impair its functioning."[19] Bishop Louis-François Laflèche in Trois-Rivières also issued a letter, instructing the clergy to read it at Sunday Mass. He advised his priests that to oppose Confederation was a sin. The debates were robust. Monsignor Thomas Cooke, the other bishop of Trois-Rivières, wrote his flock on June 8, 1867, deploring the "violence" of the Confederation debate. "Now that the project has received the support of the Imperial government and has become the foundational law of the country, we must remember our duty, as Catholics, is to end the discussion on this topic."[20] There were likely many interactions between priests and politicians, only a few of which have been documented in surviving letters. George-Étienne Cartier encouraged Curé Marquis of the Saint-Pierre-Célestin Parish to press one of his *Rouge* parishioners to drop out of the race. The same curé wrote to Jean-Charles Chapais offering to "be the representative of the government to the bishops," but said that he would need a letter of introduction from a member of the government to document this authority. Marquis even offered to send a few notes that could inspire the letter![21]

Confederation posed a threat to the Church because Ottawa would now have the final word on marriage. The very Protestant Macdonald and his allies, however, were successful in assuaging that doubt and convinced Church leaders that the intention was to ensure only that rules were followed across the country on this sensitive matter, and that the federal government had no intention of getting involved in managing holy matrimony. Otherwise, the Catholic Church's supportive position was shaped by two factors. The first was a commitment to stability, and prelates liked what they saw in John A. Macdonald. The second was his opposition. George Brown, the leader of the Liberals, had a long record of hostility, and the particular threat to Catholic schools he represented was real. Church leaders were also acutely concerned by the potential importation of American democratic ideas that Brown represented.[22]

For the Church, the debate had taken place and the government had acted. "Regardless of past opinions, the good of our country and the teachings of our religion demand that we have a duty to accept it and to submit to it,"[23] declared Monsignor Charles Larocque, the bishop of Saint-Hyacinthe, in his pastoral letter of

140    *Ballots and Brawls*

June 18, 1867. He was resolutely confident that Quebec's distinct nature could withstand any effort towards assimilation and that Confederation was likely the best bulwark against a republican regime. In his *mandement* (directive) of June 18, he urged his flock to ignore the claim that annexation was preferable to Confederation, and to remain convinced that federalism was far more likely a better guarantee of protection of Quebec's language and religion.[24] Larocque appealed to Rome for leave to publicly condemn the Liberal newspapers of his town for their "ultraliberal doctrines."[25] (Leave was granted, but only in 1868.)[26]

Not everyone saw the Church as a benign force as the election campaign got started. The writers of *Le Pays* began collecting evidence of priestly advocacy and published their findings after the election. There was an account of François-Xavier Caisse, a priest in the village of L'Épiphanie, who offered a bushel of flour to a poor man in order to entice him to vote *Bleu*. There was also the case of Sulpician Augustin-Siméon Campion, who insisted from the pulpit that citizens could form their political opinions only on condition that they consult their pastors. In his *Le Québec et la Confédération: un choix libre?*, historian Marcel Bellavance catalogued numerous instances of local priests recommending or refusing to endorse young men for employment because of their religious views.

In Bagot, for instance, former mayor of Saint-Hyacinthe and long-standing *Rouge* Maurice Laframboise was denounced as "an obnoxious idiot, slave to an annexationist party" (Laframboise lost). Alexandre-Édouard Kierzkowski, the Liberal candidate in Saint-Hyacinthe was a "foreigner" (a Polish Catholic who had immigrated to Canada in 1841) whose candidacy could only be "outrageous" (he was elected). Pierre Bachand, the Liberal candidate for the Quebec legislature in the same riding, was "a weak lawyer who speculates on the assets of widows and orphans"[27] (he was elected.) A vote for Médéric Lanctôt in Montreal East was a vote for "crime, debauchery, treason, and revolution."[28] Bellavance, drawing on the revelations in *Le Pays* after the election, makes the case that people were threatened with excommunication if they did not support the *Bleus*. He calculates that the number of people who did not celebrate Easter the following spring averaged seventy-seven in each parish of the archdiocese of Montreal, arguably as a punishment for their votes.[29] (Of course, this is highly speculative as there are many reasons not to attend church, but the data are certainly compelling.)

Benjamin Sulte, Cartier's friend and personal secretary and then an important early historian of Quebec, cited the Church's influence as critical to Quebec's support for Confederation.[30] Fifty years after the election, Lionel Groulx, the priest and nationalist historian, added some subtlety to the argument and made the point that the Church did not speak out on federalism until elections became inevitable. He also observed that the bishops mostly limited their interventions to memoranda on the proper conduct for priests and pastors as well as a call for public prayers for the success of the elections. It was not explicit support for Confederation, in his view, but an expression of support for any "government that has been legitimately established." Groulx may have easily captured the reality, but there was no denying that the Church had tacitly accepted Confederation – in Quebec as elsewhere. Officially, it observed Rome's ruling not to get involved in the affairs of politicians, but locally it was too hostile to the *Rouges* to support anything they might advocate. What was so telling of the success of Cartier's strategy was the staggering number of ridings where the authority of the *Bleus* was unchallenged. In no less than twenty, in all parts of Quebec, were Conservative candidates acclaimed.

### Dorion's Troubled Leadership

In sharp contrast, the campaign in Quebec led by Antoine-Aimé Dorion highlighted the disarray of the Liberals. This internal division, which had existed for almost twenty years, cut across regions and generations and world views. The Liberals in Quebec

142  *Ballots and Brawls*

were opposed to Confederation because it was a threat to French Canada: it promised to eliminate the French language and (ironically, certainly for them to raise it) threaten Catholicism. Second, it was going to be very expensive as the new country would assume the costs of defence (including conscription!) and the Intercontinental Railway, and inevitably levy additional taxes – taxes that would hurt workers. Third, Confederation would likely provoke American hostilities towards British North America.

The *Rouges* were always subjecting themselves to a battery of tests. The inheritors of the radical tradition in Quebec that had contested the outsized colonial influence of the British and of the Church in the 1830s and 1840s recognized that the label had become a serious disability. Most *Rouges* did not want to be seen as radicals or annexationists, or as anticlerical. Instead, they wanted a political system that recognized and respected rights, including voting and linguistic rights, and that promoted education and government run on sound principles of justice. Many looked to a future in which trade could be liberalized; for some, that could include annexation to the United States. Dorion himself was a founder of the Montreal Annexation Association in 1849, an act that showed he was friendly with the English-speaking merchant class of the city, and that alienated so many that it may have impaired his political career forever.[31]

Dorion saw an opportunity to make *Rougisme* more moderate when rumours spread that *L'Avenir,* the *Rouge* paper, was about to shut down.[32] He launched *Le Pays* in 1852 and it instantly became the party's mouthpiece under Louis-Antoine Dessaulles's able editorship (he was also the mayor of Saint-Hyacinthe).[33] It was persuasive and significant and it gave Dorion an effective platform – so much so that he succeeded the old lion, Louis-Joseph Papineau, when the leader of the *Rouges*/Liberals retired for good in 1854. Slowly, over the years, his party improved its record among the electorate, but never took more than a third of the votes. Typically, the *Rouges* were more popular among Montrealers than outside that city. Dorion gained favour and respect steadily and actually served as co-premier in 1858 (for a few days, with George Brown).

Luther Holton, a Quebec MP and an important opinion-maker in English Quebec society, reported to Brown an important meeting on the subject of a federalism between Canada West and Canada East when it was first raised in October 1859:

> We sat from three o'clock to twelve and had a great deal of desultory but in the main intelligent and high-toned discussion. The Federation scheme formed the chief topic of discussion and was generally accepted as the best if not the only practicable solution of existing difficulties though some to whom it was comparatively new desired further time for consideration before pronouncing themselves definitively. Some of our more advanced Rouges, while giving in their adhesion to the proposed movement avowed their individual preference for a continuance of the Legislative Union with Representation by population. They fear the ascendancy of retrogressive ideas and especially the effects of clerical domination in Lower Canada if separated from Upper Canada. Dessaulles, Dorion, McGee, Drummond, Laberge & Papineau pronounced themselves emphatically and unreservedly in favor of Federation.[34]

The *Rouges* published this *prise de position* in *Le Pays* on October 29, 1859, and it remained as their policy. On the island of Montreal, the *Rouges* declined heavily as the 1860s progressed. In 1861, Dorion personally lost an election against Cartier. He joined the Reformer/ *Rouge* government of Sandfield Macdonald and Louis-Victor Sicotte in 1862 but did not stay long: when the idea was proposed a few months later that the Grand Trunk Railway could be expanded into an intercolonial railway project that would link Quebec City to Halifax if enough government support was provided, he resigned in disapproval. Three months later, he rejoined the government and

144  *Ballots and Brawls*

was chosen co-premier with Sandfield Macdonald. That government would last for just over one year. In 1863, the party won barely a third of the votes against Cartier's *Bleus*. Four years later, the tally had declined by almost half, to 18 percent. In Montreal proper, the party's 42 percent share of the 1863 vote declined to 12 percent. The *Rouges* did well in Verchères, Richelieu, Saint-Hyacinthe, Rouville, Bagot, and Shefford. They were strongest in the villages of L'Avenir, Kamouraska, and Drummond-Arthabaska.[35]

Dorion's relations with George Brown were uneasy at best, and he refused to join the Great Coalition that was created after his own government collapsed. He also declined the opportunity to join the Lower Canada delegations to Charlottetown and Quebec City. On November 7, 1864, Dorion again denounced the Confederation deal and took his opposition on the road, holding major assemblies in Rouville, Verchères, Iberville, Laprairie, Drummond-Arthabaska, Chambly, Bagot, Saint-Hyacinthe, and Montreal. He brandished a long list of complaints, denouncing the proposed federal jurisdiction over criminal law and the federal government's ability to suspend provincial legislation. Opponents were skeptical that Quebec's electoral weight of sixty-five seats in the House of Commons would enable it to protect the interests of French Canadians. Dorion resented the argument that the Intercontinental Railway needed to be built for defence purposes. "The best Canada can do," he argued, "is to be peaceable and to give its neighbour no pretext for war." He condemned the inability of the new provincial government to protect its borders. Above all, he wanted a referendum on the issue. Dorion proposed a resolution in January 1865 to the effect that Canadians had no interest in creating a new nationality.[36] He gave a long speech on February 16 and was the moving force behind the *Manifeste des 20,* an anti-Confederation pamphlet signed by twenty MPs. For him, Confederation was nothing more than the evil work of British magnates who were pulling strings in order to protect their financial interests.

History weighed heavily as the Liberals prepared for an election two years later, in 1867. Just thirty years earlier, the country had experienced an uprising, and the young men who had fought the redcoats in Saint-Eustache, Saint-Charles, or Saint-Denis were now in their fifties and sixties, still active and with their memory intact. That generation might have favoured the *Rouges* but they knew that many of the *Bleus* had also fought the British in 1837–38. Now, the populace was not certain. Robert Rumilly, a French immigrant to Quebec who wrote extensively about the politics of 1867 based on interviews he conducted in the 1920s and 1930s with the direct descendants of leading intellectuals and politicians in the Confederation era, described public opinion as "indecisive and suspicious."[37]

The general apathy created conditions where Church leaders were willing to give Confederation a chance.[38] *Le Défricheur* complained about it on February 7, 1866. But there was a conviction that if they plan were put to the people, it would be defeated.[39] A number of politicians argued that the United Province of Canada should hold elections on the issue, just as New Brunswick had in the winter of 1865.[40] There were other *Rouge* newspapers scattered in the province, but their readership was sparse and their messages were often confused. *L'Électeur* in Quebec City was an example, as were *Le Journal de Lévis* and *Le Journal de Saint-Hyacinthe*.

Many among the clergy were also unconvinced by the Confederation project, in Rumilly's view.[41] Even among the English-speaking Reformers in Quebec, the Confederation idea was not popular. Luther Holton and Lucius Seth Huntington were both against it, as was the *Montreal Herald*, the Grit newspaper. The *Sherbrooke Gazette*, usually a Galt supporter, opposed it.[42] The *True Witness*, a Catholic newspaper in Montreal edited by George-Edward Clerk, a Scotsman who had converted, was horrified at the alliance struck with Brown, "the vulgar slanderer" of Catholicism and the "mortal enemy" of French Canadians; he also dismissed the notion that the Maritimes could add to Canada's security, pointing out instead that their weak defences actually made an attack more likely and Canada thus more vulnerable.[43]

And yet, at some point that remains difficult to pinpoint, many *Rouges* decided to rally to Confederation. *L'Ordre* declared on March 27, 1867, that there was no point in fighting Confederation but that the challenge was now to make it work for French Canadians. On June 1, *Le Pays* conceded that: "la Confédération est un fait accompli."[44] Essentially, all the party leaders in Quebec were agreed. It was not a "passionate" affair, according to Rumilly.[45] Rather, Dorion concluded that there was no point in fighting Confederation because there were too many forces in favour of it, not least the clergy. In the late 1850s, he had shown himself momentarily favourable to a federal arrangement between Canada East and Canada West, and he decided in early 1867 that there was no longer any point in opposing the idea of a broader confederation.

All the same, he threw himself into the race in order to unify forces and mobilize opinion. He exercised his moral authority in creating the Association de la réforme du Bas-Canada on May 30, much like George Brown, who had created a similar association in Upper Canada. The executive included Dorion as well as Maurice Laframboise, Joseph Doutre, J.A. Plinguet, and Médéric Lanctôt – representatives of each element in the Liberal spectrum, from the more conservative to the more radical. Alfred Lusignan, the editor of *Le Pays*, was the secretary. Dorion, Doutre, and Lusignan were willing to (reluctantly) accept Confederation, and this group rallied around *Le Pays*. Plinguet, editor of *L'Ordre*, a moderate publication that was notably far more friendly to the Church, declared himself sharply opposed to the presence of Lanctôt, the editor of *L'Union Nationale*, who clearly represented the more extreme wing of the party.[46] A membership list showed that this organization was composed of forty-nine men.[47]

Dorion was indisputably the Liberal leader in Quebec, but the *Rouges* were gravely divided over the question of Confederation,

*Quebec's Contest of Nationalisms* 147

not to mention atomized by it. It certainly affected his political relations. He hardly spoke with Luther Holton, the leader of English-speaking wing of the party in Canada East and Brown's key correspondent on Quebec matters. Five publications in Quebec were against Confederation. Three were based in Montreal (*L'Ordre, Le Pays,* and *L'Union Nationale*) and two were on the South Shore (*Le Journal de Saint-Hyacinthe* and *Le Franco-Canadien* in Saint-Jean). The *Montreal Herald* was a reliable Liberal organ that catered to the commercial class but often sounded Francophobic and anti-Catholic, like Brown's *Globe*. The *Witness* was liberal but very Protestant; the English Catholic paper was the *True Witness*. For a long time, it had been hostile to Confederation, but it now supported it.[48]

For all their efforts to create a program, the Liberals could not overcome the prejudices against them that had lasted for almost a generation. They were presented as anticlerical, as hostile to the Church's role in society, in policy-making, and in culture, and as annexationists with republican tendencies. The Liberals had made tremendous efforts to change their reputation since the 1850s, with Dorion trying to rein in the more radical voices in *Le Pays* and the Institut Canadien, but the hostility was unshakable. It did not help that he promoted Henri-Gustave Joly de Lotbinière as the leader of the opposition in the province in response to Chauveau's being named premier. Joly was a Protestant and had fought the idea of Confederation since its inception. His arguments were hardly original. In essence, he saw no guarantee that federalism did anything to diminish tribalism, and yet it threatened the ability of French Canadians to thrive. Beyond that, there was no proof that federalism would help the economy – and, in an original but highly prescient twist, he argued that the new union would eventually weaken the link to Great Britain.[49]

But Joly was not a radical, either ideologically or temperamentally. Like many *Rouges*, including Dorion himself, he provided an erudite critique of Confederation but technically accepted it, and, for good measure, also ran for a seat in the national parliament. He was acclaimed as the deputy for the new legislative assembly and also won the seat in Ottawa (which meant that both the premier of Quebec and the leader of the opposition sat across each other in both legislatures!). It was the task of Dorion and Joly to overcome the opposition to the Liberals in Quebec, but it was not easy. In fact, it would be thirty years before the Liberals rose to power under Wilfrid Laurier in 1896.

More importantly, Dorion also seemed estranged from the young Liberals in Quebec, who seemed on the whole against the idea of Confederation. As elsewhere across the new country, most of them could not vote, but beyond that it seems that the most outspoken opponents of Confederation were young. Arthur Buies, twenty-seven, a promising journalist and essayist who had enlisted to fight with Giuseppe Garibaldi's Red Shirts (and thus proclaimed his hostility to the Church), drafted a long article against Confederation in the winter of 1867. He returned to his beloved Paris in the spring, trying to find inspiration and outlets for his creative impulses, and found a publisher for his text, which appeared in the August issue of *La revue libérale politique littéraire, scientifique et financière.*[50] He regretted the Confederation pact, unable to conceive how it could possibly work. The English would never respect the French, and the idea that a government could be founded on antithetical entities made no sense.[51] And yet, his key worry was the grip of the Catholic Church in Quebec, which would likely disarm the critics of Confederation. He also blamed the *Rouges,* who, like Dorion, had increasingly bought into the idea.[52] Buies had nothing but respect for Dorion, "who did everything he could to rally the splintered parts of the Liberal party and opposed the iniquitous measures and the degradations of the Tory party," but could no longer fight circumstances stronger than himself and had to reconcile himself to Confederation.[53] Buies's text was probably the most sophisticated critique of Confederation to be published in

1867. He had no faith that it would be well received in Quebec, or perhaps did not care whether or not it was read there. The young man was probably more concerned about making a literary impact in France, but those hopes were dashed.

## Médéric Lanctôt's Quixotic Campaign

Médéric Lanctôt, twenty-nine, was another young *Rouge* dissenter. Like Buies, though he also still had enormous respect for Dorion, Lanctôt saw possibilities in tying the future of *Rougisme* to labour, particularly in Montreal, where working conditions were reputedly some of the worst in North America. Living conditions were particularly crushing, with widespread poverty and the highest infant mortality rate on the continent.

Lanctôt was a uniquely compelling young man. He had started work at the *Courrier de Saint-Hyacinthe* as a teenager, but left in 1858 – at the age of twenty – because it was far more conservative than he could stand. Like so many others in Quebec, he was deeply suspicious of Canada West's ambitions. When Macdonald expressed the desire for the Province of Canada to take its place "among the nations of the planet" as an independent country in London, Ontario, in July 1856, the eighteen-year-old thundered against Macdonald's French Canadian supporters, who had "sold their human dignity for big money" by applauding – at a moment when Lower Canada's independence was at hand – the vision of the attorney general.[54] And yet, in the winter of 1859, Lanctôt delivered three scintillating lectures at the Institut Canadien in Montreal that caught everyone's attention. He seemed to be a perpetually energized orator, participating in twenty-eight debates between 1853 and 1871 and sitting numerous times on the Institut's executive committee between 1853 and 1863.[55]

He then became the editor of *Le Pays,* Dorion's newspaper, but it was not an easy fit: Lanctôt liked to denounce the clergy's influence in politics and often risked getting the newspaper condemned by the Church, making Dorion, a practical politician who was convinced that the priest's support was essential to success, very uncomfortable. At the same time, Lanctôt decided to switch gears and study law at McGill University. He passed the bar exam following a clerkship in the firm led by Gonzalve Doutre and Charles Daoust (two of the most uncompromising *Rouges*) and started anew. He travelled to France for a few months, married into the Daoust family, and started his own law firm. His time at *Le Pays* revealed him to be increasingly hostile towards George-Étienne Cartier and any expansion of the Grand Trunk Railway funded by the state. He continued to express his hostility to any project of Confederation, much as he had in the *Courrier de Saint-Hyacinthe.*[56]

The young Lanctôt did not hesitate to take action. With two others, he launched a new Montreal paper, *La Presse,* on October 1, 1863, and used its pages to express outrage on a variety of issues, even though at one point in 1859 he had espoused the idea of a larger federation. He was incensed when George Brown promoted the idea in June 1864. "We thought we heard the feline voice of the great *bête noire* of cleargritism cry out 'finally I'm taking a bite out of you and I'll swallow you whole, you and your race and your religion, damned little Frenchmen,'" he lamented.[57] The follow-up editorial of was full of despair. The union agreement was judged as "the most nefarious and darkest era the lower-Canada family has ever experienced." Calling for resistance to the scheme, he asked his readers to give him the time necessary to convince them. He denounced *La Minèrve,* the Conservative mouthpiece, as the apostle of Lord Durham's assimilationist ideas and of "national annihilation." All through the summer of 1864, he blasted Confederation in one article after another, and demanded that Lower Canada be given total independence to defend French Canada, its language, and its way of life.

*La Presse* was not making money, even as Lanctôt scaled new heights of alarm as the Charlottetown Conference took place. It announced that it was shutting down on September 1, 1864 (that paper should not be confused with the daily that was launched in 1884 and still exists), but that its ideas would be carried by a new publication, *L'Union Nationale*. It first appeared two days later as delegates at Charlottetown approved in principle the idea of a Confederation of the four eastern provinces. The paper's name said it all: French Canadians had to form a strong union to fight the new proposal. Regardless of the masthead, Lanctôt's ideas were not on the agenda as the Charlottetown Conference got underway.

Lanctôt was convinced that Lower Canada's ability to declare independence was an acquired right. Dorion, in his view, had lost sight of the most important thing: the French Canadian identity.

> Where are our French Canadian politicians who will deal with this question where the stakes are most important and real: the impact on our autonomy, our national conservation! Where are the party leaders who are ready to mount an offence against confederation, the French Canadian flag in hand and the charter of our rights in hand! We need more spirit, more momentum, more national patriotism to win this victory and to break the federal link that seeks to tie a French nationality to the stock of a rival nation. To the enemy like George Brown and traitors like George-Étienne Cartier and Étienne-Paschal Taché who say "the British national interest demands confederation" our heart must respond "the national interests of French Canadians rejects it!"[58]

Lanctôt was inspired by the idea of independence for Quebec and repeal of the plan for Confederation that had been concocted by Macdonald and Cartier. Instead, he wanted a politics that united French Canadians, rights for workers and the downtrodden, and an eternal fight against assimilation as the likely product of unlimited immigration. "We want a political existence that harmonizes interests, that honours true integrity, that rewards the work of arms

152   *Ballots and Brawls*

and brains, where wisely liberal and naturally progressive institutions protect the men of the country," he pleaded. He favoured a country that would allow for enlightenments of all sorts, as well as economic prosperity that would reach the poorest in society. "Without these conditions," he argued, "we would consider any existence to be abnormal, sick and in transition, in a word it would be a national suicide."[59] His practical solution was a "compromised confederation" in which each province would declare that it was working towards independence and that Confederation was nothing more than a passing stage. Hoping for closer economic ties with the rapidly growing United States, he did not favour annexation.

Lanctôt's energies leaped beyond the printed word. He launched a variety of public demonstrations against the Confederation project in the streets of Montreal, culminating in a significant event on September 24 on Sainte-Catherine Street attended by over two thousand people, according to the *Union Nationale* (the *Montreal Gazette* estimated the audience at four hundred). Another demonstration took place four days later at the corner of Sainte-Catherine and Visitation Streets, attracting a crowd estimated at between seven and eight hundred; a third took place on October 5 at the corner of Durham and Dorchester Streets (now René-Lévesque Boulevard),[60] with Lanctôt demanding a united front of French Canadians against the union project. He called the Quebec Conference the "Quebec Conspiracy" and demanded accountability from the Canada East delegates. He condemned in particular Taché's closing speech at the Quebec Conference, which contained a plea for a new Canadian nationality.

Lanctôt persevered in his campaign to undermine the *Bleu* machine in other ways. He launched the Club Saint-Jean-Baptiste in Montreal to rally the *nationalistes.* In February 1866, he ran against a Cartier protégé in the Montreal city council election in Quartier-Est and won. His election was challenged a few months later on technicalities, but, helped by his law firm partner Wilfrid Laurier, he easily won his case. He weaponized the *Union Nationale* to undermine Cartier and his pro-Confederation campaign, publishing some of the best talent in Quebec's intellectual class, such as Laurent-Olivier David and Louis-Amable Jetté. They launched a campaign against a Montreal by-law proposed in June 1866 that seemed particularly odious – giving voters the right to vote in each riding in which they owned property. Lanctôt argued that it was a glaringly undemocratic measure that undermined the working class and deepened the hold of Cartier's faction on the city council. Lanctôt was re-elected in 1867 (elections were held annually) but was disqualified during the summer of 1867.

Lanctôt stood out in denouncing the federal project. Though short of stature, he was ceaselessly energized by the causes of the day. His oratory quickly made headlines and he could attract crowds at the drop of a hat, leaving his young colleague Wilfrid Laurier to deal with the travails of his law office.

The *Union Nationale* was merciless towards Cartier and *La Minerve,* his Montreal mouthpiece. It published a pamphlet, *La Confédération, couronnement de dix années de mauvaise administration,* as a sort of manifesto. Macdonald was condemned for his uninhibited thirst for power, for his need to fulfill Lord Durham's wish for the full assimilation of French Canadians, for denying the people a voice in crafting the Confederation arrangement, for the creation of a standing army, and for pursuing economic policies that had impoverished the country. Worse still, it argued, Confederation would bring "direct taxation." Lanctôt also supported Joseph Howe in an article published on October 15, 1866, impressed with Howe's petition of forty thousand signatures demanding that the Confederation project not include Nova Scotia.

Lanctôt was despondent as a result of the negotiations taking place in London in December 1866 and concluded that, even if Confederation were accomplished, the new Canada had to remove itself from British affairs. He withdrew to his study and crafted two new

154  *Ballots and Brawls*

works. The first, a 136-page book titled *L'indépendance pacifique du Canada,* was published as the elections were about to conclude in September 1867. It was too late, and also confusing. Had he abandoned the idea of an independent Quebec? Why was he now focused on the independence of Canada?

Marie-Marthe Filion-Montpetit, his best biographer, sees this change of tactic as emerging from his understanding of law.[61] His notion was that the tie to Britain distorted politics at home by instilling some sort of naive idea that Westminster traditions could protect Canadian liberties. He argued instead that Britain's colonialism was eroding Canada's ability to deal with, in particular, the United States. It followed that cutting the ties to the Empire was necessary to the security and "honour" of the people and would give Canada the right to conduct its own foreign policy and its own trade practices. Canada had to be seen in the United States as entirely outside the British sphere of influence. It would free Canada to pursue its own policies with its giant neighbour, as well as give it the right to protect its industries and local values.[62]

But Lanctôt was not just writing books that winter. He ran for a seat on Montreal's city council and won. Using the offices of the Institut Canadien, he also began organizing a political campaign that would draw on his personal networks as well as the disenfranchised. The idea was seeded in an article he published in his *L'Union Nationale* on March 25, 1867, that called for the organization of workers. Two days later, five thousand people attended a rally where he explained his idea and went so far as to propose a charter, a constitution for a "Grande association de protection des ouvriers du Canada" (GAPOC). The organization – the first of its kind in rallying workers – declared that it would be governed by a *Commission centrale,* and announced that it would promote protective tariffs, the creation of banking institutions for workers, and programs to help with food provision, night school, and mutual aid.[63] Lanctôt denounced inflation and announced his support for

Médéric Lanctôt, 1867
Bibliothèque et Archives nationales du Québec, Albums Massicotte, 0002735785

the teamsters and construction workers who had been on strike since early March.[64] Working with the Institut Canadien led by Gonzalve Doutre, Lanctôt mobilized action in the city. The *Montreal Herald* called their activities "seditious, not to say treasonable." The governing board of the Institut Canadien agreed and asked the GAPOC to leave its premises.[65] The Institut, after all, had refused to take a clear position on Confederation.[66]

On June 10, representatives of twenty-two of the twenty-four workmen's guilds in the city joined with the GAPOC to organize a parade through the streets of Montreal. It is estimated that between eight and ten thousand people (about 10 percent of the city's population) participated. The "Grand Procession" was impressive with its banners and slogans. It demonstrated a strong bond between Lanctôt and the working population, a loyalty he had developed over many years. To underscore his leadership, Lanctôt was placed in the last float, pulled by four robust horses. He demonstrated how well organized he was, speaking in the open air where all could see him, ensuring that the streets were sealed off to circulation.

Two days later, he ran an article in the *Union Nationale* saying that he would again campaign for a seat on the city council and would even run for mayor. He declared that the *Commission centrale*, the GAPOC's directing body, had the potential to rival Parliament in its first session, arguing that the mandate given to the members of the commission showed a certain legitimacy. "You form, so to speak, a parliament that is analogous to those political assemblies where all social classes are present or are represented," Lanctôt declared. "You represent more or less all the working classes of our city and your mission is to take the measures necessary to promote their interests by all right and legitimate means recognized by law and recommended by morality."[67] Robert Rumilly, the deeply conservative Quebec historian who was nothing if not wholeheartedly supportive of Lanctôt, bizarrely called him a "a sort of prototypical national socialist" in 1940.[68]

Lanctôt was unleashed: he gave a Saint-Jean-Baptiste Day speech, visited public places, knocked on doors, and met potential voters on church steps. He followed up with two more rallies on June 26 and July 10. On Confederation, he conceded: "We must accept this infamous work, bow our heads and submit to the fait accompli, but to which men must we rely upon to protect our interests tomorrow? Are the traitors worthy of our confidence?"[69] Lanctôt was discouraged to see Canada East's politicians abandon the fight and had concluded that the momentum now belonged to Confederationists.

The *Rouges* were divided, the Church leaders were tacitly approving of Confederation, and, most importantly, London was not going to allow the project to fail. Eager to paint the project as anti-French and anti-Catholic, he insisted that George Brown commanded the affairs of the country and that "Brownite" ideas would dominate unless *nationalistes* worked to redress the Liberal ship.[70] (The *Globe* was hostile to Médéric Lanctôt and very favourable to Dorion.)

As the formal election campaign got started, Lanctôt gathered a group in Montreal on August 8 to sign a manifesto opposing any idea of Confederation and demanding that any proposal be put to a popular vote. Among the forty-six signatories were George Edward Clerk, the editor of the *True Witness* in Montreal, even though his newspaper backed Confederation. At that point, Lanctôt declared that he would run in the upcoming federal election, against no less than George-Étienne Cartier in Montreal-Est. Comparing the *Bleu* leader to Lord Durham, he accused Cartier of "insulting workers." City authorities once again disqualified him from taking his seat on Montreal's city council on the grounds that he did not have $2,000 to his name and had not maintained a home in the city since 1866 (both of which were patently false). Lanctôt was even accused of organizing a baker's strike during the election. *L'Ordre,* a *Rouge* paper, and *La Minerve* were notably hostile, but for added power, the Conservatives launched another newspaper on August 1, *La Vérité,* a semi-weekly, to besmirch Lanctôt.

Lanctôt was excoriated in *Un Fourbe Démasqué,* a twenty-page pamphlet published during the campaign. The criticisms against him were severe: he was accused of fomenting strikes among teamsters, of being a *Rouge,* of being a Fenian sympathizer, of corruption. He was accused of competing against small businesses when the GAPOC started food banks.

On August 29, Cartier and Lanctôt met at the Marché Papineau for an open debate before a crowd estimated at six hundred. Cartier spoke first, emphasizing the good works of Confederation and the great opportunities it represented, repeating the arguments that had appeared in *Contre-Poison: La Confédération, c'est le salut du Bas-Canada*. But fighting broke out as he was pelted with rocks, and ax handles were deployed to intimate his supporters. Police and even mounted officers were called in to charge the mob, and it took forty-five minutes to disperse it. Cartier scurried home. A few days later, he organized a rally at a giant hall on Craig Street and invited all sorts of speakers to defend him. The room was filled to capacity and was noisy beyond control. The star of the evening was the eloquent young Adolphe Chapleau, who would one day become premier of Quebec and a minister in Macdonald's government.

For his part, Lanctôt continued to focus on the welfare of the working class. He organized two large meetings on September 4, attended by no fewer than five to six thousand people, according to the biased *Union Nationale*. At those meetings, Lanctôt notably declared that iron mines were found in the Mont-Royal and that up to six hundred employees would soon be hired. Laurent-Olivier David, who was seriously considering running as a *Rouge* candidate in Montmagny in 1867, described Lanctôt as unfortunately born. Had he lived in Revolutionary France, David recalled, he would have rivalled Camille Desmoulins as an agitator. Had he lived during the rebellions of 1837–38, he would have been a patriotic hero and would gladly have climbed the gallows to proclaim "Freedom!" Instead, David observed, he was destined to live in a "tranquil time" in a peaceable society where one had to keep thoughts and sentiments in check. Lanctôt was a star "lost in space," a balloon cruising the skies without fear, a steam engine without a valve.[71] Jean Hamelin, the historian who spent a career chronicling Quebec newspapers and their writers, considered Lanctôt one of the most important French Canadian thinkers of the nineteenth century, but against the likes of George-Étienne Cartier and his machine, his future in Parliament was in doubt.[72]

## Against McGee: The Irish Fight in Montreal

Another of the most-watched contests in Quebec – perhaps in the whole of the new Canada – was the fight over the riding of Montreal-Ouest, where Thomas D'Arcy McGee was challenged by Bernard Devlin. Lanctôt also fixed his suspicious gaze on McGee and sought Irish support for the anti-Confederation cause. He published two articles in March 1866 describing the "natural alliance" that existed between French and Irish Canadians, and portrayed McGee as a promoter of British interests. He made a point of protesting the suspension of the writ of habeas corpus in light of the Fenian raids, and expressed support for Devlin, a Montreal lawyer who had been consistently critical of McGee.

McGee, forty-two, who had already represented Montreal for a decade without facing much opposition, was confident of an easy victory. He was born in County Louth, Ireland, and as a young man had associated with the Young Ireland movement, demanding the establishment of an independent Irish Republic. He left for Boston at the age of twenty, and found work as a journalist at a Catholic newspaper. So anti-British was he that he advocated Canada's dissolution and its annexation by the United States. He returned to Ireland in 1845 and joined the Young Irelander Rebellion three years later. He was marked as threat to the government and escaped arrest only by leaving the country and returning to Boston.

He grew unhappy in the United States for a variety of political and personal reasons, and had a change of heart. In 1857, he moved his small family to Montreal and started *New Era,* a publication that quickly established him as a spokesman for the Irish Catholics in the city. In a year, McGee, who was without doubt a gifted orator, was elected to the legislative assembly of the Province of Canada, and decided to attend law school at McGill University. Though once a brash young Irish nationalist, he found himself at home rubbing shoulders with Canadian Conservatives, happily denouncing any attempts to use Canada to discredit the British Empire. In 1863,

160  *Ballots and Brawls*

Macdonald asked him to join cabinet as minister of agriculture, immigration, and statistics. A year later, he participated in the Great Coalition and joined the Canadian delegation to Charlottetown and Quebec City. By all accounts, McGee was supposed to continue sitting in cabinet in the new Canadian government headed by Macdonald, but, unable to find room for him, Macdonald apologized for letting down his good friend, leaving posterity with the legendary line: "Look, McGee, there's no room for two drunks in this cabinet; it's either you or me, and you have to go." Needing to shore up his support in Nova Scotia, particularly among the Irish Catholics of that province, Macdonald felt he had no choice but to appoint Edward Kenny and bypass Charles Tupper, who also had every right to expect a cabinet neat. It was a sacrifice Tupper was willing to make. Inspired by Tupper, McGee agreed to bide his time, and sought election to the House of Commons.

For people like Bernard Devlin, forty-three, a well-connected criminal lawyer and leading figure of Irish nationalists in Montreal, McGee was "a foul informer, a corrupt witness, a knave and hypocrite."[73] Trained as a doctor, Devlin had migrated from Ireland to Quebec City in 1844 and launched himself into journalism before commencing his legal studies. Admitted to the bar three years later, he built a large criminal law practice and was known to support Liberals. In 1864, he was hired to represent the American government in the prosecution of the St. Albans Confederate raiders.

Devlin's eloquence matched McGee's, and he used it effectively. He raised every subject imaginable pertaining to his adversary's past actions and did not hesitate to raise the issue of McGee's drinking and disorderly conduct. As the campaign opened, McGee received a letter threatening his life if he disclosed any details of how various individuals were attempting to establish Fenianism in Montreal. The letter came with an illustration of a gallows and coffin that had been published in the *Buffalo Fenian Volunteer* of July 27, with the inscription underneath: "You rich traitor, if you oppose Devlin by God such will be your fate!"[74]

The race was off to a bitter start when fights broke out early during a McGee rally on Saint-Laurent Boulevard on August 1.[75] McGee was called a traitor and was forced to flee a hail of rotten eggs. His headquarters in Mechanics' Hall was attacked and the windows of the neighbouring houses were broken in a show of force. McGee responded by threatening to expose the Fenian network in Montreal, and he was in turn threatened with murder. The unconditional *Rouges* lent their influence as the *Union Nationale* urged French Canadian voters to support the Irish in getting rid of McGee.[76] In mid-August, the *Montreal Gazette* published three of his articles on Fenianism in Montreal. One of Devlin's partisans, Patrick James Whelan, took things personally and publicly declared that he would "go up & blow McGee's bloody brains out."[77] Undaunted as ever, McGee organized a meeting for 8 p.m. on August 9 at the corner of St. Lawrence and St. Catherine Streets, and about seven hundred people attended. He was introduced in French, but the master of ceremonies was booed off the stage. The second speaker was treated just as rudely. McGee stepped up and quickly realized that his supporters had been drowned out by Devlin partisans. A "storm of hooting and groanings" greeted him and for once McGee was speechless, looking bewildered. He stepped down and tried again when the commotion appeared to die down. Adolphe Chapleau attempted to soothe the audience, but he soon gave up also, and McGee and his party left.[78] The *Montreal Daily News* described the actions as the work of "anarchists" and "ruffians," "toughs" of the Griffintown neighbourhood.[79]

The campaign against McGee remained controversial and was covered across Canada.[80] The election finally took place on September 5–6. McGee did well on the first day, taking a lead of over five hundred votes as the eligible men were polled in three wards.

Friday, September 6, brought out a different crowd as Devlin whipped up his supporters. Some of McGee's poll attendants were assaulted, and a police officer was nearly killed by protesters. Two of Devlin's men were hurt by gunfire. Devlin's tactics on the second day worked and he won the day, but McGee's lead proved insurmountable, and he defeated Devlin by 262 votes.[81] McGee left for Kingston immediately to attend a grand dinner in honour of Macdonald (a dinner also attended by Cartier) and gave what the *Kingston Whig-Standard* called a "great speech."[82] The election had been sobering for him (well, not entirely). He had narrowly held on to his seat in Montreal but was humbled and decided to withdraw from the provincial race in the riding of Prescott (Ontario). Days later, he was accosted on a Montreal street by Devlin, who called him a "damned scoundrel" and spat in his face. McGee retaliated by throwing a punch and the two men started a brawl.[83]

### The Fiasco in Kamouraska

Most campaigns in Quebec, as elsewhere in Canada, were conducted peacefully, but there were occasions when disruptions and brawls did break out. It was reported that, at one point in the campaign, the new premier of Quebec, Pierre-Joseph Chauveau (who, incidentally, was also running for a seat in the House of Commons) personally got involved in disrupting a group of young "rowdies." He was on the steamer travelling to Montreal when he heard that the gang was about to step off at Trois-Rivières to intimidate voters in the upcoming poll. He ordered their arrest on board, and charges were laid when they landed in Montreal.[84]

But the race that caught the most attention took place in Kamouraska, the small village on the south shore of the St. Lawrence River, about 175 kilometres north of Quebec City. It was bitterly divided and probably the dirtiest election in Canada's history because there were so few rules, and even those were routinely broken. Kamouraska had been the scene of electoral violence before, notably in 1854.

Jean-Charles Chapais, the Conservative (and minister of agriculture in Macdonald's government), had been the member of the legislature for the riding since 1855. The man who sought to deny him election was the "Liberal nationalist" Luc Letellier de Saint-Just, who had just been named senator for the region, which he had represented in the Legislative Council of the United Province of Canada. Letellier also enlisted Pantaléon Pelletier, a former *Bleu*, to run provincially for the Liberals. The *Bleus* decided to fight back.

The pastor of the parish of Sainte-Julie, Curé Joseph Martel, called the Liberals his "enemies."[85] The election commissioner, who apparently was related to Chapais, also favoured the *Bleus*, going so far as to tie blue ribbons on his cow's horns and a red ribbon on its tail. Citing irregularities, he summarily declared that Sainte-Julie and two other parishes would be disenfranchised. It turns out they were suspected of Liberal leanings. In revenge, Pelletier supporters tried to steal key reporting documents on election day and assaulted the returning officer because he refused to accept the poll results in a few parishes. Fights broke out at 10 a.m. on September 2, noses were broken, and there was blood everywhere. The returning officer escaped to his house in fear of his life, and barricaded himself with the help of a few friends. His house and that of his neighbour were nearly destroyed. Two people died and the election was cancelled (a by-election was held eighteen months later). People blamed the riot on Pelletier and his friends, treating it as utterly unjustifiable. Serious injuries, it was stated, had been suffered by several of the inhabitants of the riding.[86] A second explanation for the riot was that the returning officer kept hearing the name of the Conservative candidate even when the vote was obviously going to the Liberal, and was going to declare Chapais elected by acclamation as a result. The House of Commons condemned the official and suspended

164 *Ballots and Brawls*

elections in Kamouraska, during which time the riding was without representation in either Quebec City or Ottawa.[87] Chapais kept his seat in cabinet temporarily, but Pelletier won it in the by-election in 1869.

The race in Quebec was particular. From the beginning, twenty districts were acclaimed for Conservatives and three were given to the Liberals so that a third of the sixty-four seats were uncontested. The rest of the races were more divisive, with both *Bleus* and *Rouges* tearing at each other on the hustings, in the press, and, in some instances, on the street. There weren't many seductive reasons to join Confederation, but the opposition had no compelling alternative. In the end, it might have come down to the influence of one man. As Lionel Groulx wrote long ago, "All historians agree: only one man, Georges[sic]-Étienne Cartier, could make his province agree to the significant political changes of 1867."[88]

# 5

# The Clash of Imperialisms
# in Nova Scotia

NOVA SCOTIA GREETED Confederation with a decidedly divided heart. The Halifax *Morning Chronicle* was not very enthusiastic about the new Canada that Nova Scotia had joined. On July 1, 1867, it announced: "Died! Last night at 12 o'clock, the free and enlightened Province of Nova Scotia."[1]

In the capital, a parade organized by the provincial government was attended by about six hundred people, and the absence of important trades and prestigious societies was glaring. Glebe House, the Catholic archbishop's home in Halifax, posted a bullish pro-Canada sign that proclaimed, "To-day we span a Continent, make two Oceans meet, and must soon become connected with 30,000 miles of Railroad." The *Colonist,* the newspaper owned by Charles Tupper, the leader of Nova Scotia Confederationists, devoted a short paragraph to enumerating the businesses that participated in the celebratory evening "illumination" for the occasion. The Halifax Hotel, which had hosted the Charlottetown delegates in September 1864, was chief among them. Sandford Fleming, the chief government surveyor of the province, who was directing the hotly debated railway line linking Halifax, Pictou, and Truro, was up at 5 a.m., greeted by a very cloudy and rainy day in the new provincial capital; he was, however, happy to report in his diary that the clouds soon dissipated and "Halifax very gay, a perfect sea of flags. Beautiful day. The demonstration went off splendidly."[2] A few days later, he received a letter from John A. Macdonald promising that his name would be considered for the position of chief engineer of the new Intercolonial Railway.[3]

At the same time, however, flags were flown at half-mast everywhere in the new province, and the festivities did not last long. The few bonfires burned out quickly, a few fireworks were launched, and one reporter noted a grim reality in Nova Scotia: the real test of convictions was upon its citizens, and the elections for both provincial and federal governments were likely to be divisive. He noted that "a prescience of public danger seems to have settled upon the public mind."[4]

The election in Nova Scotia would be different from those in the rest of the country. It was scheduled by Tupper to be the last one, to take place when the results in Canada and New Brunswick would be known. It was probably a mistake to hold the election so late, as it gave ample opportunity to the opposition to spread its views, but Tupper clearly hoped to give himself as much time as possible to rally electors around the Confederation project. Nominations were held much later than in the other provinces, with the vote scheduled for September 18. An election for the provincial legislature would be held simultaneously, as in Quebec and Ontario.

It was a far more bitter contest than in the rest of the new country, with higher stakes. The idea that a new "nationality" could be born from the Quebec Resolutions of 1864 was repulsive and was contested by none other than Joseph Howe, the champion Nova Scotia Liberal, promoter of responsible government, and former premier. For him, the "new nationality" was phony, American, and divisive. "Every young fellow who has had a taste of the license of camp life in the United States will be tempted to have a fling at it," he wrote.[5]

Howe saw no hope in this new Canada, pointing to the likely schisms in anglophone ranks ("as the English will split and divide, as they always do"), which would "inevitably allow French Catholics to be masters of the situation."[6] As one Howe-friendly journalist put it, "the electors of Nova Scotia owe it to their self-respect that they should reject candidates who have treated them not only with disrespect but with contempt."[7]

As in New Brunswick, the election of 1867 was also about the incumbent government and political revenge. In 1863, the Tupper Tories had won fifteen of the nineteen seats in the colony, a resounding victory over the Joseph Howe Liberal Reformers.[8] It was a fairly easy victory, as Howe had undermined his position by his aggressive campaign to abolish the manhood suffrage that had been established in 1854 and by his increasingly anti-Catholic pronouncements on questions of education.[9]

Tupper's record in office was mixed. He had alienated many people with his "free schools" education act of 1864, and his failure to get the Pictou railway and the Windsor-Annapolis extension finished also rankled.[10] There was a great deal of concern in Nova Scotia over the failure to renew a trade agreement with the United States, but the economy was hardly ailing. In fact, trade with the United States was prospering. Imports went from £47,000 in the early 1860s to £808,000 in 1866, and exports rose from £266,000 to £645,000. Coal, a source of prosperity in the province, constituted a third of the exports by 1865.[11] The wealth was not evenly distributed, however. Halifax, Hants, Colchester, Cumberland, Pictou, and Cape Breton controlled 75 percent of the province's industrial capital. Halifax was slowly becoming a bastion of free-traders, to the point where merchants formed an Anti-Confederation League.[12] With anti-Confederation sentiment building since early 1865, Tupper knew he would not replicate the result of 1863 in 1867.

The argument in favour of Confederation was simple: it promised an economic union with a much larger country that would be advantageous. It would be a modern idea – unionists could point to the various unions in the anglosphere, such as England, Scotland, and even Ireland and the United States – but that view was rejected.[13] "Surely the number of people in Halifax County who are not for Confederation must be small indeed, if they have any regard for the prosperity of the county, as well as that of the entire Province," one writer noted. "Will our tradesmen lose or gain by the Union? Will our carpenters, joiners, smiths, and other artisans have less work when there is ten or twentyfold greater demand for it? Will our clothiers, shoemakers, and other tradesmen, amid a more teeming and industrious population, have less to do?" The writer noted that producers received higher prices for their goods in bigger markets, pointing to London in particular.[14]

But there was far more at stake than economics in this election campaign. It was also a question of identity, loyalty, and belonging. As with its neighbour to the west, Nova Scotia's political labels also faded in the 1867 election campaign. It would not be a fight between Liberals and Conservatives, but between "unionists" or "confederates," who supported Charles Tupper and Sir John A. Macdonald, and the "antis" of the Nova Scotia Party who followed Joseph Howe. For the writers of the *Eastern Chronicle,* it was not a question of party but a battle of the people against a treasonable attack. That publication, hostile as ever to Confederation, deeply resented the fact that the proposal had not been voted upon directly by the people, and made a personal appeal to the men who were entitled to vote. "The polls are a great corrector of public wrongs," wrote its editorialist. "Our country may yet be saved from the degradation to which we would be assigned by those who propose to transfer us to the control of our Canadian neighbors. Now is our day of power. Rise, electors, in the dignity of your manhood, and exercise your privilege at the polls."[15]

It was also a time for reprisals, and the *Eastern Chronicle* did not hesitate to point its finger:

The Clash of Imperialisms in Nova Scotia 169

Verily, the men who have consummated the Confederation Scheme – the men who have forced it upon the people – John A. McDonald [sic], Cartier, Galt, McGee, Archibald, Tupper, Henry, Tilley – they are responsible for the riots, the bloodshed, and the loss of life, which occurred in Montreal last week. People of Nova Scotia, be warned in time. Condemn Confederation, reject the men who have sought to force it upon you, and, ere it be too late, shake yourselves clear of an alliance which must bring ruin and distress to your country.[16]

The links with Central Canadian parties would also be uneven. Macdonald would remain the reference for the unionists, but George Brown and the Liberals held little sway in Nova Scotia. They did not bother to craft a Liberal ideology that could welcome Reformers in the Bluenose province or to make the argument that Confederation could meet regionalist expectations.

The fight in Nova Scotia featured two champion imperialists who had diverging views of the link that should exist between London and the new Canada. Joseph Howe, at sixty-three one of the oldest men caught in the Confederation battles, was born in Halifax, the son of American Loyalists who inherited a deep sympathy for the British Empire. In his view, Nova Scotians had to invest their identity in the culture and ideas of London, not become subsidiary to hyped-up Canadian politicians whose track records in managing politics, the economy, and social peace were mediocre. In his view, Nova Scotia would be inheriting Canadian problems and paying for it by giving up its own sovereignty. Charles Tupper, who was introduced earlier in this book, was so much in love with England that he would spend much of the last thirty years of his long life there.

Tupper made a bold decision to resign on the eve of Confederation, intending to join the Conservative cabinet in Ottawa and hopefully win the kinds of concessions from the new federal government that would convince Maritimers that they would prosper in Canada. Hiram Blanchard was asked to form a new Conservative government, something that did not sit well with many newspapers in the province, which considered the Blanchard government illegitimate. Impatient for change, they demanded that Sir William Fenwick Williams, the new Lieutenant-Governor, show his "manliness" and his "patriotism" and install an "efficient and honest executive" until the election could be held. "Our rights and interest have a long enough played 'second fiddle' to those of Canada," raged the editor of the *Eastern Chronicle,* based in Pictou. "The people now demand that they should be heard. Will the imbecile administration any longer dare deny them that right? Are we living in a free country in an enlightened age? And are people Britons or are they too ignorant to speak for themselves. The time, we hope, is not far distant, when Nova Scotians will assert the dignity of their manhood, and sweep from existence a corrupt an imbecile administration."[17]

Tupper was an early champion of the view that Nova Scotia would benefit from Confederation while remaining a vital part of the British Empire. He had been an enthusiastic delegate at the Charlottetown Conference and then again at Quebec City. When he returned from the London Conference in early 1867, he was received with a "solemn, sullen, and ominous silence." The mood had changed. Tupper had his enemies. The *Halifax Chronicle,* for one, routinely referred to the Nova Scotia premier as the "arch-traitor," who was "such a beaten man that he bribed people."[18] The paper was owned by William Annand, a man dedicated to the political destruction of Charles Tupper. Historians have been more kind.

## The Rise and Fall and Rise of Joseph Howe

Joseph Howe was the prime mover of that change of heart towards Confederation. In fact, he was incensed by the whole project. He hammered away at the Nova Scotia government's failure to put the Confederation pact to the people and blamed everyone he could

The Clash of Imperialisms in Nova Scotia    171

think of, especially Tupper. Tupper was aware of Howe's impact. He "had a deep impression upon the masses to whom the people of the Upper Provinces were utter strangers." In his *Recollections,* published almost fifty years later, Tupper cited Howe:

> The people of Nova Scotia are determined to defeat this idea of erecting a new Dominion in British America. They are determined that not a pound of their capital should go to paying the debts of Canada, that not an acre of their province shall go under Canadian rule, and that not a man of their militia shall be liable to be marched up to the backwoods of Canada to fight the battles of faction, or to prevent Canada from burning down parliament building or pelting governors through the streets.[19]

Born and raised in the province, Howe did not attend school beyond what was strictly necessary, and instead launched himself in the newspaper business. He bought a small newspaper, the *Weekly Chronicle,* in early 1827, and within the year also purchased the *Novascotian* in Halifax, unceasing in his devotion to his adoptive city.[20] He was twenty-four years old. A few months later, he married and started a family, but domestic responsibilities did not slow him down. Always restless, he used his newspaper to disseminate his notion that government had to change. Loyal to a fault to Britain, he held it to the highest standards and demanded that its representatives in Nova Scotia be respectful of the needs of the people and end their arbitrary habits. He distinguished himself as a reformer, attacked corruption at all levels, and demanded responsible government.

A fine writer, Howe became the dominant orator of his generation. A populist who championed free speech (but who was suspicious enough of the common man to insist on the franchise being subject to property ownership so that less than 10 percent of men could vote), he defended early on the rights of the Irish Catholics.

Joseph Howe, circa 1864–65
Library and Archives Canada, C-021463

He was convinced early of the need to speak in defence of industry, particularly against the evil of taxation and in favour of building transportation infrastructure, notably roads and railways. He was devoted to the British Crown and to the very idea of a Great Britain and what it represented in terms of government, culture, the arts, and the sciences.[21] He wished Nova Scotia would imitate that source of wisdom, and dedicated himself to promoting its culture and its book industry.[22] In 1836, he ran for office to represent the county of Halifax in the legislature and was distinguished by his unceasing campaign to make elementary school freely available throughout the colony, as well as to establish Mechanics' Institutes, devoted as they were to helping workers educate themselves.[23] Focusing on what was happening in Lower and Upper Canada, he echoed the concerns of the radicals and demanded change. After being elected, he immediately tabled twelve resolutions that sparked fury but none of the violence known in the Canadas.

Howe made his points, and in 1840 was appointed to the Executive Council as part of a coalition government with Conservatives. He was not universally popular, as many of his reformist colleagues thought he was legitimizing the status quo, but he persisted. The following year, he was out of the Executive Council but was named speaker of the Legislative Assembly, where he articulated further demands for responsible government – that the executive be held accountable to the people for its policies, taxation, and expenditures. He worked to promote those views and won his race in the 1848 election, which brought to power a reformist administration under James Boyle Uniacke. Howe was given the post of provincial secretary, in which portfolio he suddenly became a formidable champion of railways within the province, stretching to the Canadas, and plunging into the United States.

The Reform Party lost to the Conservatives in the election of 1857, and Howe lost his seat to Tupper. Looking for lessons, he concluded that the Catholics in his district had turned against him unfairly. He was re-elected in 1860 and returned as provincial secretary under William Young. When Young opted to become chief justice of the province in the summer of 1860, Howe was appointed prime minister. Tupper hammered away against the government. It was not an easy time, and Howe welcomed the opportunity to leave when he was offered a seat on the Imperial Fisheries Commission, based in London, in 1863. He was not involved in the Charlottetown or Quebec Conferences.

He was not happy with the conclusions of those conferences and with the idea that Nova Scotia would become a part of Canada. For sure, he considered that his community had much in common with Canada, declaring (perhaps in jest) before the Charlottetown Conference in 1864 that "I am not one of those who thank God that I am a Nova Scotian merely, for I am a Canadian as well."[24] Because he was still linked with the Imperial Fisheries Commission, he expressed his initial opposition anonymously through the *Botheration Letters,* a series of twelve editorials that appeared in the *Morning Chronicle* between January and March 1865. It was the sort of contradiction that was always held against him, and that he ultimately could not surmount.

It was Tupper's resolution in the legislature in April 1866 that Nova Scotia join Confederation that roused Howe to action. He travelled to London and furiously lobbied all his acquaintances to oppose any legislation that would enable the union of the North American provinces, arguing that it would ultimately undermine the British Empire.[25] He wrote that "we are powerless to do anything but punish if we can the rascals who have sold the country. If our people can, they could clear them out of the local and general representation, place the provincial affairs in the hands of honest men who will command respect and give us some chance of fair play."[26] That spring, Howe returned to Nova Scotia after completing his stint at the fisheries commission, resolved to return to active politics and to organize a campaign against the Macdonald coalition so that the new system could work "fairly." On March 27, two days before the British North America Act received royal assent, the Anti-Confederation League, dominated by merchant and banking interests in Halifax, met in that city to organize for the upcoming election at both provincial and federal levels. The Nova Scotia Party was formed and local riding associations were created. Howe started his campaign. In contrast, Tupper created the Canada Party, promising a rosy future and progress in the new Confederation.

The Clash of Imperialisms in Nova Scotia 175

Howe did not trust the Canadian Liberals. In turn, the Reformers from Central Canada were frustrated with Howe, who was known above all as politically liberal.[27] He was unmoved by overtures from any party. Both the Conservatives and the Liberals had shown "equal barbarity" towards Nova Scotia and could not be trusted. Howe began a speaking tour, hinting that he would favour an armed confrontation. "I would take every son I have and die on the frontier, before I would submit to this outrage," he declared. He made fun of Adams Archibald, memorably mocking his alliance with Tupper: "Is there an honest woman in Colchester, if she had proclaimed another woman a strumpet, would breakfast with her, dine with her, sup with her, and sleep with her afterwards?"[28] Halifax politics was practised with sharp insults.

Howe had alienated the Catholics in 1857 but was a good friend of Thomas L. Connolly, the archbishop in Halifax, who begged him again in 1867 not to "excite our Catholic people ... who were inflamed enough."[29] However, this did not keep him from accusing Connolly of not being a Nova Scotian (he was, in fact, Irish and had worked in the Maritimes for almost twenty-five years), "nor is it to be expected that he can feel or resent, as Nova Scotians do, the attempt to break down the institutions of the country."[30] Howe opted to play a positively dangerous game of identity politics, forgetting that 25 percent of the citizens of Nova Scotia were Catholic. On September 18, Connolly declared his support for Confederation and wished "my whole Catholic people to follow my example."[31]

## Arguments against Confederation in Nova Scotia

The first argument was one of process. In the view of the antis, Nova Scotia had been forced into Confederation without a mandate for the government to negotiate such an agreement. At the very least, the government should have submitted a resolution to the people. In this, Howe's supporters were very much in tune with the *Rouges* of Quebec. The *Halifax Chronicle* put it slightly differently

176   *Ballots and Brawls*

in highlighting the helplessness that had been created by Charles Tupper and his party: "As cattle driven to the market, so have we been driven into this union."[32] "Political treachery should be punished," argued the *Weekly Citizen* in Halifax, "the hideous doctrine that representatives, against the clearly expressed and well understood wishes of their constituents, can vote away the rights and powers entrusted to them for four years only, should be effectively repudiated. Punish the wicked, is the first commandment in our political decalogue."[33] Voting for a unionist candidate was to support the overthrow of Nova Scotian institutions, "and our revenues have been given over to the control of another people," argued the *Halifax Chronicle*.[34]

The second argument was the loss of self-determination. Joseph Howe argued that Nova Scotia had had its own parliament for 108 years and had achieved responsible government long before Canada. Its citizens were being asked to yield those accomplishments to a majority of Canadians who had "never invested a pound of capital." Nova Scotia, holding 19 seats in a parliament of 181, would never be in a position to determine its own destiny. In terms of representation in the House of Commons, there was no doubt that Nova Scotian interests would come third, after Ontario and Quebec. The mode in which senators would be appointed left Maritimers with no voice. "They can do what they choose in snapping their fingers in our faces," wrote one anonymous commentator. "They may be weak minded and stupid, greedy and dishonest or ambitious and reckless, but we cannot call them to account or turn them out of office. Is it right that the men who have the governing of our country, the disposing of our revenues, and the making of our laws in their hands should be that absolutely independent of us?"[35] The likely outcome would be "undying hatreds and ultimate annexation."[36]

Another argument was the contamination of "coalitions" that was embodied in Macdonald's approach. "The country has had enough of Coalitions," wrote the *Weekly Citizen*. The Halifax newspaper recalled that the reformist coalition of the 1850s had doubled the debt of the province in one mandate, and the same thing was likely to happen in Ottawa under John A. Macdonald. "Give us a coalition with an overwhelming majority in parliament ... and we will show you a country rushing to bankruptcy and ruin as fast as reckless managers can drive it."[37] Confederation was promoted by men who had proven disloyal to Britain in the past. "How can you be loyal if you are supporting Mr. Cartier of Canada who had 500 pounds placed on his head a few years ago for conspiring at the head of the foreign element to wrest a British colony from the crown?" asked the *Eastern Chronicle,* which also pointed to the fact that Thomas D'Arcy McGee was also subject to a bounty when he left Ireland. Furthermore, that paper pointed to Alexander Galt, who had signed the Annexation Manifesto.[38]

Howe could not have painted a darker picture. Nova Scotia would be "a mere spectator of the doings of that legislature," he predicted. He argued that Nova Scotians saw themselves as belonging to their own country, and wanted their own country. The deal was "a detestable confederation that has been attempted to be forced upon us ... a union brought about by corrupt and arbitrary means." "Our nationality would be merged into that of Canada."[39] In fact, the British North America Act robbed Nova Scotia of any of its independence, the argument ran. It would be reduced to a dependency of Canada. The *Morning Chronicle* declared: "We are almost shamed to silence facing such an attempt to reduce us to the rank of slaves."[40] It was also a means of sending a protest to London, "to the mother country against her very harsh treatment of, what has often been deemed, her favorite child –to make us feel that there are some men at Ottawa who will always vote right; and to give Nova Scotia some influence in the House of Commons." The hope was that London's intervention would give the province an opportunity to drive a better bargain with its "big brother."[41]

There was concern about the loyalty of judges in this regard, with some fearing that they would uphold Ottawa's statutes – "the tyranny and usurpation of Canada," as one put it – over those emerging in Halifax. There was a demand for a provincial constitution. Judges, as much as the politicians, were "under the obligation manfully to assert the rights of the people, who will accept no excuse for their hostility or even lukewarmness in the cause of our freedom and dependence."[42]

The fourth main argument against Nova Scotia's joining Confederation was that it was unnecessary. The colonies were sufficiently united by a common bond inside the British Empire, and any economic need for cohesion and concert could be achieved through simple accommodations. Ottawa would now have the upper hand on railroad policy, again putting Nova Scotia in a disadvantageous position. Nova Scotia's needs would always be secondary to those of Central Canada. Outside Confederation, Nova Scotia would at least have the right to negotiate. In joining Confederation, however, the colony would lose any privilege to engage in discussion. The same fear prevailed in terms of defending Nova Scotia in international trade. There was a fear, for instance, that a Canadian government could negotiate poor terms with the United States on the fisheries of Nova Scotia in return for better ones for New Brunswick, or Quebec or Ontario.

The Nova Scotian segment of the Intercolonial Railway, in this view, could be constructed without endangering the financial position of the province. It could be efficient and responsive to local needs. However, the Canadian idea of eventually joining it to the Grand Trunk Railway in Canada would distort its mission and saddle it with the debts of an inefficient system. "It will prove to be a mill stone around the neck of confederation, a rock on which the good ship 'union' will be hopelessly wrecked."[43]

Not least was the matter of taxation, and the numbers on this issue were designed to create alarm.[44] One correspondent calculated that Nova Scotia would have to send an extra $369,400 to Ottawa within the year. Ottawa would then impose a tariff on imports, none of which would go to provincial coffers, but which would have an inflationary effect. Another pointed out that Ottawa was likely to collect an extra $500,000 in tariff revenues from Nova Scotian points of entry. None of this new money was likely to be returned to the citizens of the province. The argument was that Nova Scotia's revenues (mostly drawn from the tariff on imports) were sufficient to meet the colony's expenses. With Confederation, Nova Scotia would lose revenues of over $1,119,400. On top of that, Ottawa could impose its own taxes, such as export duties or even an income tax.[45] "Our revenue will not be ours, but Canada's," ran the lament. It would be difficult for the province of Nova Scotia to borrow, as it was now deprived of its own sources of revenue. The impact of Confederation on Nova Scotia would inevitably be poverty, "if she succeeds in her scheme of enslaving us."[46] Joseph Howe's argument resonated: "All our revenues are to be taken by the general government, and we get back 80 cents per head, the price of a sheepskin."[47]

The editor of the *Charlottetown Examiner* noted that the antis were increasingly divided between those who simply wanted a repeal of the British North America Act and those who wanted annexation to the United States. In his view, the annexationists had the upper hand: "They are determined at all costs, to sever their connection with Canada." He also reported that Howe had been "astonished" by the "strength and intensity of the anti-union feeling." Howe had discovered "a bitter hatred of Canada."[48]

### The Campaign

The editor of the *Charlottetown Examiner,* a supporter of Confederation, wrote from Halifax that "the country is very much excited" and that "men everywhere, and of all classes and parties, use very strong language."[49] The election campaign in Nova Scotia was

180   *Ballots and Brawls*

probably the most bitter since the fight for responsible government. As the *Morning Chronicle* crudely put it: "Let us decide ... by our votes whether Nova Scotia is to be owned by four lawyers and a doctor or by her own people."[50]

In the election campaign of 1867, Howe ran in Hants, while Tupper ran in Cumberland, but they had started their campaign of mutual destruction months earlier. On June 4, they had met in a head-to-head debate in Truro, and Tupper fought hard against Howe's nativist appeals, highlighting his opponent's inconsistency in sometimes arguing that he was "Canadian" while campaigning against Canada. They met again six times between June 27 and July 13. "The campaign was an extremely bitter one," remembered Tupper.[51] Howe made it personal, aiming to defeat Tupper in his own county, and aggressively campaigned in the four corners of Cumberland. No less than William Annand, Howe's old friend who had also been minister of finance in Howe's government between 1860 and 1863, decided to run against Tupper and put him seriously on the defensive. Annand, who was described as "clever but sly and unscrupulous,"[52] was the owner of the *Morning Chronicle*. Tupper invoked two of Charles Dickens's characters to denounce Howe and Annand – whom he also called Siamese twins – likening them to Mr. Pike and Mr. Pluck: "Whatever Mr. Pike says, Mr. Pluck uniformly swears to. Who have their modern counterparts in these two worthy patriots, Messrs. Howe and Annand, with this difference that the latter are prepared to swear to anything, or swear against anything, provided it will 'save the country' or please the Junto."[53]

The anti-Confederationists were confident of a triumphant victory because the Unionist party was poorly organized. At the end of August, it had no candidates in nine of the seventeen electoral counties for the House of Commons, and four antis won by acclamation. Those who were nominated were not perceived as having much of a chance. The Conservatives tried to appeal to Liberal voters, but the "coalition" aspect of Confederation Toryism seemed to have a repellent aspect.[54]

From the beginning, the campaign appeared to be a path to victory for the antis. "Know that nothing is more certain than that," regretted Brown in the *Globe,* who saw his chances of forming a strong opposition to Macdonald evaporate as Nova Scotians were poised to go their own way.[55] The Halifax *Sun and Advertiser* was confident by the end of August that the Anti-Confederation Party (sometimes also known as the Nova Scotia Party) would sweep the province even though "neither money nor labor is spared by the Unionists."[56]

There were allegations of corruption. On Wednesday, August 7, 1867, the *Eastern Chronicle* republished a story about the unionists in Pictou that it considered revealing of the "most unblushing corruption, sufficient to make the blush of shame mount to the cheek of every honest Nova Scotian." It also thought that the story should raise in "every honest man the deepest indignation against the men, the government, the party who are those prostituting the public offices and using the people's money to bribe electors of the province in support of a scheme of confederation which the people instinctively hate." The practice was rampant, the *Eastern Chronicle* warned, though it felt somewhat reassured by the thought that "honest farmers" would not be bought for $20 or a "paltry road commission."[57] There were also allegations that the postmaster general had threatened post office employees with dismissal if they voted for Howe's party, and that Tilley, as minister of revenue, had sent similar orders to customs house officials.[58]

By mid-August, there seemed little doubt that Howe and the anti-unionists would win election by a very large majority. Howe's campaign was mostly limited to the Halifax area, Cumberland County, where he spent three weeks touring the communities in order to personally defeat Tupper and his own riding of Hants.

Tupper, for his part, campaigned little outside his Cumberland riding, which William Annand toured relentlessly. He was preoccupied with finding candidates. The unionists, in contrast, still had not chosen candidates in half the counties, and there was talk about local Conservatives rejecting converts to the Confederation idea and sticking with old "Tories" who were unwilling to join Howe. There was also evidence that old Liberals were willing to support Howe out of personal loyalty, even though they favoured Confederation.[59] Howe's influence must have surprised his opponents. Like any deeply experienced politician, he had accumulated enemies. In 1867, however, his popularity had much to do with the strength of the anti-union party. As one journalist observed, even those who wanted Nova Scotia to join Confederation wished to see him in the House of Commons. Many Nova Scotians, he wrote, "believe that under such circumstances he would soon acquire a good position in the federal parliament, and do credit to himself and to Nova Scotia."[60] It was a point of view that must have caught the ear of Sir John A. Macdonald.

# 6

# The Outcome

**THE ELECTION RESULTS** were announced on September 20, 1867.[1] There was no surprise as local wins and losses had been declared for weeks already, and only the (mostly predictable) results of the election in Nova Scotia were being awaited. John A. Macdonald's coalition of Conservatives and Liberal-Conservatives were elected to a majority government with 100 seats, with the Liberal-Conservatives collecting 29 seats and the Conservatives 71. The Liberals took 62 seats, while the Anti-Confederation Party picked up 17 seats, all from Nova Scotia.

In Canada's first election, 360,792 men were eligible to vote and 268,677 did so, for a 74.5 percent turnout rate. That degree of participation was surpassed only fourteen times over the course of the next forty-three elections. With a population of about 3.25 million, this means that about 11.1 percent of the population was eligible and 8.3 percent made key decisions in this election – and arguably for Canada's destiny. There is a distortion of the results in this calculation, however, in that the eligible population in the forty-two ridings that were won by acclamation was not counted in the official record. (Had all ridings voted, and assuming that roughly the same proportion of the local population was eligible, the rate would have

184  *Ballots and Brawls*

been close to 14 percent.) This is significant, but the participation rate among eligible voters is more important. It showed that the campaign was legitimate, and the results confirmed that even though many people challenged the existence of Canada, that conviction did not lead to a boycott of the election.

The election set another record: 46 seats (25 percent of the total) were decided by acclamation. The Conservative coalition took 29 of those: 20 in Quebec, 7 in Ontario, and 2 in New Brunswick, which certainly pointed to a solid degree of support in certain areas. The Liberals won 13: 8 in Ontario, 3 in Quebec, and 2 in New Brunswick. The Anti-Confederation Party in Nova Scotia won 4 seats by acclamation.

The first elected House of Commons in the history of Canada counted 54 lawyers on both sides of the aisle (and 5 notaries from Quebec), at least 40 merchants/dealers/traders of all sorts, 17 farmers, 9 businessmen, 9 printers/editors/journalists, 4 engineers, 2 Crown Land agents, 2 land surveyors, 1 manufacturer, 1 investor and promoter, 1 druggist, and 1 tanner. The biggest news was undoubtedly the defeat of the editor George Brown in the riding of South Ontario (Whitby-Pickering-Oshawa). Disheartened, Alexander Mackenzie pressed Brown to run again, but in light of the general loss, Brown declined. His heart was not in it and, as hard as it was to accept the rejection (he lost bids for both a federal and a provincial seat), he secretly rejoiced that his destiny was not Ottawa but the comforts of home in Toronto, his Bow Park farm in Brant County, and the *Globe*. The opposition would be redoubtable all the same. Antoine-Aimé Dorion, Luther Holton, Timothy Warren Anglin, Alexander Mackenzie, Edward Blake, and Joseph Howe all won their seats.

The Halifax *Morning Chronicle* naturally interpreted the result as a mandate for Nova Scotia to withdraw from Confederation. "We should be freed from the connection forced upon us. If we be not ... we fear strange consequences," it declared.[2] Howe told the new

British secretary for the colonies, Lord Stanley, that if any obstacles were to interrupt Nova Scotia's efforts to withdraw, "we shall cease to regard England as the fountain head of justice and begin to study foreign affairs on our own account."[3] A summit of all new Nova Scotia Members of Parliament and Members of the Legislative Assembly held in Halifax on October 5 put them on the warpath, with orders to have the British North America Act repealed and Lieutenant-Governor Sir William Fenwick Williams sent home. The new Nova Scotia government under Premier William Annand also quickly resolved to get the province out of Canada.[4]

Macdonald, fully convinced that Reform was "split up and demoralized," had expected a big victory. In Quebec, he had hoped to win 50 of 65 seats, and he took 47 of 64 (since Kamouraska's election was cancelled) – 73 percent of the seats. He did well in Ontario also, winning 49 of 82 seats (60 percent). But he really miscalculated in the Maritimes. He thought the Conservatives would win 12 of the 15 seats in New Brunswick, but they actually *lost* 12 of the 15. He had hoped for half the seats in Nova Scotia but got only one lone seat: Charles Tupper in Cumberland. There was another source of sourness in the easternmost province: the only loss of a cabinet member, Adams Archibald.[5]

The popular vote tells a very different story, however. J. Murray Beck's classic account indicates that Macdonald's men took just over 50 percent of the vote but does not indicate how he came to that count. The source of the confusion lies in the official report of the election, which does not recognize party affiliation. In terms of identifying the winner, the task is fairly easy in that winners became easily recognizable by where they sat in the House of Commons a few weeks later. But the losers in the election were not identified by any label. One has to assume that if a "government" candidate took a seat in the House of Commons, he would do so as a Conservative, and if an "opposition" candidate won, he was likely a Liberal. In New Brunswick and Nova Scotia, however, it was not so

186    *Ballots and Brawls*

obvious who came in second. The party labels from the United Province of Canada had little resonance in those ridings. Party discipline was loose, and the leaders did not always seem to be in control of what was happening locally, as it was not uncommon for Conservatives or Liberals to challenge each other. Regardless, it is impossible to determine precisely because party labels (if any) were not recorded. The work necessary to clarify this would require an exhaustive study of each individual riding that would go beyond the mandate of this short book and may still not yield much clarity.

By my count, in tabulating the results collected by the government of Canada, the Conservative coalition took 94,997 votes (35.4 percent), the Liberal Party of Canada collected 59,456 votes (22.1 percent), the Anti-Confederationists 21,239 votes (7.9 percent), and the catch-all category of "unknowns/independents" 92,985 votes (34.6 percent). Put differently, the non-Liberal, non-Conservative vote amounted to 42.5 percent of the tally, by far the largest share.

### New Brunswick

New Brunswick saw a decisive Liberal victory, with the party securing 80 percent of the seats (twelve of fifteen). Timothy Anglin returned home to Saint John from his trip to Gloucester predicting that he would win three-quarters of the vote, but had to be satisfied with 61 percent. He complained that holding the election on a Wednesday discouraged the many Liberal fishers in his riding, and he may well have been correct.[6] The question is whether the Liberal voters were expressing anti-Confederation sentiment in the way Anglin and Smith interpreted it – namely, opposition to the project as in 1865 – or were tacitly accepting the new order of things. It is impossible to say, but the resounding proportion of the anti-Conservative vote was impressive.

The Liberal-Conservatives took two seats: Leonard Tilley, who won by a large margin in the city of Saint John (almost 70 percent) and John Costigan in Victoria (58 percent). The only "Conservative" seat (Saint John City and County) was won by acclamation by long-time party activist John Hamilton Gray. The Conservative/Liberal-Conservative coalition wins were in the province's westernmost riding and in the Saint John area. Remarkably, the ridings of Gloucester, Victoria, and Westmorland, all of which had strong Acadian proportions, voted against the Conservative pro-Confederation coalition.[7]

The turnout across the province was 71.1 percent (19,581 voters out of 27,535 eligible), slightly below the national average. The numbers varied by number of eligible voters in a riding. The ridings with the highest turnout tended to be those with fewer than or around 2,500 eligible voters; all these ridings had roughly 80 percent turnout, within a few percentage points. The highest was Albert at 84.5 percent turnout (1,492 voters out of 1,766 eligible). Ridings with over 3,000 eligible voters all had much weaker turnouts, with a low of 57.9 percent in Charlotte (only 2,132 voters out of 3,685 eligible). The one exception to this was Westmorland, which had 69.3 percent turnout in spite of its population of 3,842.

Four of the province's races, accounting for about a quarter of the seats, were won by acclamation, including the only Conservative victory. The Liberals took three seats by acclamation, but their overall performance was commanding even excluding these. Charles Fisher decided not to run as a Conservative and returned to his Reformist roots, and he was acclaimed in York, just north of Fredericton. Charles Connell, a merchant, was named MP for Carleton, in the western part of the province. Another merchant, John Farris, was acclaimed in the centre-east riding of Queen's.

The popular vote told a similar story. The Liberals took 49.5 percent of the vote and the Conservative coalition took 11.1 percent. A staggering number of votes – 39.3 percent – went to independent/unidentified candidates, even though New Brunswick had few competitive races. In five races, the winner received 60 percent or more

188   *Ballots and Brawls*

of the vote. In Westmorland, former Liberal premier Albert J. Smith won 82.9 percent, defeating his opponent 2,207 votes to 454. Only three ridings saw winners get less than 55 percent of the vote. In Albert, the Liberal, John Wallace (listed as a farmer), took 778 votes to 714 (52.1 percent). In a hotly debated contest, King's was won by Liberal George Ryan (also a farmer), with 1,303 votes to 1,083 (54.6 percent).

In Kent, one of two four-way races, Liberal Auguste Renaud, a farmer and the only Acadian candidate in the election, won with 876 votes (41.3 percent). His three opponents received 757, 485, and 4 votes, respectively. Robert Barry Cutler, who placed fourth, ran as an independent. In 1872, he reversed the score entirely and won the riding for the Liberal Party, narrowly defeating Renaud. The other four-way race was in the riding of Victoria, where, as mentioned earlier, John Costigan won 778 votes (58 percent). The third-place candidate received only 16 votes and the unfortunate James Tibbetts received zero votes – he clearly did not even vote for himself! (He got his revenge in 1872 when he won the riding.) Any candidate in New Brunswick who was not a Liberal had poor odds, and it was felt keenly by these men in particular.

The MPs sent to Ottawa by New Brunswick were quite diverse in terms of their professions. Four were farmers, four were lawyers, and three were merchants of various descriptions. There was a businessman, an editor, a druggist, and a judge. The three races that were particularly close were all won by Liberals whose professions were listed as farming.

The results were a big disappointment for Tilley, now fifty, but he more than made up for it. He got married again, to Alice Starr, on October 22, and then left for a honeymoon in Bangor, Maine. He joined his colleagues in Ottawa for the opening of Parliament. New Brunswick had elected a Liberal opposition, but it was not an anti-Confederation opposition as Anglin might have wished it to be. Its signals were confused and confusing. Peter Mitchell was made a senator in October 1867 and given the marine and fisheries portfolio. There was no provincial election, as in Nova Scotia, Ontario, and Quebec; the next one was held in June-July 1870.

## Quebec

Macdonald's coalition won big in Quebec, claiming 47 seats – almost 75 percent of the ridings. The Liberals took 17 seats, 9 of which were either in Montreal or its surrounding areas. The most spectacular races – those where Antoine-Aimé Dorion, Thomas D'Arcy McGee, and George-Étienne Cartier ran – were nail-biters. Dorion won Hochelaga by only 23 votes. McGee won his seat in Montreal-Ouest by 197 votes. The election in Montreal-Est saw Cartier take a huge lead with 571 votes on September 5, only to have Médéric Lanctôt collect 979 votes against Cartier's 756 the next day. In the end, Cartier won by 348 votes (2,433 against 2,085). Brown's *Globe* conceded that while he was "something very like a jobber," Cartier had "at times, achieved something which could fairly be called statesmanship," which deserved some recognition.[8] Early on, the Conservatives appeared to be giving Luther Holton a major challenge. Complaining that the Catholic clergy was against him, Holton conceded that he "was fighting as if for dear life." In mid-August, Cartier and McGee held a rally in Sainte-Martine to take the fight to Holton, arguing that Holton had never done much for Quebec's interests and praising, in contrast, the accomplishments of various Tory administrations. Dorion and Joseph Doutre organized a counter-rally in support of Holton and emphasized the Liberal contribution to the abolition of the seigneurial system; the subject of Confederation hardly came up.[9] The rally may well have helped, as Holton won his seat of Chateauguay by getting almost double his opponent's votes.

The turnout in Quebec was generally lower than average at 68.6 percent. It varied by region, ranging from 51.1 percent in the riding

190   *Ballots and Brawls*

of Quebec-Centre to 82.6 percent in Verchères, where the Liberal Félix Geoffrion defeated Gaspard-Aimé Massue, the *seigneur* of Varennes, who ran as an independent (but perhaps as a Conservative) by only ninety-one votes.[10] Because twenty-three ridings were decided by acclamation – the Conservatives/Liberal-Conservatives taking twenty and the Liberals three – these figures are not indicative of the breadth of the Macdonald coalition's victory. Given the relatively low turnout (though still impressive by modern standards) and the number of acclamations, the Quebec election seems to have been affected by indifference more than in the other provinces.

The vote percentage is more difficult to evaluate, however, because so many "opposition" candidates were not labelled with partisan tags in the returns. Murray Beck is confident that the Conservative coalition took 53.6 percent of the vote in Quebec, beating the Liberals' 45.1 percent by more than 8 percentage points and giving "independents" 1.3 percent, but it is not clear how he could have arrived at such a conclusion.[11] Jean-Paul Bernard's painstaking calculations show the *Bleus* taking 60 percent of the federal vote, the Liberals 15.3 percent, and the independents 24.4 percent. My calculations produced a much different result: the Conservative/Liberal-Conservatives taking 42.5 percent of the vote, the Liberals 24.9 percent, and the independents/unlabelled 32.6 percent. Here is an added complication: Normand Séguin examined the Liberal Party's performance in the Montreal region in an excellent Master of Arts thesis at the University of Ottawa in 1968. His study of the twenty-six ridings yielded a slightly different result for the province. By his count, the Conservatives would have garnered 50.5 percent of the vote in the province (midway between Beck's estimate and mine), the Liberals would have taken 30.2 percent (again midway between Beck and me), and independents 32.6 percent (exactly my result). The problem is that Séguin, like Bernard, does not show enough research to indicate how he labelled those individuals who did not win. Bernard's brave attempt also yielded a strange result, in that he recorded 78,195 voters exercising their right to suffrage, almost 6,000 more than the actual records indicate.[12]

Averaged out, Bernard, Séguin, and I conclude that the non-Conservative/non-Liberal support amounted to a quarter of the vote (25.3 percent). There is a temptation to argue that the quarter of voters who voted for neither of the openly federalist parties were expressing an anti-Confederation sentiment, but proving this would require a detailed micro-political study of every riding.

Regardless of how the count is sliced and diced, it is clear that the *Rouges* continued their decline among voters. In 1863, the last election in the United Province of Canada, they had relinquished 4 seats (managing to retain 25), and they lost all their by-elections in 1864–67. In 1867, they were reduced to 17 seats. Only five MPs who had voted against Confederation in 1865 were re-elected.[13] The *Rouges* kept their support in some towns on the eastern shore: Verchères, Richelieu, Saint-Hyacinthe, Rouville, Bagot, and Shefford, and to some degree in L'Avenir and Drummond-Arthabaska, the area where Wilfrid Laurier had just settled and for a time in 1866 had assumed the editorship of *Le Défricheur*. They did scarcely any better in the simultaneous Quebec provincial election, in which Pierre Chauveau and the Conservative Party won 51 of 63 seats and 53.5 percent of the vote.

In the days following the election, a few Protestant representatives complained that they were underrepresented. In the Quebec City area, the *Quebec Gazette* noted that forty thousand French Canadian Roman Catholics had elected four members and ten thousand Irish Roman Catholics had two representatives, but that the fifteen thousand English, Irish Protestants, and Scots had no representation. "There was a time when the majority of the citizens of Quebec used to show their respect for the Protestant minority by allowing them to elect one of the two members to be returned to Parliament," it noted.[14] A much stronger argument could have been made regarding the inequality in riding population that was especially pronounced in Quebec. Electorates ranged from those of Trois-Rivières, with 561 eligible voters, to Montreal-Ouest, with 7,860. This disparity meant that a voter in the former riding had a vote fourteen times as powerful as that of a voter in the latter. There were several tight races for some of the sixty-five seats contested in Quebec. In fifteen, the winner received under 55 percent of the vote. A few were won by a single percentage point. In general, three-way races in Quebec were effectively two-way, with the exception of Richelieu. In Berthier, the Liberal physician Anselme Homère Paquet won by a few dozen votes. A three-way race in Richelieu had Thomas McCarthy, a Conservative businessman, claiming victory against two other candidates with a simple plurality: he won 777 votes (41.6 percent of the total), while Joseph-Xavier Perrault, a hardline opponent of Confederation, took 625 and Pierre Gélinas, also a Conservative, took 450.[15] Several races were won by less than 100 votes, and seven of them were claimed by Liberals, a strong overrepresentation given their overall performance.

The other two races featuring a third candidate were mere formalities. One candidate received 2 votes in Quebec-Centre, and a third candidate in Portneuf got only 1 vote (his own, one would assume). Two-way races featuring independent candidates varied in their margins but were won by candidates representing a party. The riding of Drummond and Arthabaska offered a close race between Conservative financier Louis-Adélard Sénécal and an independent whose only listed name was "Houle." Sénécal defeated Houle by 24 votes (1,135 to 1,111). In L'Islet, the Conservative candidate running against an independent received 92.1 percent of the vote. Independent candidates were most often defeated soundly, the most staggering example being a three-way race in Quebec-Centre, where the winner, Conservative manufacturer Georges Honoré Simard, got 1,291 out of 1,298 votes. One of his opponents obtained 5 votes, while the other took 2. Although some independents fared better, none was able to win a single seat against candidates belonging to either the Conservatives/Liberal-Conservatives or the Liberal Party.

The vote distribution offers only a few clues in terms of regional preferences. Montreal was split, with the ridings to the east a little more Liberal than to the west. The areas most proximate to Montreal, to the northeast or on the south shore, tended to support the Liberals. Otherwise, the southern shore of the St. Lawrence was blue; the only exceptions were the Geoffrion win in Verchères and Henri Joly de Lotbinière – the Liberal leader in the simultaneous provincial campaign – being acclaimed for the Liberals in his home riding of Lotbinière (he would sit in both legislatures until 1874, when double mandates were abolished). Quebec City seemed indifferent: the Liberal Philéas Huot was acclaimed in Quebec-Est and Thomas McGreevy was acclaimed in Quebec-West on a Liberal-Conservative ticket. The only race, really a non-contest in the end, was the three-way match in Quebec-Centre, already mentioned, in which the Conservative, Simard, pulverized his opponents. The Quebec MPs came from different walks of life, though 20 of the 64 were lawyers. There were also 9 merchants, 8 physicians, 7 farmers, 5 notaries, 3 businessmen, 2 contractors, a financier, a militia captain, and a flour and feed dealer.

It is worth noting that the Conservative success in winning the general election was replicated in the provincial election. Chauveau's Conservative government crushed the Liberals, taking fifty-one of the sixty-three seats, and would be re-elected in 1871.

### Ontario

Ontario, like Quebec, was a victory for Macdonald's coalition: It took forty-nine of the eighty-two seats (60 percent). The Conservative coalition was strongest in the eastern half of the province, taking practically every seat, as well as most ridings that touched Lake Erie and Lake Ontario. The western half told a different story, with Liberals dominating in all areas west of Whitby, including Toronto and the Hamilton area, Brantford, and the ridings touching Lake Huron. The Liberals were acclaimed in nine seats, three more than the Conservative coalition. It was a bitter result for the Liberals. In South Ontario, George Brown notably lost by 69 votes to the Liberal-Conservative merchant Thomas Gibbs (1,292 votes to Brown's 1,223). Brown also lost his bid for a seat in the Ontario Provincial Parliament. In the eastern Ontario riding of Russell, even J.L. O'Hanley, "Brown's fourth and last 'catholic friend'" (he was an Irish Catholic, mocked the *Ottawa Times*), was defeated.[16] In Ontario, as in the other provinces, unknowns and independents secured no seats.

The Tory win belied the number of very tight contests, however. As in Quebec, there is a contrast between the results Murray Beck reported and those collected for this book. Beck indicated that the Conservative coalition took 51.1 percent of the vote, and that the "opposition" Liberals would have earned 48.4 percent. My count indicates that the Conservative coalition took 39.6 percent of the vote, the Liberals running under a "Liberal" ticket took 22.7 percent, and the independent candidates took 37.2 percent. In Ontario, as in Quebec, independents took far more votes than the Liberals. It is entirely possible that over a third of voters rejected the two federalist parties as an expression of anti-Confederation sentiment, but it is not certain. What is clear is that six of ten voters did not support the Macdonald coalition in its drive for Confederation. It hardly seems likely, but again, as in Quebec, this would require a detailed micro-history research into each riding. The point is that independent candidates (or unlabelled ones) did manage to obtain a sizable share of the vote, far more than in the eastern provinces.

In thirty-five races (nearly half of the total number of seats), the winner secured less than 55 percent of the vote in the riding. Ontario was much more of a battleground than the other provinces in this respect. Of these, a few stand out as particularly interesting.

Algoma featured a three-way race, narrowly won by the Conservative trader Mackenzie Simpson with 250 votes, with his opponents receiving 241 and 38. Brant North was remarkably close, barely won by Liberal-Conservative physician John Young Brown with 672 votes, only 2 more than his opponent. Bruce North was won by Conservative Alexander Sproat with 862 votes, 10 more than his opponent. Essex saw Conservative lawyer John O'Connor win 1,439 to 1,432. Grey South went to Conservative Crown lands agent George Jackson, 1,560 votes to 1,547. Huron North was not strictly close, but the winner, Liberal railway contractor Joseph Whitehead, received a total of 49.32 percent of the vote in this three-way race. He won 1,940 votes to his opponents' 1,318 and 675. Leeds South was taken by Conservative lawyer John Crawford with 1,393 votes to 1,364. Middlesex West went 1,063 to 1,044 in favour of Conservative contractor Angus Peter McDonald. Norfolk North was won by Conservative civil engineer Aquila Walsh with 1,026 votes to his opponent's 990. Wentworth South had another close race, 1,015 to 988 in favour of Liberal farmer James Pearson. Several other races were close, within a percentage point or two of flipping, in this competitive province.

Generally, three-way races mostly ended poorly for third candidates in Ontario (as opposed to other areas of the country), with the exception of Huron North, where the third-place candidate received 675 votes. Otherwise, nearly every other three-way race saw the third-place candidate receiving votes in the single digits. Four-way races were even more pitiable; the two fourth-place candidates across the province received one vote each, likely their own. In Addington, there were seven candidates, but the fifth, sixth, and seventh received zero votes each. No party outside the Liberals, Conservatives, and Liberal-Conservatives won a single seat in Ontario.

Turnout in Ontario averaged 75.1 percent, above the national average and second only to Nova Scotia, but varied greatly in different ridings. The low point was Ottawa, the despondent new national capital, where 34.9 percent of eligible voters turned out. This race was an uncompetitive four-way race, with Liberal-Conservative lumberman Joseph Merrill Currier winning 96.9 percent of the vote. This poor result can be explained only approximately: public servants were prohibited from voting (laws were hardly needed – most would have been highly uncomfortable in openly declaring their allegiance) but might have been counted as eligible. Currier's high prestige – alluded to earlier in Chapter 3, on Ontario – made the race a foregone conclusion.

In contrast, the riding with the highest turnout, Middlesex East (East London and its eastern environs) at 89.1 percent, had a close race of 1,896 votes for Liberal-Conservative farmer Crowell Wilson to 1,756 for his opponent, the winner managing to obtain 51.9 percent of the vote. This pattern generally repeated itself across the province; while turnout rate seems unrelated to eligible voting population, the victory margin of the winner was tightly linked with the turnout of the riding, suggesting either that people were more likely to vote when they believed a race would be close or that higher turnout led to closer races. There was one big exception: John A. Macdonald decisively won his riding of Kingston with 83.8 percent of the vote, even though only 39 percent of the eligible voting population of the riding turned up to vote.

Ontario necessarily sent a variety of MPs to Ottawa, given the size of the province. The new delegation would include 19 lawyers and 15 merchants. Five each of contractors and farmers also won their races, and 4 each of physicians and businessmen. There were 3 civil engineers, 2 millers, 2 Crown lands agents, 2 tanners, 2 editors, 2 lumbermen, 2 lumber dealers, and 1 each of several other professions. Notable among the last was a brewer, John Carling, founder of the Carling Brewery. Ontario also had the only candidate with two occupations listed, a merchant who was also a sawmiller.

The results were not so encouraging in the Ontario provincial election, where Sandfield Macdonald (who was branded by the Brantford *Expositor* as "having no rival in history for treachery except Judas Iscariot")[17] split the eighty-two seats with Archibald McKellar, the Liberal leader. Because he took over 50 percent of the vote, Macdonald won the right to try to form a government, and succeeded in forging a coalition that would govern until 1871, when it was narrowly defeated by Edward Blake's Liberals.

## Nova Scotia

In the flush of enthusiasm for Confederation felt in some corners of Nova Scotia, Adams Archibald thought the Tupper unionists would be lucky to hold half of the nineteen seats in the province, a view that was widely shared, but Senator Edward Kenny predicted to Macdonald that the "antis" would likely win the provincial race.[18] Voters turned out in droves on September 18 – 32,322 of them out of 41,291 eligible men, for a turnout rate of 78.3 percent, the highest recorded in the country. As elsewhere, participation varied between a high of 87.5 percent in Colchester and a low of 66.5 percent in Inverness. It is thought that participation was a little lower in the areas where Conservatives had traditionally been strong.[19] No clear pattern in terms of turnout emerges; smaller ridings like Richmond, where 824 out of 1,232 (66.9 percent) eligible voters turned out, can be compared with larger ridings like Inverness.

Four races were won by acclamation. While not nominally important compared with other provinces, this did represent over 21 percent of ridings in Nova Scotia, and all of these ridings went to anti-Confederationist representatives. Given their performance in actual races, the likelihood that another party would take these seats was slim. The most striking aspect of the Nova Scotia election was the dominance of the anti-Confederationists across the entire province, where they won nearly 90 percent of races. They did so nearly unchallenged; the other parties ran very few candidates anywhere in the province. Judging from the party labels that were reported, only three Conservatives and one Liberal-Conservative ran against anti-Confederationists. All others were independents and lost by varying margins.

In terms of the popular vote, the anti-Confederationist perform-ance was imposing. Howe's Nova Scotia Party took 21,131 of 36,463 votes (58 percent), while the Conservatives took 18.1 percent. Independents, as elsewhere, took more votes than the official second party, winning 24.2 percent. Combined, the voices expressed against Howe and his party amounted to a very sizable 42.3 percent.

Nova Scotia saw the most lopsided result of all the provinces. Joseph Howe's anti-Confederationists won all the seats except one: Charles Tupper's. At the provincial level, on the same day, the anti-Confederationists won thirty-six of thirty-eight seats. The biggest victories were along the coasts. In his own riding of Hants, Howe crushed his opponent, Jason King.

The results "proved that the people of Nova Scotia would not be trampled upon; it showed that here traitors are held in no more esteem than they deserved," declared the *Halifax Chronicle;* "people were true to themselves, that no scoundrelly threats could intimidate them, that no money could buy them."[20] Bonfires were lit across Halifax and Dartmouth and many other parts of the province. A mock advertisement announced: "'Missing' – A polit-ical party, heretofore known in this Province as the Confederate Party, disappeared very suddenly at 5pm on Wednesday, the 18th September, and has not since been heard of."[21]

Tupper was humiliated. In his riding of Cumberland, the west-ernmost electoral district, every effort was made to get out the vote and 87.1 percent of those eligible voted. Tupper held off the direct challenge from William Annand by only 97 votes (1,368 to 1,271). He was strongest in the towns that were likely to benefit most from railway traffic, in areas with important Catholic populations,

The Outcome   199

and along the coasts. A loss for the Tupper team was Adams Archibald, who sat in Macdonald's cabinet. He faced A.W. McLelan in Colchester. Archibald was most popular in railroad towns, but McLelan's strength along Cobequid Bay carried him to victory.[22]

D.A. Muise has argued that support for Confederation in Nova Scotia came from more progressive types – more open to industrialization and the infrastructure required to sustain a modern chain of production and reach to markets. Others, more tied to classic industries like shipbuilding ("wood, wind and sail") and the Maritime trade tended to see Confederation as an undermining of the provincial economy.[23] Six of the nineteen seats in Nova Scotia were won by margins of less than 5 percent. In Annapolis and Pictou, respectively, the winning Anti-Confederation candidates received 53.5 percent and 54.9 percent of the vote. William Hallett Ray won the race in Annapolis by 155 votes (1,171 to 1,016), while James William Carmichael won by a slightly more comfortable margin of 358 votes (2,011 to 1,653). Of greater interest were the races in Cumberland, Digby, and Halifax. Tupper won Cumberland by only 97 votes. Digby was the only three-way race in the province, with two candidates of undeclared party affiliation running against the victorious Alfred William Savary, who won 47.97 percent of the votes in the riding, 792 to his competitors' 497 and 362. Halifax was a riding with two MPs and proved to be a close race. It seems as though urban dwellers in Halifax voted for the Tupper formation, while county voters supported Anti-Confederation candidates. The two winners were merchants: Patrick Power with 2,267 votes, and Alfred Gilpin Jones with 2,381.

The professions of the men who would represent Nova Scotia in Ottawa while simultaneously protesting their very presence in the House of Commons were more varied than their party affiliations: six merchants, five lawyers, a farmer, three physicians, two shipowners, and two newspaper editors (including Joseph Howe). Their mission was to undo Confederation. Timothy Anglin thought that the Nova Scotia results were significant but very likely would not have a long-term impact. "We believe that ... for generations to come the recent Nova Scotia elections will be a subject of interest with thoughtful men," he wrote. "We believe that generations of the future of Nova Scotia when reading the History of their Country will wonder that their ancestors had submitted for a day to be governed by men who betrayed the trust reposed in them by the people."[24]

Did Catholics make the difference, or did they split their votes? Muise pointed out that the ridings of Antigonish and Inverness, both of which had Scottish Catholic majorities, voted against Confederation.[25] In general, however, the answer can be as affirmative as (in a Canadian sense) "probable under the circumstances." There is no doubt that Catholics in Ontario, for instance, did support the Conservative coalition, but it is not possible to determine to what degree. Catholics in Quebec certainly did also, but it is equally obvious that they supported Liberals and all sorts of independents. Catholics certainly did not make much difference in Nova Scotia or New Brunswick, though they may have held the balance of power that would have swayed votes, probably towards the Conservative side. Religion aside, the new Parliament would feature enough parties to vie for the attention of voters – and the attention of 3.25 million new "Canadians": Liberal-Conservatives, Conservatives, Liberals, and Anti-Confederationists.

The humiliation of the idea of Confederation was accentuated at the provincial level. In that contest, William Annand led the Anti-Confederation Party to a crushing victory, taking thirty-six of thirty-eight seats and nearly 61 percent of the vote. Hiram Blanchard led the Confederation Party as best he could, and took almost 40 percent of the vote. He actually won his riding in Inverness but was later disqualified.

# Conclusion

**Politics is the art of the possible.**

– Otto von Bismarck, August 11, 1867[1]

**DESPITE HER BEST INTENTIONS,** Agnes Macdonald stopped jotting entries in her new diary in mid-July 1867 and did not write again until September 29. It was not without guilt that she returned to her pastime: "When I think over the eventful two months that have past [sic] since last I wrote in this pretty book I am angry with myself for my negligence and indolence in not putting some of our doings in its papers." (She clearly had no inkling that historians one day would be triply angry!) Agnes wrote that she had been overwhelmed with visitors, engagements, parties, letters, and all sorts of excitement.

All through the intensely hot summer days & far in the close breathless night my work went on & seeing my husband so busy, being cognizant of the enormous machinery he was setting in motion, watching hour after hour the results of his marvellous skill in the diplomatic line – all this helped to weary and yet excite me – a novice in this kind of life.[2]

Two months later, she confessed to being afraid of revealing in her diary what was being discussed in cabinet. Every day, she encountered "the men who are now making part of the History of their country." She was now living in "the atmosphere of 'head quarters.'"[3] Sir John A. Macdonald is not much help to students of history either. He stopped sending letters starting in mid-August. He wrote again on September 28 to the secretary of the Orphan's House in Ottawa to express his profound regret in not being able to be present at a soirée, and pleaded exhaustion.[4] Is it possible that the events of that seven-week hiatus kept him entirely away from his desk? Politics, it is often said, is a contact sport, and the couple may well have been too consumed with the task of pressing the flesh in order to win this first election (it is also possible, though not likely, that this tranche of mail was lost).

## What the 1867 Election Accomplished

The 1867 election was the most important one in nineteenth-century Canada, and one of the most significant political events. It could have gone in a completely different direction. Three big arguments were made during this first Canadian election. Some held that the constitutional arrangements were proper and that the country's progress would depend on their application. For them, it was important to vote Conservative/Liberal-Conservative or Liberal. Some thought that the British North America Act was defective but could be made to work. They tended to vote Liberal, especially in New Brunswick, but also in Quebec and Ontario and probably in Nova Scotia. Then there were some who believed it was all wrong. They would vote for Joseph Howe and his party in Nova Scotia or for the more radical *Rouges* in Montreal. Anywhere between a quarter and a third of Canadians may have supported independent candidates for precisely that reason.

In the end, and by the conventional measures of a parliamentary system, the Conservatives won the election and the cabinet proposed by Sir John A. Macdonald on July 1 was confirmed in power. Canada survived its first test and today can boast of being one of the longest-standing democracies anywhere in the world. But in 1867, it took a lot of convincing, no small measure of clever political maneuvering, and a strong element of luck. Canada was not brought about by a coup d'état, but it was certainly born of a *coup de force,* brought on by a *coup de tonnerre* from the business community and the British establishment that no longer wanted Canada listed in its tally of vulnerabilities. All these forces were powerfully heard in the first election. The election, however, was about more than electing mere Reformers (or Liberals) or Conservatives (or Liberal-Conservatives). It was also a referendum on whether the Confederation project should proceed.

The election was at once an act of political bullying and an enormous gamble. It provoked a realignment of political parties in Canada by pushing the formations that had shaped politics in the individual colonies to express themselves differently. In Quebec, moderate elements of the *Rouge* reformers joined with the *Bleus* and the Conservatives led by Macdonald and accepted the new constitutional arrangements, and the results of the election weakened the resolve of even the most convinced anti-Confederationists. In Nova Scotia, the supporters of Confederation were Conservatives and the opponents were mostly Liberals. It was the same in New Brunswick, though the party lines were harder to perceive. In the Maritimes, the most important political phenomenon was the split among Liberals, depending on whether or not they favoured Confederation. After all, the most ardent defender of Confederation was Leonard Tilley, a New Brunswick Liberal. This discouraging electoral result did not stop Tilley from joining Macdonald's cabinet and staying for much of the next twenty years. The reverse happened in Nova Scotia: the most ardent opponent of Confederation was Joseph Howe, also a former Reformer.

The Canadian federal election that concluded in the last week of the summer of 1867 legitimized what had been wrought at Charlottetown and at Quebec almost exactly three years earlier. The road to Confederation had been hectic. It was hardly a road at all, more of a confusing choice of political trails, detours, unmarked paths, and rickety suspended bridges. The best way to forge a route was, to borrow from Bismarck, to take advantage of the local political environment at hand, to use the politics of the possible. (Macdonald was hailed as the "Bismarck of Canada" by the *Republican*, a newspaper in the American West following the election.)[5] The winners would be the practical politicians, those with the best sense of the political compass.

The election of 1867 established Sir John A. Macdonald as the dominant political figure of his age. His brand of moderation worked in 1867 – at least, it worked better than others. Richard Cartwright, a Kingston Conservative, remembered that 1867 had "extraordinarily altered" the position of the new prime minister of Canada. "In the Parliament of 1863, he had appeared as a defeated and, to say the truth, as a rather discredited politician" who depended on the *Bleus*. "In 1867 he had blossomed out into the first Premier of the Dominion, with absolutely no opponent or opposition worth the name."[6]

The cabinet Macdonald had formed on the eve of Dominion Day thus lasted long enough to survive the first election. Then, in early November, the capital was shaken by the news that Macdonald had effectively fired Finance Minister Alexander Galt over a grave disagreement on banking regulation.[7] Macdonald appointed John Rose, an old friend based in Montreal and London, who occupied the post for almost two years. Fergusson Blair died two months later, in late December 1867, and Howland retired in the summer of 1868, due to illness. When Archibald retired from the position of secretary of state for the provinces at the end of April 1868, Macdonald left the post vacant until Howe could be convinced to finally and frankly join the government.

Macdonald clearly dominated the politics of his day. His ability to convince colleagues, to see the most positive things in the most negative scenarios, had won over a plurality of voters, but far from all of them. George-Étienne Cartier had to be satisfied in a secondary role; within three months, Galt was gone, George Brown was a spent force, and Antoine-Aimé Dorion had been forced into silence. That left Howe.

Macdonald's political ability was in shaping the country's first "big tent" party, and this was surely one of the revelations of the 1867 election. He appealed to Catholic and Protestant – even Orangist – voters, to Grit and Clear Grit supporters, to *Bleus* and even to some *Rouge* militants. He had old-time nationalists on his side, as well as former annexationists. He could claim support in almost all reaches of the country. There were limits, of course, particularly in the Maritimes, where any such pretensions would die hard. Confederation had won favour as a solution for stagnation, real or imagined. It was, in Ontario, a solution to a flaw in the United Province of Canada's democracy, namely, that Quebec (or Canada East) had equal numbers of Members of the Provincial Parliament as Ontario even though it had a far smaller population. There was no patience left for a parliament where stability was always held to ransom. Breaking the deadlock, however, would force the Liberals into almost permanent opposition. It was especially galling for Ontario Liberals that Macdonald's brand of Toryism could give him a lock on power because he harnessed the *Bleus* in Quebec. Ontario could have militated for a separation, but, except by a small minority, that option wasn't seen as workable. A federated system was also a possibility – where there would be two provinces united by some weak central government, but again there was little support for that option.

It was the results in the provinces of Quebec and Ontario that elevated Macdonald. For all its successes in Central Canada, the Conservative coalition was unpopular in the Maritimes. Nova Scotia was a grave problem, but Macdonald waxed optimistic. "We all deeply regret the result of the elections in your province," he wrote to Philip Carteret Hill, the provincial secretary in Hiram Blanchard's now defeated government. "Our majority is so overwhelmingly strong in the rest of the Dominion that it [the Nova Scotia result] won't seriously embarrass us here, but we cannot but sympathize with those who fell in the good cause."[8]

Confederation certainly appealed to people who liked to think big and who wanted British North America to be as vast as the continent. The commercial class wanted to be more ambitious and saw potential in seeking some sort of alliance with the other British colonies that sat north of the United States. It did not take too much imagination to conceive of a grand territory, running from one coast to the other, ideally linked by the emerging new technologies of railways. But that argument raised all sorts of opposition. It was expensive, unlikely to be cost-effective, and possibly ruinous to the Maritime economy as it would facilitate imports (the argument that it could facilitate exports was downplayed). Rupert's Land, the vast stretch of land that spanned the shores of Hudson Bay to the Great Lakes and to the Rockies, was widely seen as uninhabited except for a few tens of thousands of migrant Indigenous peoples and Métis, and could be easily appropriated.[9] To those who thought in terms of natural resources, markets, government revenue, and geopolitics, the project made sense. While the United States was tearing itself apart, new countries were emerging – India was being consolidated, and so were Germany and Italy.

*Conclusion*  207

The United States loomed large in the minds of Ontarians in particular as it emerged from its Civil War: it had an important army ready for action, and the fear of a repeat of 1812 was real. The second factor was an act of Congress, in March 1865, weeks before Lincoln was assassinated, that gave notice of abrogation of the reciprocity treaty between Great Britain and the United States. Britain and Canada were caught off guard, having done nothing to kickstart new talks, even thinking that the secessionist South had a chance of victory. There were very few working contacts between the two countries, and it seemed that the Americans saw no need to reach out. They were more interested in the inevitability of annexation. In the geopolitical realities of the day, the project of Canada was an instinctive process of risk management. The bonds of the various colonies were fetching better prices than ever (the same could be said of American bonds).[10] For the advocates of a stronger union, it was an opportunity to develop economies of scale that could give government credit.[11]

The Conservative victory aside, the votes gave enormous support to candidates who were not official representatives of the dominant parties. Nevertheless, especially in the eyes of the leaders, the turnout gave the project legitimacy, and the support for both the Conservatives/Liberal-Conservatives and the Liberals who supported a broad federal union was unquestionable. In what amounted to a victory banquet at the fashionable Burnett House in Kingston two weeks before Nova Scotia voted, Macdonald was apparently seized by this realization. In the middle of a long speech, he recounted the ups and downs on the road to Confederation. Between the "cheers" and "prolonged cheering," he invoked another ancient fable: the tale of the tortoise and the scorpion.[12] Macdonald presented himself as the tortoise, a quiet but determined creature with a hardened shell that could withstand the attacks of his enemies. The invectives did not matter – it was in the nature of the opposition to try to sting. What mattered was that he, fortified by his supporters, was headed in the right direction, and so was the "scorpion" opposition. His remarks again elicited "loud cheers," according to the reporter of the *Ottawa Citizen*.[13]

There is no doubt that as the men gathered around Macdonald's desk in the East Block of Parliament Hill in Ottawa in late September, their worries went to the heart of a new national unity question: how could Timothy Warren Anglin's anti-Confederation acolytes be held in check? How can we win Nova Scotia? Macdonald's answer was simple and instructive: keep building and Maritime opinion will eventually be won over. Perhaps he saw in the actual results of those elections a real softness in the support for anti-Confederation politicians. Good deeds, he mused, could still win hearts and minds, but time was of the essence. Macdonald could look to his own caucus for some support: both the premiers of Quebec (Pierre-Joseph Chauveau) and Ontario (Sandfield Macdonald) were backbenchers!

### Nova Scotia's Secessionism

In Nova Scotia, there was no fear of helplessness before the might of the United States. Upon his victory in September 1867, Howe immediately began a campaign to repeal Nova Scotia's participation in the new Dominion. In February 1868, Martin Wilkins, the Nova Scotia attorney general, who was described as "very clever though eccentric," proposed a resolution in the House of Assembly that a delegation be sent to London to renegotiate Confederation. He argued that the cause of Nova Scotia's self-determination was honourable and that the Crown would be reasonable. "But," he warned, "if the Imperial Government should refuse our prayer, we shall then have to appeal to another nation to come to our aid."[14] He called Charles Tupper a Lazarus, denouncing his "rodomontading homily" on union, particularly because it opened with the "hackneyed truism 'Union is Strength'" and the rest was "philosophical twaddle."[15]

Wilkins himself denounced the notion of union as inevitably "logical, conclusive, and irrefragable."[16] "There is nothing like union men to unite to make railroads, telegraphs, and steam navigation," he said, "so we would remind [ourselves] they sometimes unite to rob, to defraud, and to betray. Nations also, like individuals, may unite for good, or they may unite for evil. They may unite to defend, or they may unite to destroy the liberty of their neighbors." He compared the efforts of Ontario and Quebec to Russia and Prussia, who had united to carve up Poland, and predicted that the Canadians "will unite to rob and oppress Nova Scotia."[17]

Howe produced petitions and travelled to London to make the case to British parliamentarians. Macdonald seemed unfazed at first. "I am pretty well satisfied that now that Howe and his friends have done their revenge, they will not assume a very hostile position here, when we get them away from local influence and surrounded by representation of all the rest of the British America – indeed I shall be very much surprised if many of the representatives of Nova Scotia do not give their adhesion to confederation and submit to the inevitable." For Macdonald, there was no question that Tupper had done the right thing in pressing on because he had a majority in government. He went further in his prediction: "In a very short period, when the success of the Union is no longer doubtful, men will be ashamed of having ever been counted among those opposed to it," and Conservatives would win the right to govern again in Nova Scotia.[18]

Nevertheless, Macdonald pressed Tupper to go to London also in order to lobby both the Gladstone government and Howe himself. The *Globe*, speaking on behalf of Liberals, hoped that Howe would see the light, or at least the benefits of remaining in Confederation. The message had been heard: Nova Scotians were a people eager to defend their self-determination, but independence was not a safe option. "Now that the Anti-Unionists have won their victory – and so overwhelmingly a victory too – we hope that they will 'accept the situation' in the fullest sense of the term," Brown wrote. "Let them reap the legitimate fruits of their victory, and make the best of the Union."[19] Tilley's newspaper in Saint John suggested that Howe accept a post in cabinet, perhaps the secretaryship of the Dominion. He could aid Nova Scotia in the cabinet as nowhere else. After all, it said, Sandfield Macdonald opposed Confederation to the last in Ontario, "but when that measure was finally settled by the action of the British parliament, he accepted it and resolved to make the best of it."[20]

Howe was quickly told in London that his cause was lost. The House of Commons refused, by a vote of 181 to 87, to appoint a Royal Commission to investigate the Nova Scotia claims.[21] The British would not support a return to the status quo ante, and the best he could hope for was to negotiate "better terms" on Confederation with the Macdonald government. Howe had seen enough of the new prime minister of Canada to know that he was "trenchant, animated and effective."[22] Macdonald also worked on a strategy to convince each Nova Scotia MP and, most of all, redoubled efforts to make progress on the Intercolonial Railway and live up to the constitutional commitment provided by section 145.

Macdonald took Nova Scotia's protest seriously. He was invited to appear before the Committee of the Provincial Convention of Nova Scotia, also known as the Repeal Committee, in early August 1868. He accepted, and asked Cartier, Peter Mitchell of New Brunswick, and Senator Edward Kenny to accompany him. The idea of receiving the Canadians was not unanimous, and many of the members categorically refused to meet the Canadians and New Brunswicker. Others argued that "London was unlikely to repeal if Nova Scotians did not make a show of goodwill."

Macdonald and his colleagues landed in Halifax on August 6 and met with the committee at 4 p.m. the next day. Things did not go well. Macdonald and his colleagues were greeted by "noisy insulting demonstrations," "coldness," and a "refusal to meet them in society."

The committee was nothing if not hostile. The Lieutenant-Governor had organized a dinner for the Canadians but the committee members refused to attend.[23] There is no indication that Macdonald gave a speech or that he used his visit to Halifax to campaign. The hostility was such that he simply turned on his heels, convinced that his presence would likely do nothing more than envenom negotiations. Macdonald's presence seemed to have triggered strong emotions.

Macdonald, for his part, treated Howe with kid gloves, and employed a clever strategy. Even though Adams Archibald had been defeated in the election, Macdonald kept him in cabinet. He could easily have replaced him with Charles Tupper, who had more than earned the recognition, but Macdonald thought that would be provocative. It took just a little over a year, but by early 1869 – sixteen months after the vote – Macdonald convinced Howe to join the cabinet. By that time, at least twelve of the eighteen Nova Scotians elected in 1867 on the "anti" ticket now fully supported the Macdonald government.[24] Parties were not "constant institutions," Howe observed in justifying his change of heart. "They form and reform, fuse and divide in all free Countries as opinions change and new issues and exigencies arise."[25] Howe, a Conservative Reformer, according to his best biographer, had much in common with Macdonald.[26]

It was an instance when Macdonald, the dominant policy entrepreneur of his era, also showed his exceptional political *doigté;* he had the ability to make practically anything politically possible. "Sir John Alexander Macdonald is a man of resources and he has made precedents for himself which if followed will exactly suit the present emergency," the *Montreal Herald* observed after the election.[27] Touched with no small dose of cynicism, its correspondent had good advice now that the election campaign was over. Macdonald "has only to find out which of the 'antis' are to be bought and then to buy them. We do not see why it should be any harder to take

212  *Ballots and Brawls*

Mr. Howe into the combination, supposing he will go, than it was to take Mr. John Sandfield Macdonald, or at an earlier day Mr. George Brown." The journalist recalled Macdonald's ability to work with people who had previously battled him: D'Arcy McGee, "Yankee" Howland, "Washington" McDougall, and Sandfield Macdonald. "Howe was not likely to be much different."[28]

Macdonald did not abandon the task of convincing Maritimers, and the results of the 1872 election reflected his progress in that region. While his coalition lost support in Quebec and Ontario, it took five of sixteen seats in New Brunswick and thirteen of the twenty-one seats in Nova Scotia, a big improvement over the 1867 results.

### The Liberals on Trial

If Macdonald was barely in control of the Conservative coalition, the election of 1867 was a disaster for the Liberals. George Brown proved to be a short-sighted, even myopic leader, his party unable to open doors. The listless leadership aside, the Liberals had no real program to carry Confederation to its next steps. It suffered the disastrous decisions of Brown, who had left the governing coalition in 1865 and thus could claim no credit at all for the consummation of the Confederation pact. His kind biographer held that "the problem was beyond his control," and that the "the times were simply out of joint for him," but it was clear that he had none of the attributes of a statesman.[29] Brown was an ideologue with a local following, and could not rally people around a vision beyond the narrow confines of his clan. In Quebec, even the Liberals were ready to pronounce their party dead. The *Franco-Canadien,* a moderate paper that accepted Confederation in principle but on the condition that Quebec be given maximum autonomy, described the "complete disappearance of the old rouge party," and it seemed everyone wanted a divorce from *Le Pays,* which had been denounced as the "*journal des sans-culottes.*"[30] Médéric Lanctôt's *Union Nationale* soon closed its doors. If anything, the 1867 election had shown that any radicalism on the part of the Liberal Party in Quebec would be unsaleable electorally.[31] It would take almost thirty years to shake off that poor reputation, even though the party did demonstrate time and again that it had lost its zeal for bold ideas.

The Liberal Party was gravely divided as it entered the first election, but perhaps more than that it was disoriented by the Confederation project and especially bedevilled by Macdonald's political wiles. Under Brown's leadership, the party in Ontario – the Grits and Clear Grits – had come to champion Confederation, but it had enormous trouble translating that vision to the other provinces. In *The Present and Future of Canada*, Henry Olivier Lacroix described it as obsessed with the idea of annexation, only to suddenly discover that a powerful antidote (Confederation) had been found for it. The Grits essentially had nothing to complain about. "The strongest objections which they can bring against Confederation, are all questions of form, rather than of foundational principles," Lacroix argued. In his view, the Liberals would need a long time to recover.[32]

Its leadership was largely to blame. Brown had reason to believe that Reform/Liberals could do well, but he could not extend his authority beyond the borders of Ontario. Combative and irascible, he had no patience for politics. Intensely convinced of his own views, he was insensitive to the consequences of alienating people, notably Catholics – hardly a desirable quality in the game of persuading voters. As the election campaign began, he observed condescendingly that "there are plenty of ignorant people that have votes, whom a little judicious talk might be enlighten, and a little kindly attention and urgency might warm into something of interest, and prompt to earnest and effective activity." The Conservatives feasted on such remarks. The *St. Catharines Constitutional* noted that any voter could thus legitimately see himself as one of Brown's "ignorant people," who would "stand in need of a little judicious talk and a little hunting up." The editor at the *Constitutional* turned it around wittily: "In fact, to be seen talking even with the emissaries of the Opposition is almost enough to write oneself down as 'an ass.'"[33] The *Ottawa Times* said that he pursued a "miserable mire of personal politics in which George Brown continues to grovel, and with instinctive consciousness of the meanness of his cause, he frantically calls upon his friends to hunt up the 'ignorant voters' to sustain it."[34]

There was another face to Ontario's Liberalism, moreover, personified especially by the three men ("turncoats" in the Liberal press) who joined Macdonald's government in the early summer of 1867 – William McDougall, William Howland, and Fergusson Blair – as well as Liberals from New Brunswick such as Leonard Tilley, Peter Mitchell, and even Thomas D'Arcy McGee, who had changed his political allegiance years ago but could not escape the label.

The position of a Liberal like Joseph Howe was an embarrassment for Brown, who expected like-minded politicians to see the benefits of Confederation and compete against Conservatives on that basis. The *Quebec Gazette* wrote:

> Mr. Brown, however well disposed to fraternise with Mr. Howe, the self-vowed destroyer of Confederation, and with M. Dorion the Annexationist, could not but see that unless his friends changed their attitude very materially and very speedily he stood a good chance of being left almost alone. We say he could not but see this, and fight as he would through the *Globe,* scream as he would at public meetings, there was that terrible Howe demon grinding at him, and through the incredulous eyes of readers and bearers staring at him, and showing they could not be brought into such unholy partnership.[35]

The *Rouge* Party of Quebec was equally divided. At its core was a reluctant acceptance of Confederation. Dorion, the formal leader of the Association de la Réforme, had grudgingly accepted the project mostly because he had no practical strength to fight it. Yet many in the *Rouge* family vehemently opposed Confederation even if they were pushed aside or simply ignored. There is little doubt that many simply boycotted the elections, and the infighting sapped Dorion's energies. He had neither the words, the imagination, nor the troops necessary to fight the good fight. "The object of [the *Rouge*] association, it is said, is to protect the interest of Lower Canada, and to prevent by all constitutional means, the evil effects which may be feared from the new Constitution which has been forced upon the people of [that] province without their consent," wrote the *Sarnia Observer*. This was red meat for the likes of McDougall, who charged Dorion and his followers with being disloyal and being "determined to destroy Confederation if they could."[36]

If Macdonald came out strong as a result of the 1867 campaign, George Brown did not. Certainly, their strategies contrasted sharply. Macdonald was often on the move, and though he might have dropped in on his Kingston riding a few times at the most, he won it handily. Brown picked South Ontario, a place he barely knew, as his riding and campaigned assiduously. The *Globe* echoing his every word, he canvassed the large riding repeatedly. His performance on polling days was nothing if not frantic, pleading his case from one station to the next. Yet he was crushed, defeated in his run for federal office as well as for the Ontario Provincial Parliament. This proved to be the last day he was of any consequence. His subsequent career was limited to managing his newspaper. Politically, he was broken.

That said, the Liberal Party of Canada performed well in Ontario (federally and provincially), and in New Brunswick under the leadership of Albert J. Smith and Timothy Anglin, even though the Liberals there were not convinced that Confederation was the best solution for their province. "Truly this is a queer world, and a queer lot are those men who wish to be called unionists," reflected Anglin in the last weeks of the election.[37] The campaign forced that transformation. In mid-August, the *Headquarters,* a small publication

216    *Ballots and Brawls*

in Fredericton, wrote that "political bands are being thrown out, and political parties in one province are developing affinities for parties in another."[38] It worked better for the Conservatives than for the Liberals.

The same self-contradiction bedevilled the Liberals in Quebec. Federalism in that camp was accepted without enthusiasm, *à contre coeur,* and many Liberals openly challenged Dorion's compromise. In Nova Scotia, old Liberals and Reformers of Howe's ilk were now facing an ideological quandary. Behind the façade of *Rougisme* and anti-Confederationism, the Liberal Party's reformist spirit was quietly collapsing. George Brown, the driving force behind liberalism in Canada West, decided in the aftermath of the election that he had had enough of politics. The Liberal Party had gone into this vitally important election with no real leader. Brown may well have been considered the party's leader, but he hardly campaigned except in his own riding, and when he did, he did so poorly. "We confess that the result is not a satisfactory one," he wrote in the *Globe* on September 21. He gradually retreated from politics, but the Liberals did not learn their lesson, going into the 1872 campaign without clear leadership once again. It was only when Macdonald was brought down by self-inflicted political wounds during the Canadian Pacific Railway scandal and had to yield power that Alexander Mackenzie was chosen to head the party and almost immediately became prime minister.

Of course, in the aftermath of defeat, some Liberals looked for explanations and consolations. They casually pointed to the "Macdonald corruption fund," particularly money spent on pro-Tory ridings in the first stages of the elections ("precisely how that fund was made up is not yet known").[39] They blamed defectors; they blamed the Church in Quebec; they blamed double representation.[40] *Le Pays* launched a post-mortem search for examples of how priests had forced their parishioners to vote for the Conservative coalition. The strident campaign further fractured Liberalism in Quebec.[41] Others blamed the wealth and influence of the Bank of Montreal and the outsized power of the Grand Trunk Railway.[42]

One comforting thought was that the dozen former Liberals who were now sitting on the government side of the House of Commons might be able to rein in Macdonald. Others, noting that the Conservative hold on power was far weaker than it appeared, were satisfied that Confederation had been legitimized and easily discerned better days ahead for their party. "The prospect, indeed, is much brighter now than it was six weeks ago," wrote the *Canadian Champion* in Milton, Ontario. "We see no reason for despondency, but on the contrary, much ground for Hope: all will yet be right, and 'all's well that ends well.'"[43] There was suspicion that the "antis" in the Maritimes would recover their reformist impulses and naturally fortify the Liberals in the House of Commons. This proved to be correct. In Quebec, Ontario, and the Maritimes, the "anti" vibe translated into a "provincial-rights" rhetoric that became a hallmark of Liberal Party ideology for at least three generations. The unionists of the Maritime provinces, regardless of whether they had been Reformers or Conservatives in the past, seemed in sync with the government parties in Quebec and Ontario. To give the Liberals their due, they performed very well in New Brunswick in 1872, taking ten of sixteen seats, though their performance in Nova Scotia was relatively disappointing, with eight of twenty-one seats.

### Aftermath

Rumours abounded following the campaign. The Ottawa *Daily News* circulated the idea that the government was about to create a court of appeals and that Macdonald would be named its chief justice.[44] The new political creation north of their border was a concern to some Americans. The Montreal correspondent of the *New York Herald* commented that provinces uniting were "laying

218   *Ballots and Brawls*

the foundation of a power far more dangerous, more inimical, more disastrous and deadlier than the power built up in the South by the slaveholders before the break of our national civil war." The new Canada had wealth, a capacity for political action, and an ability to organize. "The triumph of the Conservative or Tory party of Canada means certainly war ... on the part of Great Britain and Canada towards the United States."[45]

Many of the ideas articulated during the campaign had a long afterlife. Macdonald's program of a Liberal-Conservative blend of ideas and impulses actually captured the political culture of the country – to this day perhaps. The idea of Confederation, of a country called Canada, was the winner in the election of 1867. "Formerly, the idea of nationality was only a sentiment, but now this idea has grown, and has become an intellectual power," wrote Lacroix. "Formerly, this idea was wrapped in swaddling bands; now it is freed from its trammels; it has attained a body, a movement, a future, because circumstances are favourable to its development, and this state of things is due, in part, to the conservatives of to-day, who, before, were progressionists."[46]

The claims made by Howe and the anti-Confederation movements were translated to the Maritime Rights Movement, which persisted until the Second World War and arguably still continues today. Lanctôt's idea of Canadian independence has also cast a long shadow. His founding of the Grande association de protection des ouvriers du Canada – the first union of its kind, preceding by far the Toronto Trades Assembly – showed that populism could find fertile ground. His ideas about protecting the French Canadian identity were echoed by Honoré Mercier's Union Nationale party (the name was partly an homage to Lanctôt, who had died eight years earlier at the tender age of thirty-nine) and transplanted into the twentieth century by Henri Bourassa. Within his lifetime, Lanctôt could have read some English Canadians who advocated similar ideas. William Norris, a very obscure lawyer and pamphleteer from southwestern Ontario, advocated in the 1870s for full Canadian independence from Britain in his *The Canadian Question* (1875); later, John S. Ewart expressed similar thinking in his books *The Kingdom of Canada* (1908) and *Canadian Independence* (1911).[47]

Canada's first election gave a jump-start to an entirely new politics and was thus a key turning point in North American affairs. As imperfect as it was, it remained a turning point in the history of democracy, in Canada and in the world. More than that, it was also a confirmation of the new direction for the British colonies. The combination of the two made this a turning point in Canadian political history. It also signalled the creation of a new, enterprising authority and a new resolve for peoples who had much in common and just as much to tear them apart. For many who witnessed the event, it was an exceptional experience, but for most, it was a bland exercise that attracted little but apathy and few swells of opinion.

Seen today, the election of 1867 may appear trivial, and yet it was not. It was an election given to distinctively local issues that were intimately and inexorably tied to the new national project. At its heart, this was an election about the existential needs of the population, and it was about defence. It was about guaranteeing rights, and having a hand – and a say – in self-determination. "The future of a nation, like that of an individual, is in the hands of Providence," wrote Lacroix that summer. The men who campaigned in 1867 all agreed.[48]

When the result of the Nova Scotia vote was revealed on September 19, there were calls to reform the system so that all elections are held on one day, not two. There were also calls for the elections to be held on the same day across the country, as in Great Britain and the United States, for adoption of the secret ballot, and for the abandonment of double mandates, where one man could sit in both a provincial and federal legislature.[49] Those reforms would have to wait for the election of 1874.

220   *Ballots and Brawls*

It was now time for Canada's first government to get to work. Narcisse Belleau, whom Macdonald had appointed Lieutenant-Governor of Quebec, sent quiet congratulations on the "extraordinary amount of work" Macdonald had accomplished during the election. He hoped to see Macdonald "make use of those resources of which nature has been so lavishly prodigal in your favour, which never forsook you in the numerous difficulties which you had to encounter." He told Macdonald that his tact and "appreciation of the human character will, at once, be put into requisition," and closed by writing that "I am anxious to see you at work."[50] Every citizen in the new country could have written that letter.

Parliament was called into session on November 10, a brief Speech from the Throne was read by Governor General Viscount Monck, who announced, much like Cartier had done in the 1865 debate, "the foundation of a new Nationality" as well as his belief that it would "extend its bounds from the Atlantic to the Pacific."[51] Macdonald also included a line in the speech promising that the right to vote would be broadened. In his maiden speech in the House of Commons, Joseph Howe told his colleagues that Nova Scotia had "been tricked into this scheme." He spoke for about an hour and forty minutes, and was warmly applauded when he resumed his seat. Charles Tupper responded, regretting that Howe's many talents were not to be "available for the advancement of the common interest of the British North American Provinces now united under one Dominion." He reviewed the policy environment that had prompted the idea of Confederation and admitted that he and the Union Party had been "thoroughly and handsomely beaten at the recent general election," but declared that there were no grounds to believe that "an overwhelming majority of the people of that Province are determined to obstruct and break down the Union which has been formed."[52] Tupper shared the view of the cabinet and would have agreed with the *Montreal Herald's*

*Conclusion* 221

editorialist: "Bygones should be bygones, and though there must be parties and divisions and strife, these should be based upon principles, not upon men, so that friends and foes many no longer be confounded."[53]

Once the first week of Parliament was behind him, Macdonald finally came to rest, even on Sundays. Agnes had been praying for months that he would at least take the Lord's Day off, and it finally happened. On November 17, she confided to her diary that the day had been "very quiet, happy." "He – my own dear, kind husband – has been mercifully taught to see the right in this thing and now we have so much happy rest after our morning service."[54] Macdonald could be excused for feeling a sense of accomplishment as the year 1867 came to an end. The work ahead was nothing short of extraordinary: establishing the governance of a new country, negotiating the expansion of territory, arranging for the creation of Manitoba in 1870, triggering the creation of the Canadian Pacific Railway, negotiating with the United States and Great Britain for a new trade regime. It would prove to be one of the most accomplished governments in the history of Canada.[55]

But for now came the routine of governing. Macdonald's brother-in-law, the Reverend Professor Williamson, wrote him a note on New Year's Eve, congratulating him again on his "success in the conduct of public affairs in the first and critical Parliament of the United Provinces," and hoped that the first prime minister would be able to win some holidays from work. This was but a preamble: what he really wanted was funding for an observatory for Queen's University, especially given that Quebec and Toronto had been identified as recipients. "Kingston ought to be included," he told the MP for Kingston. "The oversight can be easily remedied, and I earnestly trust it may yet be so."[56] For Macdonald, it was back to the business of negotiating demands for money. Being chosen as president of the Ottawa Rowing Club after it was founded

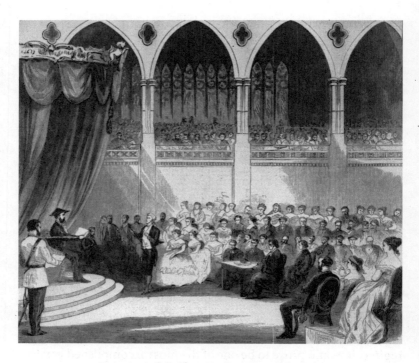

Opening of the first Parliament of Canada
Sketch by Alfred Jones, *Harper's Weekly*, November 30, 1867,
Library and Archives Canada, 2933884

in August 1867 was easy. Winning the first election and becoming prime minister had been difficult. Now Macdonald had to hope he would be as adroit (and as lucky) in governing.

A year later, Macdonald sent Cartier and McDougall to London to quickly negotiate the acquisition of Rupert's Land, just as had been planned in London in 1866.[57] The idea that animated him gave Confederation even more promise. The colonies were bound to a common cultural ribbon that united them: their British heritage and their Protestantism. They spoke a common language and were at ease in their respective local cultures – this was a reality that even a crusty Nova Scotian nationalist could recognize – even as they talked about creating a new nationality. Charles Ritchie, the distinguished Canadian diplomat who maintained (and later published) a compelling diary, recalled that he was raised in an atmosphere "in which everything British was best and 'Upper Canada' was a remote and unloved abstraction" forty years after the Confederation debates. His family had been anchored in Halifax for nearly one hundred years and it was devoted to "Crown and Empire" with a "romantic fidelity." "They were Nova Scotians first, Canadians second ... they belonged to Nova Scotia, the land where memories are long, legend, loyalties and grudges unforgotten, a land where a stranger should tread warily."[58] That feeling, a sound echo of Nova Scotian opinion in 1867, would persist for at least two more generations.

Canada was not the only country to come together in 1867. A historic compromise in Central Europe established the dual monarchy of Austria-Hungary that year under Franz Joseph and that marked the start of an intellectually vibrant and elegant era.[59] On a distant other continent, Canada, an incoherent political duckling, started to stretch its legs and outlasted its Austro-Hungarian cribmate by a over a hundred years. In 1867, its first election featured four internecine contests: nationalists in Quebec, Liberals in New Brunswick, Imperialists in Nova Scotia, and Scotsmen in Ontario. In its continued struggle to find identity and to reconcile religions, cultures, geographies, and politics, it proved to be much more than a mystery, as the fantastic dreamer Henry Lacroix had written. It became a miracle.

# Appendix 1
## Key Players

*Anglin, Timothy Warren* (1822–96): A native of County Cork, Ireland, he immigrated to New Brunswick in 1848, where he founded the *Morning Freeman*. He won election to the Legislative Assembly of the colony in 1861. He was an ardent campaigner against Confederation but was elected to the House of Commons in 1867 as a Liberal, representing the riding of Gloucester. He was made Speaker of the House of Commons when the Liberals formed the government (1874–78). He lost his seat in 1882 and moved to Toronto, where he edited the *Toronto Tribune*.

*Annand, William* (1808–87): Born into a well-heeled Halifax family and educated in Scotland, he was first elected to the Nova Scotia House of Assembly in 1836 on a bold platform demanding responsible government. Defeated in the election of 1843, he bought and began to edit both the *Novascotian* and the *Morning Chronicle*. He returned to active politics in 1851 and won the seat of Halifax County. Nine years later, he was appointed financial secretary in Joseph Howe's government. Annand fought the idea of Confederation and headed the Nova Scotia delegation to London in the summer of 1866. In 1867, he ran against Charles Tupper in the riding of Cumberland. Defeated, he was named

_List of Key Players_ 225

premier of Nova Scotia that November, a position he held until 1875. He was then named agent-general to London by the Alexander Mackenzie government. He died in London in 1887.

_Blake, Edward_ (1833–1912): Born on a farm in Adelaide Township in Upper Canada, he was educated at Upper Canada College and started a legal practice in 1856. In 1867, he was the Liberal candidate in the provincial riding of Bruce South (Ontario) and in the federal riding of Durham West, and won both contests. He was named leader of the Ontario Liberal Party in 1868 and became premier when his party won the 1871 election, but resigned in 1872 in order to focus on national affairs. In 1874, he was named to the Alexander Mackenzie cabinet. He succeeded Mackenzie after the Liberal defeat of 1878 and led the Liberals in the 1882 and 1887 elections, but without success. He resigned the leadership and remained an MP until 1891. He moved to Ireland at that point and was elected to the British House of Commons for the riding South Longford, Ireland. He served as an MP until 1907, and then returned to Canada for his retirement.

_Brown, George_ (1818–80): A native of Scotland, he emigrated with his family to the United States in 1837. He followed his father in the newspaper business, and in 1843 moved to Toronto, where they first published the _Banner_. In 1844, he founded the _Globe_ newspaper and soon thereafter launched himself into the politics of Canada West. He was a founder of the Reform Party, making increasing demands for reform to the governance of the United Province of Canada. He lost his bids for a seat in both the House of Commons and the Ontario legislature in 1867, and effectively resigned from political life. He was made a senator by Alexander Mackenzie in 1874, but his influence was limited. He was killed by a disgruntled employee in Toronto.

_Cartier, George-Étienne_ (1814–73): Born in Saint-Antoine-sur-Richelieu, he began practising law in 1834 and gravitated to

226   *Appendix 1*

*Patriote* circles. He fought at the Battle of Saint-Denis then escaped to Vermont. In the 1840s, he resumed politics and associated with Louis-Hippolyte La Fontaine. He was elected to the Legislative Assembly of the Province of Canada in 1848 and was appointed to cabinet in 1854. Cartier was easily one of the most important legislative leaders for the next twenty-five years. From 1858 to 1862, he was co-premier, with Macdonald. He was named minister of militia and defence by Sir John A. Macdonald and was re-elected. He died in London, England, in 1873 while seeking medical treatment for Bright's disease.

*Chauveau, Pierre J.O.* (1820–90): Born in Charlesbourg, he studied law and was elected to the Legislative Assembly of the Province of Canada in 1844. Chauveau was known as a writer and promoter of French Canadian culture and a *Bleu* supporting Louis-Hippolyte La Fontaine. He was named premier of Quebec in 1867, and was elected as a member of the Legislative Assembly of Quebec in 1867, as well as to the House of Commons. He resigned the premiership in 1873 and was named a senator.

*Connolly, Thomas-Louis* (1814–76): Born in Cork, Ireland, he joined the Order of Capuchins as a teenager. He studied in Rome and was ordained a priest in France in 1838. He arrived in Halifax in 1842 and served the Church there until he was appointed bishop of Saint John, New Brunswick, in 1852. He returned to Halifax in 1859 to lead the Church as archbishop in the Nova Scotia capital. He openly supported Confederation in 1867.

*Dorion, Antoine-Aimé* (1818–91): Born into a *Patriote* family in Sainte-Anne-de-la-Pérade, he became a lawyer in 1842 and was elected to the Legislative Assembly of the Province of Canada in 1854. He served briefly as co-premier with George Brown in 1858, and then again with John Sandfield Macdonald in 1863–64. He denounced the Great Coalition led by John A. Macdonald as well as the meetings that shaped Confederation in 1864. He was elected to the House of Commons in 1867, where he remained until he was named chief justice of the Court of Queen's Bench of Quebec. He died in Quebec City just a few days before Sir John A. Macdonald.

*Galt, Alexander T.* (1817–93): Born in Chelsea, London, England, and educated at Reading School, he arrived in North America in 1828 and was educated at the Anglican seminary in Chambly, Lower Canada. He joined the British American Land Company soon after, working in both London and Canada East, and honed his business skills in land use, industrialization, and railway development. He was elected by acclamation in Sherbrooke to the Legislative Assembly of the Province of Canada in 1849 but resigned a year later. He was known to be a Liberal. He returned to the Legislative Assembly in 1853 and Sherbrooke continued to support him. In 1857, he switched his support to John A. Macdonald. He was acclaimed as the member of Parliament for the riding of Sherbrooke in 1867. In 1867, Macdonald named him as minister of finance, but he disagreed with Macdonald on a banking policy a few months later, and was forced to resign. He was named Canada's first High Commissioner to the United Kingdom in 1880 and served until 1883.

*Howe, Joseph* (1804–73): Born into a strongly Loyalist family in Halifax, he apprenticed as a printer in his father's shop and launched himself in journalism 1827 by purchasing the *Novascotian*. In 1835, he distinguished himself in his defence against a charge of seditious libel and won the case by invoking the principle of press freedom and by attacking the government for corruption. The next year, he was elected to the Nova Scotia House of Assembly as a Reformer and dedicated himself to the cause of responsible government. He served as premier of Nova Scotia from 1860 to 1863, resigning his post for one on the Imperial Fisheries Commission. In 1867, he ran and won in Hants on the Anti-Confederation ticket. On April 24, he crossed the floor and declared himself a Liberal-Conservative, joining Macdonald's

228   *Appendix 1*

government. He was named Lieutenant-Governor of Nova Scotia in May 1873, but died only a few weeks later.

*Holton, Luther* (1817–80): Born near Brockville in Upper Canada, he was raised and educated in Montreal and joined an uncle's business as a teenager. By the time he turned thirty, he was a senior partner in a transportation company, focused on the waterways of the St. Lawrence and the Great Lakes. He was attracted to the railway industry and became interested in the affairs of the Grand Trunk Railway (GTR). He formed a company with Alexander T. Galt, a Conservative, to build the GTR's tracks from Toronto to Sarnia. He was elected to the Legislative Assembly of the Province of Canada as a Montreal Reformer in 1854 and served as minister of finance in the Sandfield Macdonald–Dorion government in 1863. Active in all sorts of Montreal charities and business societies, Holton was elected in Chateauguay that same year and was re-elected in 1867. He remained an MP until his death.

*Lacroix, Henry Olivier* (1826–97): Born in Monroe, Michigan, he was the son of Dominique Lacroix. He was orphaned in 1834 and sent to live with relatives in Montreal. An avid itinerant even as a teenager, he left his aunt to roam the lands of the Hudson's Bay Company or to live in New York City. In 1844, he became a sailor aboard the *Commodore Morris* and travelled the world. He returned to Canada in 1848 and married Eliza Wilbrenner, with whom he had fifteen children (five of whom survived past eighteen months). He worked for the customs office of Province of Canada for twenty years and was also the treasurer of the Institut Canadien for a few years. He became fascinated with spiritualism and mesmerism and declared himself a medium, able to speak to the dead, and he apparently earned a living providing such services. He wrote eleven pamphlets and books, most notably *Mes experiences avec les esprits,* published in 1889. He died at the Hôtel-Dieu de Montréal on February 26, 1897.

*Lanctôt, Médéric* (1838–77): Born in Montreal to an English mother and a condemned *Patriote* father, he was raised to idolize the 1837–38 rebellions. Though a brilliant student, he drifted in his studies and eventually dropped out of school to find work and to follow the Institut Canadien-français de Montréal. He became a journalist and began studying law at McGill University. He worked at *Le Pays* and launched *La Presse* (1863–64) and then *L'Union Nationale* (1864–65), through which he denounced the Confederation project as he became increasingly radical. In 1867, he launched the Grande association de protection des ouvriers du Canada and challenged George-Étienne Cartier in vain. He left Canada soon thereafter to start newspapers in the United States, but returned in 1870, unable to commit his career in any direction. He died at a farm he had just purchased in Aylmer, Quebec, in 1877.

*Lotbinière, Henri-Gustave Joly de* (1829–1908): Born in Epernay, France, he was the son of a Huguenot father and Canadian mother, and returned with the family to Lower Canada soon afterwards. He studied in Paris from 1836 to 1849, and returned to Canada in 1850. He started a law practice and then gradually assumed the direction of the Lotbinière seigneury he inherited from his mother (and added that distinction to his name). He was elected the Legislative Assembly of the Province of Canada as an independent in 1861 but gradually moved to support the *Rouges*. He became leader of the Quebec Liberals in the provincial election of 1867, and was acclaimed in the riding of Lotbinière, both in the House of Commons and in the Legislative Assembly. He was premier of Quebec for eighteen months (1878–79), leading the Liberal Party. In 1896, he returned to the House of Commons until he was named Lieutenant-Governor of British Columbia in 1900, a post he held for six years.

*Lynch, Archbishop John Joseph* (1816–88): Born in County Fermanagh, he was raised in Dublin, entered the seminary of

230   *Appendix 1*

Saint-Lazare in Paris in 1837, and was ordained a priest in Maynooth in 1843. He served as an itinerant priest from Houston, Texas, for two years, in 1846–48. He also served in Missouri and in Buffalo, New York, where he founded the Seminary of Our Lady of Angels. Lynch was named bishop of Toronto in 1860 and was elevated to archbishop in 1870. He died in harness in 1888.

*Macdonald, Agnes* (1836–1920): Agnes Bernard was born just south of Montego Bay, Jamaica, the daughter of a British plantation owner who likely owned enslaved Black people until he left the island in 1831. She moved to Barrie, Ontario, in 1854 to live with her brother, Hewitt Bernard, who eventually became a close working associate of John A. Macdonald. She married Macdonald in London on February 16, 1867 and became Lady Macdonald on July 1 that year. She departed for London soon after Macdonald died in 1891 and never returned to Canada. She died in Eastbourne, England, in 1920.

*Macdonald, Sir John A.* (1815–91): Born in Glasgow, Scotland, he migrated with his family in 1820. He attended school in Kingston, Ontario, and drifted into a legal apprenticeship with his uncle. He was elected to the Kingston Municipal Council in 1843 and attracted the interest of the business community. He was elected to the Legislative Assembly of the Province of Canada in 1844 and served in Parliament until his death in 1891. He was elected in the riding of Kingston in 1867.

*Macdonald, John Sandfield* (1812–72): Born in Glengarry County in Upper Canada into a Roman Catholic Highland Scots family, he trained as a lawyer and was elected to the Legislative Assembly of the Province of Canada for Glengarry in 1841, gradually associating himself with the Reformers demanding responsible government. He continued to represent the riding and was co-premier with George-Étienne Cartier in 1862–64. He became an ally of John A. Macdonald, who appointed him to be the first premier of Ontario. He won the riding of Cornwall at both levels (federal and provincial) in the 1867 election and went on to form a coalition government. The support of the staunch Reformers gradually eroded and the government was defeated in 1871.

*Mackenzie, Alexander* (1822–92): Born in Logierait, Scotland, he trained as a stonemason and immigrated to Canada in 1839. He launched a construction company and edited the *Lambton Shield* as a Reform newspaper. He was elected to the Legislative Assembly of the Province of Canada in 1862 and won election to the House of Commons in 1867. He was named leader of the Liberal Party in 1873 and became prime minister when the Macdonald coalition collapsed. The Liberals won the general election in 1874 and Mackenzie served as prime minister for the next four years. He retired as leader in 1880, but remained a Member of Parliament until his death in 1892, ten months after Sir John A. Macdonald passed away.

*McDougall, William* (1822–1905): Born north of York (today's Lawrence Park) into a family of first-wave Loyalist stock, he was educated at Victoria College and started a law practice in 1847. His office soon became the rallying point for a group of the most radical Reformers in Toronto, who called themselves Clear Grits. He was elected to the Legislative Assembly of the Province of Canada in 1858, served as commissioner of Crown lands and provincial secretary at different times, and gradually won the confidence of leading ministers as he abandoned his anti-Catholic rhetoric. He joined the Great Coalition and participated at both the Charlottetown and Quebec Conferences. He broke with the George Brown Liberals for good in 1867 and joined the Macdonald cabinet as minister of public works. He was elected to the House of Commons for Lanark North in 1872. Macdonald appointed him Lieutenant-Governor of Rupert's Land and the North-West Territory in 1869–70. He was defeated in the 1872

232  *Appendix 1*

election and ran for a seat in the Ontario legislature three years later, serving as MPP for Simcoe South from 1875 to 1878. He retired in Ottawa.

*McGee, Thomas D'Arcy* (1825–68): Born into a Catholic family in Carlingford, Ireland, he emigrated to the United States at the age of seventeen and launched a career as a journalist in Boston. He returned to Ireland in 1845, became active in the Young Ireland Movement, got married, and started a family. Wanted on suspicion of criminal activity, he returned to the United States in 1848. McGee underwent a conversion of sorts in the 1850s, gradually abandoned his republicanism, and came to see Canada as a better place to raise a Catholic family. He moved to Montreal in 1857 and entered politics on the strength of his extraordinary oratory. He was elected to the Legislative Assembly of the Province of Canada in 1858, registered to study law at McGill University, and gradually converted to Conservatism. In 1863, he was made minister of agriculture, immigration, and statistics. He participated in the Great Coalition and in both the Charlottetown and Quebec Conferences, and was elected in the riding of Montreal West in 1867. He was killed in Ottawa by Fenian terrorists in 1868.

*Monck, Lord* (1819–94): Born in Templemore, Ireland, into a vice-regal family, Charles Stanley Monck inherited the title in 1849. He was elected MP for Portsmouth in 1852 and served in Palmerston's government as Lord of the Treasury. He was appointed Governor General of British North America and Governor of the Province of Canada in 1861, and became Governor General of Canada in 1867. He made Rideau Hall the residence of the Governor General. He left Canada in 1869 and died in his native Ireland.

*Smith, Albert J.* (1822–83): Born into a well-to-do family in Shediac, New Brunswick, and trained as a lawyer, he was elected to the New Brunswick Legislative Assembly in 1852 as an advocate of responsible government, and served as attorney general in the Tilley government in 1861. In 1865, he turned against the Liberals and led the anti-Confederation forces to victory in the election. He was named premier but lost the election in the spring of 1866. In 1867, he won the riding of Westmorland and served as MP until 1882.

*Tilley, Leonard* (1818–96): Born into an ardently Loyalist family in Gagetown, New Brunswick, he apprenticed as a pharmacist and soon began retailing medicines. Based in Saint John, he was active in a wide variety of care organizations and in the temperance movement. He was elected to the New Brunswick Legislative Assembly as a Liberal in 1850. When the Liberals formed the government in 1854, he was named provincial secretary. In 1861, he became premier and distinguished himself as an advocate for Confederation. He participated in both the Charlottetown and Quebec Conferences. He called an election in January 1865 but he and his party were defeated. In 1867, he ran and won as a Liberal-Conservative in Saint John. He was part of every Macdonald cabinet thereafter until he retired in 1885 to become Lieutenant-Governor of New Brunswick.

*Tupper, Charles* (1821–1915): Born in Amherst, Nova Scotia, he studied medicine at the University of Edinburgh and graduated in 1843. He returned to Canada, started a practice, and was elected to the Nova Scotia Legislature in 1855, serving on two occasions as provincial secretary in the governments led by James W. Johnston. In 1864, he became premier of Nova Scotia and quickly gravitated to the defence of Confederation. He participated at the Charlottetown, Quebec, and London Conferences in 1866–67. In 1867, he resigned as premier to run in the riding of Cumberland, and was elected. He served as MP until 1884, when he was named Canadian High Commissioner to the United Kingdom. He returned to the House of Commons in 1887–88 and again in 1896, but this time to lead the Conservatives. He

234   *Appendix 1*

was prime minister for sixty-eight days in 1896, leading the Conservative Party in the election that year. He was the Conservative leader in the 1900 election, lost, and then retired to England in 1900 and died there.

# Appendix 2
## Timeline of Events

### 1864

| | |
|---|---|
| March 28 | Nova Scotia House of Assembly approves a resolution in favour of Maritime Union. |
| June 22 | Great Coalition formed in the Province of Canada. The ministers of the Great Coalition are sworn in on June 30. |
| September 1 | Charlottetown Conference on Maritime Union begins. Nova Scotia, New Brunswick, Prince Edward Island, and the United Province of Canada attend. |
| October 10–24 | Quebec Conference. Four provinces agree on the fundamentals of federalism. |
| October 19 | St. Albans raid. A party of Southern Confederate agents based in Canada raids the town of St. Albans, Vermont, in an attempt to humiliate the Lincoln administration. Canada is shown to be vulnerable. |

## 1865

| | |
|---|---|
| January–February | Publication of the *Botheration Letters* in the *Morning Chronicle,* written by Joseph Howe under a pseudonym, denouncing the Quebec City scheme. |
| March 6 | Pro-Confederation Tilley government is defeated in New Brunswick. |
| March 11 | United Province of Canada votes for Confederation. The Legislative Council of the Province of Canada adopts an address urging the Imperial Parliament to enact legislation to achieve the union of British North America. |
| April 10 | Premier Charles Tupper of Nova Scotia announces that there will be no vote on the Quebec Resolutions. |
| May | Canadian delegates travel to London to seek the British government's help. |

## 1866

| | |
|---|---|
| April 10 | Smith government in New Brunswick resigns. |
| April 14 | Fenian scare on Indian Island, New Brunswick. |
| April 16 | Lieutenant-Governor Arthur Hamilton-Gordon appoints Peter Mitchell premier of New Brunswick and dissolves the legislature. |
| April 18 | Nova Scotia legislature votes for Confederation (thirty-one for, nineteen against). The League of the Maritime Provinces (also called the Anti-Confederation League or the Anti-Union League) is created. |

*Timeline of Events*  237

| | |
|---|---|
| June 12 | New Brunswick elects thirty-three Confederation Party candidates versus eight Constitutionalists led by Albert James Smith. |
| June 30 | New Brunswick legislature votes in favour of Confederation. |
| December 4 | London Conference: Sixteen delegates from the Province of Canada, Nova Scotia, and New Brunswick meet with the British government in London. During the three-month conference, delegates review the Quebec Resolutions, creating a document that would form the basis of the British North America Act. They choose "Canada" as the name of the new country and designate it as a Dominion. |

### 1867

| | |
|---|---|
| March 8 | British North America Act is passed by the British Parliament. It is given royal assent by Queen Victoria on March 29 and comes into effect on July 1. The act joins the colonies of Canada, Nova Scotia, and New Brunswick in one federal union. |
| March 18 | Amor De Cosmos's resolution in the British Columbia legislature calling for "the admission of BC into Confederation on fair and equitable terms" is given unanimous support by the colony's legislative council. |
| March 25 | Grande association de protection des ouvriers du Canada (GAPOC) is created in Montreal. |

| | |
|---|---|
| March 27 | Anti-Confederation League is founded in Halifax. |
| April | George Brown creates the Reform Association of Upper Canada. |
| | Charles Tupper founds the Canada Party in Halifax. |
| May 22 | A royal proclamation declares that the Dominion of Canada will come into existence on July 1. |
| May 30 | Association de la réforme du Bas-Canada is formed in Montreal. |
| June 27–28 | Reform Association of Upper Canada holds conference in Toronto. |
| August 7 | Official start of election campaign. |
| Late August–mid-September | Voting takes place in Ontario, Quebec, and New Brunswick. |
| September 18 | Voting day in Nova Scotia. |
| September 20 | Electoral results are announced. |

### 1868

| | |
|---|---|
| July 31 | Rupert's Land Act is passed, allowing the Crown to declare Rupert's Land part of the Dominion of Canada. |

### 1869

| | |
|---|---|
| December 1 | Hudson's Bay Company surrenders Rupert's Land. |

*Timeline of Events*  239

## 1870

| | |
|---|---|
| July 15 | The British Crown officially transfers Rupert's Land and the North-West Territory to Canada. These lands comprise present-day Manitoba, most of Saskatchewan, southern Alberta, southern Nunavut, and northern parts of Ontario and Quebec. |
| July 15 | Manitoba joins Confederation. |

## 1871

| | |
|---|---|
| July 20 | British Columbia joins Confederation. |

## 1873

| | |
|---|---|
| July 1 | Prince Edward Island joins Confederation. |

# Appendix 3
## Data Tables

**TABLE 1: RESULTS OF THE 1867 ELECTION**

|  | Conservative | | Liberal-Conservative | | Liberal | | Anti-Confederation | | |
|---|---|---|---|---|---|---|---|---|---|
|  | Seats | % of seats in province | Seats | % of seats in province | Seats | % of seats in province | Seats | % of seats in province | Provincial total |
| Ontario | 33 | 40 | 16 | 20 | 33 | 40 | – | – | 82 |
| Quebec[1] | 36 | 56 | 11 | 17 | 17 | 27 | – | – | 64 |
| New Brunswick | 1 | 7 | 2 | 14 | 12 | 86 | – | – | 15 |
| Nova Scotia | 0 | 0 | 1 | 5 | 0 | 0 | 18 | 95 | 19 |
| TOTAL | 70 | | 30 | | 62 | | 18 | | 180 |
| % of seats in the House of Commons (180) | 38 | | 16 | | 34 | | 10 | | |

*Note:*

1  The election in Kamouraska was cancelled due to violence. It was won by the Conservative Party in 1868.

## TABLE 2: POPULAR VOTE IN THE 1867 ELECTION

| | Eligible | Actual | Turnout | Conservative | | Liberal-Conservative | | Liberal | | Anti-Confederation | | Other | |
|---|---|---|---|---|---|---|---|---|---|---|---|---|---|
| | | | | Votes | % | Votes | % | Votes | % | Votes | % | Votes | % |
| New Brunswick | 27,535 | 19,581 | 71.1 | 0 | 0 | 2,180 | 11.1 | 9,699 | 49.5 | – | – | 7,702 | 39.4 |
| Nova Scotia[1] | 41,291 | 32,322 | 78.3 | 5,390 | 14.6 | 1,289 | 3.5 | 0 | 0 | 21,239 | 57.7 | 8,907 | 24.2 |
| Ontario | 186,345 | 139,859 | 75.1 | 52,125 | 37.3 | 3,220 | 2.3 | 31,743 | 22.7 | – | – | 52,771 | 37.7 |
| Quebec | 105,621 | 72,412 | 68.6 | 22,002 | 30.4 | 8,791 | 12.1 | 18,014 | 24.9 | – | – | 23,605 | 32.6 |
| TOTAL | 360,792 | 268,677 | 74.5 | 79,517 | 29.6 | 15,480 | 5.8 | 59,456 | 22.1 | 21,239 | 7.9 | 92,985 | 34.6 |

*Notes:* Percentages are rounded off and so may not add exactly to 100.

1 Nova Scotia's vote is complicated by the fact that Halifax was a dual riding; in other words, individual voters had the opportunity to vote for two candidates. A total of 32,322 people voted, but 36,825 votes were cast.

# Notes

**Preface**

1 "The Victory," *Sun and Advertiser,* September 20, 1867.

**Introduction**

1 Henry Olivier Lacroix, *The Present and Future of Canada* (Montreal: John Lovell, 1867), 21. There were precious few exclamations of national pride. J.D. Edgar's poem "This Canada of Ours" has often been pointed to, but while it glorifies the new country's British and Irish ancestry, it completely ignores French Canada. Henry Morgan published *Bibliotheca Canadiensis* (Ottawa: G.E. Desbarats, 1867), a volume that identified every book published in the country until the new birth in 1867.

2 Lacroix, *The Present and Future of Canada,* 21.

3 Lacroix, *The Present and Future of Canada,* 19. Lacroix gave a talk at the Institut Canadien in December 1867 titled "Excursion to the Holy Land of Thought," a "rather original title, promising originality of thought," announced the *Gazette* on December 14, 1867, 2. See also "Institut Canadien," *Gazette,* December 17, 1867, 2. The writer, Aegidius Fauteux, profiled Lacroix in *La Patrie,* May 3, 1934, 16–17, 19.

4 Lacroix, *The Present and Future of Canada,* 32.

5 See *Annuaire de l'Institut Canadien pour 1867* (Montreal: Imprimerie du Journal *Le Pays,* 1868), 5.

6 *Grand River Sachem,* August 21, 1867.

*Notes to pages 6–18* 243

7 Ramsay Cook, "The Meaning of Confederation" (1965), reproduced in Ramsay Cook, *Watching Quebec: Selected Essays* (Montreal and Kingston: McGill-Queen's University Press, 2005), 160.

8 Cited in *Weekly Citizen* (Halifax), August 24, 1867.

9 John A. Macdonald to Brown Chamberlin, July 1, 1867, Library and Archives Canada, John A. Macdonald Fonds (JAMF-LAC).

10 P.B. Waite, ed., *The Confederation Debates in the Province of Canada, 1865* (Montreal and Kingston: McGill-Queen's University Press, 2006), 45.

11 Macdonald expressed his support for it in a letter to Isaac Cairns (?) (Goderich), July 4, 1867, JAMF-LAC.

12 *Ottawa Times,* August 8, 1867.

13 *St. Catharines Constitutional,* August 8, 1867, 4.

14 *St. Catharines Constitutional,* August 8, 1867, 4.

15 Lacroix, *The Present and Future of Canada,* 29.

16 Egerton Ryerson, *The New Canadian Dominion: Dangers and Duties of the People in Regard to Their Government* (Toronto: Lovell and Gibson, 1867), 8.

17 A good summary of the origins of the parties is Frederick Engelmann and Mildred A. Schwartz, *Canadian Political Parties: Origin, Character, Impact* (Scarborough, ON: Prentice-Hall, 1975).

18 To avoid confusion, I have chosen to avoid the use of the word "Confederate" to describe Confederation's defenders. That moniker has long been applied to defenders of the American South during the run-up to the Civil War and ever since.

19 John Gray, *A Letter on the Disgraceful Riot in the Catholic Church in Prescott* (Ogdensburg, NY, 1867), 6. The incident was covered in the *Montreal Herald,* September 17, 1867, 4.

20 Cited in *Montreal Herald,* August 19, 1867, 3.

21 Alexander Mackenzie to George Brown, July 17, 1867, Library and Archives Canada, George Brown Fonds (GBF-LAC).

22 *Advertiser and Eastern Townships Sentinel,* August 8, 1867, 4. Note: sometimes this issue is dated August 15, 1867.

23 W.H. Kesterton, *A History of Journalism in Canada* (Toronto: McClelland and Stewart, Carleton Library Series, 1967), 39.

24 Cited in *Montreal Herald,* August 19, 1867, 3.

25 France introduced the secret ballot during the French Revolution. Greece, the Netherlands, Italy, and Sweden had made the act of voting private in the 1860s.

244 *Notes to pages 19–22*

26 See John Garner, *The Franchise and Politics in British North America, 1755–1867* (Toronto: University of Toronto Press, 1969), 214; Jean and Marcel Hamelin, *Les moeurs électorales dans de Québec de 1794 à nos jours* (Montreal: Les Éditions du jour, 1962), decries the corruption of elections in the United Province of Canada but makes no mention of the 1867 campaign. See also Ian Radforth, *Expressive Acts: Celebrations and Demonstrations in Streets of Victorian Toronto* (Toronto: University of Toronto Press, 2022), which devotes a chapter to "the press and electoral culture" but which makes no specific reference to 1867.

27 Reprinted in *Grand River Sachem*, August 21, 1867.

28 "The Elections in Ottawa – a Wretched Business," *Quebec Gazette*, August 28, 1867, 2.

29 Cited in "Correspondence," *Ottawa Times*, September 7, 1867.

30 *Sarnia Observer*, September 6, 1867, 1.

31 "The Brown Coalition," *Ottawa Times*, August 20, 1867.

32 *L'Union Nationale*, September 12, 1867, estimated the cost of Cartier's election at somewhere between $40,000 and $50,000. Brian Young, *George-Étienne Cartier, bourgeois Montréalais* (Montreal: Boréal, 1982), 109, 105.

33 Kenneth G. Pryke, *Nova Scotia and Confederation, 1864–1974* (Toronto: University of Toronto Press, 1979), 57.

34 Richard Gwyn, *The Life and Times of John A. Macdonald*, vol. 2, *Nation Maker; Sir John A. Macdonald: His Life, Our Times* (Toronto: Random House Canada, 2011), 209.

35 The *Globe* argued that Macdonald won because Indians had not been allowed to vote at some point. The *Montreal Herald*, September 23, 1867, 1, opined that the Indigenous should not have the right to vote, as they lived "upon Crown reservations." After the election, Macdonald told a correspondent that he "really forgot all about the Indians. Had they occurred to my mind I should certainly have excluded them." The letter, dated October 10, 1867, is cited in D.G.G. Kerr, "The 1867 Elections in Ontario: The Rules of the Game," *Canadian Historical Review* 51, 4 (1970): 377. I am grateful to Roger Hall for drawing this to my attention.

36 Dennis Pilon, "The Contested Origins of Canadian Democracy," *Studies in Political Economy* 98, 2 (2017): 105–23.

37 Bellavance claims that this explains why forty-two of sixty-five districts were won by acclamation. See Marcel Bellavance, *Le Québec et la*

*confédération: un choix libre? Le clergé et la constitution de 1867* (Quebec: Septentrion, 1992), 136.

38 *Cleveland Herald,* August 30, 1867, cited in *Ottawa Times,* September 3, 1867.

39 Normand Séguin, "L'opposition canadienne-française aux élections de 1867 dans la grande région de Montréal" (MA thesis, University of Ottawa, 1968), 110–11.

40 *Le Pays,* September 5, 1867, cited in Séguin, "L'opposition canadienne-française," 112.

41 John Garner reproduced a number of oaths of allegiance in the appendix to *The Franchise and Politics in British North America, 1755–1867* (Toronto: University of Toronto Press, 1969), 215–16. Dennis Pilon makes the point that the 1867 election was undemocratic; see Pilon, "The Contested Origins of Canadian Democracy."

42 *Advertiser and Eastern Townships Sentinel,* August 22, 1867, 2.

43 *Advertiser and Eastern Townships Sentinel,* August 8, 1867, 4. (Strangely, this edition is also dated August 15, 1867.)

### Chapter 1: The Battlefield, the Wheels, the Flies, and the Flywheels

1 Ged Martin, "The Case against Canadian Confederation," in *The Causes of Canadian Confederation,* edited by Ged Martin (Fredericton: Acadiensis Press, 1990).

2 See Lee A. Farrow, *Seward's Folly: A New Look at the Alaska Purchase* (Fairbanks: University of Alaska Press, 2016), and Joseph A. Fry, *Lincoln, Seward and US Foreign Relations in the Civil War* (Lexington: University of Kentucky Press, 2019).

3 *Year-Book and Almanac of British North America for 1867; Being an Annual Register of Political, Vital and Trade Statistics, Tariffs, Excise and Stamp Duties; and All Public Events of Interest in Upper and Lower Canada; New Brunswick; Nova Scotia; Newfoundland; Prince Edward Island; and the West India Islands* (Montreal: Lowe and Chamberlin, 1866).

4 See Statistics Canada, "Canadian Statistics in 1867," https://www65.statcan.gc.ca/acyb07/acyb07_0002-eng.htm.

5 Cited in William F. Rannie, *Wines of Ontario* (Lincoln, ON: Rannie, 1977), 48.

6 These statistics were offered in a strong pro-Confederation pamphlet. See A. Cosmopolitan, *A Letter to the Electors of Nova Scotia in Which*

246  *Notes to pages 31–35*

*Certain People and Pamphlets Are Reviewed, and Certain Facts and Arguments Stated* (Halifax, July 1867), 27.

7  Ralph C. Nelson, Water C. Soderlund, Ronald H. Wagenberg, and E. Donald Briggs, "Canadian Confederation as a Case Study in Community Formation," and Ged Martin, "The Case against Canadian Confederation, 1864–1867," in Martin, *The Causes of Canadian Confederation*, 57, 61. Robert Rumilly's description of Quebec's economy in 1864–67 makes the case that it was far from dynamic: *Histoire de la Province de Québec*, vol. 1, *Georges*[sic]*-Étienne Cartier* (Montreal: Éditions Bernard Valiquette, 1940).

8  Cited in D.A. Muise, "The Federal Election of 1867 in Nova Scotia: An Economic Interpretation," *Collections of the Nova Scotia Historical Society* 36 (1968): 338.

9  See Gil Remillard, "Les intentions des Pères de la Confédération," *Les Cahiers de droit* 20, 4 (1979): 800.

10  See A. Cosmopolitan, *Has the Country Been Sold? A Letter to the Electors of Nova Scotia, by a Cosmopolitan* (Halifax, July 1867); L.F.S. Upton, "The Idea of Confederation, 1754–1858," in *The Shield of Achilles: Aspects of Canada in the Victorian Age*, edited by W.L. Morton (Toronto: McClelland and Stewart, 1968), 184–85.

11  See Yvan Lamonde and Jonathan Livernois, *Papineau: Erreur sur la personne* (Montreal: Boréal, 2012).

12  On Taché, see Jean-Guy Nadeau, "Taché, Joseph-Charles," in *Dictionary of Canadian Biography*, vol. 12 (Toronto/Quebec: University of Toronto/ Université Laval, 2003). On the importance of his articles, see P.B. Waite, "The Quebec Resolutions and the *Courrier du Canada*, 1864–1865," *Canadian Historical Review* 40, 4 (1959): 294–303.

13  Marie-Marthe Filion-Montpetit, "Médéric Lanctôt, journaliste engagé (1838–1877): Une biographie intellectuelle" (PhD diss., University of Ottawa, 2003), 102–4.

14  Filion-Montpetit, "Médéric Lanctôt," 108.

15  D.L. Macpherson to John A. Macdonald, June 23, 1864, in Sir Joseph Pope, *Correspondence of Sir John A. Macdonald* (Toronto, 1921), 12. L.F.S. Upton argued that the idea of a federation was hardly a new one in the Maritimes, and that the idea of uniting all the loyalists north of the United States was as old as the arrival of loyalists themselves. L.F.S. Upton, "The Idea of Confederation, 1754–1858," in Morton, *The Shield of Achilles*, 184–204.

*Notes to pages 37–56* 247

16 His biographer is quite persuaded that the pettiness of New Brunswick affairs wore Hamilton-Gordon down. See J.K. Chapman, *The Career of Arthur Hamilton Gordon, First Lord Stanmore, 1829–1912* (Toronto: University of Toronto Press, 1964), 23–24.

17 Carl M. Wallace, "Sir Leonard Tilley: A Political Biography" (PhD diss., University of Alberta, 1972), 387.

18 See Laurence S. Fallis, Jr., "The Idea of Progress in the Province of Canada: A Study in the History of Ideas," in Morton, *The Shield of Achilles*, 184–85, 169–83.

19 Anonymous, "Biographical Foreword," in Charles Tupper, *Recollections of Sixty Years in Canada* (London: Cassell and Company, 1914), 2.

20 P.B. Waite, *Canada 1874–1896: Arduous Destiny* (Toronto: McClelland and Stewart, 1971), 84–85.

21 Waite, *Canada 1874–1896*, 24.

22 Waite, *Canada 1874–1896*, 28.

23 Waite, *Canada 1874–1896*, 38.

24 Kenneth G. Pryke, *Nova Scotia and Confederation, 1864–1974* (Toronto: University of Toronto Press, 1979), 5.

25 See Raymond B. Blake and Melvin Baker, *Where Once They Stood: Newfoundland's Rocky Road towards Confederation* (Regina: University of Regina Press, 2019), 22–23.

26 This detail was reported by the *Charlottetown Islander* on the day the delegations left the province, September 9, 1864. See W.H. Kesterton, *A History of Journalism in Canada*, Carleton Library Series (Toronto: McClelland and Stewart, 1967), 38.

27 Donald Creighton, *John A. Macdonald, The Young Politician* (Toronto: MacMillan, 1965), 360.

28 See John A. Macdonald, "A Toast to Colonial Union, 1864," in *Canada Transformed: The Speeches of Sir John A. Macdonald*, edited by Sarah Katherine Gibson and Arthur Milnes (Toronto: McClelland and Stewart, 2014), 141–47.

29 Both delegates, Ambrose Shea and Frederic Bowker Terrington Carter, quickly became converts to the cause of Confederation and were featured in Robert Harris's famous 1884 painting, *Conference at Quebec*. See Blake and Baker, *Where Once They Stood*, 24–32.

30 See Rachel Chagnon, "The Fathers of Confederation and the BNA Act: Constitutional Visions and Models," in *The Quebec Conference of 1864:*

248  *Notes to pages 57–63*

*Understanding the Emergence of the Canadian Federation*, edited by Eugénie Brouillet, Alain-G. Gagnon, and Guy Laforest (Montreal and Kingston: McGill-Queen's University Press, 2018), 29–48.

31 See David A. Wilson, *Canadian Spy Story: Irish Revolutionaries and the Secret Police* (Montreal and Kingston: McGill-Queen's University Press, 2022); Barr Sheehy and Cindy Wallace, *Montreal, City of Secrets: Confederate Operations in Montreal during the American Civil War* (Montreal: Baraka Books, 2020), 177–85.

32 Macdonald to Gowan, November 1864, Library and Archives Canada (LAC), Sir James Robert Gowan Papers, cited in J.K. Johnson and P.B. Waite, "Macdonald, Sir John Alexander," in *Dictionary of Canadian Biography*, vol. 12.

33 Tilley to Macdonald, February 12, 1865, cited in Wallace, "Sir Leonard Tilley," 207.

34 See C.P. Stacey, "Confederation: The Atmosphere of Crisis," in *Profiles of a Province: Studies in the History of Ontario*, edited by Edith G. Firth (Toronto: Ontario Historical Society, 1967), 75.

35 Cited in Stacey, "Confederation: The Atmosphere of Crisis," 75–76.

36 Richard Cartwright, *Reminiscences* (Toronto: William Briggs, 1912), 58.

37 See Ben Forster, *A Conjunction of Interests: Business, Politics and Tariffs, 1825–1879* (Toronto: University of Toronto Press, 1986), 48–51.

38 Cartwright, *Reminiscences*, 45.

39 Forster, *A Conjunction of Interests*, 66–67.

40 See Peter J. Smith, "The Ideological Origins of Canadian Confederation," *Canadian Journal of Political Science* 20 (1987): 3–29.

41 *La Minerve*, September 9, 1864.

42 Marie-Marthe Filion-Montpetit, "Médéric Lanctôt, journaliste engagé (1838–1877): Une biographie intellectuelle" (PhD diss., University of Ottawa, 2003), 184.

43 P.B. Waite, ed., *The Confederation Debates in the Province of Canada, 1865* (Montreal and Kingston: McGill-Queen's University Press, 2006), 172.

44 I used the translation provided by Guy Laforest and Félix Mathieu in their essay "The Trustee, the Financier, and the Poet: Cartier, Galt, and D'Arcy McGee," in Brouillet, Gagnon, and Laforest, *The Quebec Conference of 1864*, 117–41.

45 Dorion's anti-Confederation manifesto of 1864 can be found in P.B. Waite's *The Life and Times of Confederation (1864–1867): Politics, Newspapers and*

*the Union of British North America* (Toronto: University of Toronto Press, 1962), 125. See also Stéphane Kelly, "The Economic Arguments of the Quebec Opponents of Confederation," in Brouillet, Gagnon, and Laforest, *The Quebec Conference of 1864,* 233–51.

46 Macdonald to Brown, April 11, 1865, Library and Archives Canada, John A. Macdonald Fonds (JAMF-LAC).

47 Cited in Richard Gwyn, *The Life and Times of John A. Macdonald,* vol. 1, *John A.: The Man Who Made Us* (Toronto: Random House Canada, 2007), 358.

48 Copy of a Report of a Committee of the Honourable the Executive Council, approved by his Excellency the Governor General on the 24th March 1865. In *Papers Relating to The Conferences which have taken place between Her Majesty's Government and a Deputation from the Executive Council of Canada appointed to confer with Her Majesty's Government on Subjects of Importance to the Province Presented to both Houses of Parliament by Command of her Majesty, 19th June 1865,* Parliamentary Archives (UK), HL/PO/JO/10/9/568. https://www.parliament.uk/about/living-heritage/ evolutionofparliament/legislativescrutiny/parliament-and-empire/ collections1/parliament-and-canada/london-conference-papers/.

49 P.B. Waite, *The Life and Times of Confederation (1864–1867): Politics, Newspapers and the Union of British North America* (Toronto: University of Toronto Press, 1962),

50 Ben Forster, *A Conjunction of Interests,* 57. On Howe's free-trade views generally, see J. Murray Beck, "Joseph Howe: A Liberal, but with Qualifications," in *The Proceedings of the Joseph Howe Symposium,* edited by Wayne A. Hunt (Sackville, NB: Centre for Canadian Studies, Mount Allison University, 1984), 13.

51 See Charles Tupper, *Recollections of Sixty Years in Canada* (London: Cassell and Company, 1914), 44. Those meetings inspired Richard Rohmer to write a novel, *John A.'s Crusade and Seward's Magnificent Folly* (Toronto: Dundurn, 2013). Highclere Castle doubles as the location in the popular television series *Downton Abbey.*

52 Alexander Galt to Anne Galt, January 14, 1867, Library and Archives Canada (LAC), Galt Papers, ID8, vol. 3.

53 "The North West," *Ottawa Times,* August 8, 1867.

54 See his letter to Louisa Macdonald, December 27, 1866 (reprinted in J.K. Johnson, *Affectionately Yours: The Letters of Sir John A. Macdonald and His Family* [Toronto: Macmillan of Canada, 1969], 102–3).

250　*Notes to pages 68–78*

55 Brown to Holton, January 17, 1867, in Alexander Mackenzie, ed., *The Life and Speeches of Hon. George Brown* (Toronto: Globe Printing Company, 1882), 210.

56 See Joseph Howe, William Annand, and Hugh McDonald, *Letter Addressed to The Earl of Carnarvon stating their Objections to the Proposed Scheme of Union of the British North American Provinces* (London, February 8, 1867).

57 Letter from Joseph Howe to W.J Stairs, March 29, 1867, cited in Kenneth G. Pryke, *Nova Scotia and Confederation, 1864–1974* (Toronto: University of Toronto Press, 1979), 40.

58 Dale Thomson, *Alexander Mackenzie: Clear Grit* (Toronto: Macmillan of Canada, 1960), 102.

59 Tupper, *Recollections of Sixty Years in Canada,* 53.

60 Donald Creighton, *John A. Macdonald,* vol. 2, *The Old Chieftain* (Toronto: University of Toronto Press, 1998), 36.

61 Macdonald to James O'Reilly (Kingston), July 4, 1867, JAMF-LAC.

62 See Creighton, *The Old Chieftain,* 12.

63 Andrée Désilets, "Chapais, Jean-Charles," in *Dictionary of Canadian Biography,* vol. 11, http://www.biographi.ca/en/bio/chapais_jean_charles_11E.html.

64 W.A. Spray, "Mitchell, Peter," in *Dictionary of Canadian Biography,* vol. 12, http://www.biographi.ca/en/bio/mitchell_peter_12E.html.

65 See Tupper, *Recollections of Sixty Years in Canada,* 54.

66 *Montreal Herald,* September 23, 1867, 1.

67 *Morning Freeman,* July 6, 1867, 1.

### Chapter 2: The Third Liberal Showdown in New Brunswick

1 *Morning Freeman,* July 2, 1867, 1.

2 *Morning Freeman,* July 16, 1867, 2.

3 *Morning Freeman,* July 20, 1867, 3.

4 *True Humorist,* June 22, 1867, cited in Alfred G. Bailey, "Railways and the Confederation Issue in New Brunswick, 1863–1865," *Canadian Historical Review* 21, 4 (1940): 383.

5 *Morning Freeman,* July 9, 1867, 4.

6 Carl M. Wallace, "Sir Leonard Tilley: A Political Biography" (PhD diss., University of Alberta, 1972), 215.

7 Tilley to Galt, 11 November 1864, Library and Archives of Canada (LAC), Galt Papers.

Notes to pages 79–81   251

8  Tilley to Hamilton-Gordon, January 30, 1865, LAC, New Brunswick Dispatches, cited in Ray Argyle, *Turning Points: The Campaigns That Changed Canada* (Toronto: White Knight, 2004), 52. Though tensions between Catholics and Protestants had calmed down significantly by the 1860s, they still existed. See Scott W. See, *Riots in New Brunswick: Orange Nativism and Social Violence in the 1840s* (Toronto: University of Toronto Press, 1993).

9  The issue of links to Great Britain is discussed by Philip Buckner in "Canadian Constitution-Making in the British World," in *The Quebec Conference of 1864: Understanding the Emergence of the Canadian Federation,* edited by Eugénie Brouillet, Alain-G. Gagnon, and Guy Laforest (Montreal and Kingston: McGill-Queen's University Press, 2018), 70–100.

10  Edward Whelan, *The Union of the British Provinces* (1865; reprint Gardenvale, QC: Garden City Press, 1927), 77–78.

11  P.B. Waite, *The Life and Times of Confederation (1864 -1867): Politics, Newspapers and the Union of British North America* (Toronto: University of Toronto Press, 1962), 235.

12  *Morning Telegraph,* November 3, 1864, cited in Wallace, "Sir Leonard Tilley," 192–93 (emphasis in original).

13  Macdonald to J.H. Gray (PEI), March 24, 1865, Library and Archives Canada, John A. Macdonald Fonds (JAMF-LAC), cited in Wallace, "Sir Leonard Tilley," 197.

14  Macdonald to Tilley, October 8, 1866, JAMF-LAC, cited in Wallace, "Sir Leonard Tilley," 196.

15  Wallace, "Sir Leonard Tilley," 205.

16  *Morning Telegraph,* February 1, 1865, cited in Wallace, "Sir Leonard Tilley," 204.

17  Cited in C.M. Wallace, "Smith, Sir Albert James," in *Dictionary of Canadian Biography,* vol. 11 (Toronto/Quebec: University of Toronto/Université Laval, 2003). Carl Wallace considered Albert Smith "backward looking." See Carl Wallace, "Albert Smith, Confederation and Reaction in New Brunswick: 1852–1882," *Canadian Historical Review* 44 (1963): 285–312.

18  *Fredericton Headquarter,* December 14, 1864, cited in Alfred G. Bailey, "The Basis and Persistence of Opposition to Confederation in New Brunswick," *Canadian Historical Review* 23, 4 (1942): 378.

19  New Brunswick, *Journals of the Legislative Assembly,* June 6, 1865, 223, cited in Bailey, "Basis and Persistence," 384.

252  *Notes to pages 81–87*

20 *Fredericton Headquarter,* December 7, 1864, cited in Bailey, "Basis and Persistence," 381.

21 Tilley to Macdonald, February 13, 1865, JAMF-LAC, Confederation Correspondence, file 6, cited in Bailey, "Basis and Persistence," 378.

22 Tilley to Hamilton-Gordon, May 17, 1865, cited in Wallace, "Sir Leonard Tilley," 211.

23 Wallace uses the correspondence of Lieutenant-Governor Arthur Hamilton-Gordon; see Wallace, "Sir Leonard Tilley," 219. See also J.K. Chapman, "Arthur Gordon and Confederation," *Canadian Historical Review* 37 (1956): 141–57.

24 Macdonald to Gray (PEI), March 24, 1865, JAMF-LAC, Confederation Correspondence, file 6, 66, cited in Bailey, "Basis and Persistence," 387.

25 Tilley to Galt, May 18, 1865, cited in Wallace, "Sir Leonard Tilley," 212.

26 Fisher to Macdonald, April 5, 1865, JAMF-LAC, Confederation Correspondence, file 6, cited in Bailey, "Basis and Persistence," 388.

27 C.P. Stacey, "Confederation: The Atmosphere of Crisis," in *Profiles of a Province: Studies in the History of Ontario,* edited by Edith G. Firth (Toronto: Ontario Historical Society, 1967), 76.

28 See Argyle, *Turning Points,* 54–55.

29 Bailey, "Basis and Persistence," 390.

30 Fisher to Macdonald, August 13, 1865, JAMF-LAC, Confederation Correspondence, file 6, cited in Bailey "Basis and Persistence," 391.

31 Fisher to Macdonald, November 1865, JAMF-LAC, Confederation Correspondence, file 6, cited in Bailey, "Basis and Persistence," 393. See also D.M.L. Farr, *The Colonial Office and Canada, 1867–1887* (Toronto: University of Toronto Press, 1955).

32 Letter in Saint John *Globe,* September 27, 1865, cited in Wallace, "Sir Leonard Tilley," 389.

33 *Morning Freeman,* February 3 and 6, 1866, cited in William M. Baker, *Timothy Warren Anglin: Irish Catholic Canadian* (Toronto: University of Toronto Press, 1977), 107.

34 Anglin to Arthur Hill Gillmour, February 9, 1866, cited in Baker, *Timothy Warren Anglin,* 100.

35 Anglin to Hamilton-Gordon, February 15, 1866, cited in Baker, *Timothy Warren Anglin,* 100.

36 Tilley to Macdonald, April 14, 1866, cited in Wallace, "Sir Leonard Tilley," 237.

Notes to pages 87–96  253

37  Tilley to Macdonald, April 17 and 20, 1866, cited in Wallace, "Sir Leonard Tilley," 238.
38  Tilley to Galt, undated, JAMF-LAC, cited in Wallace, "Sir Leonard Tilley," 215.
39  Tilley to Macdonald, April 14, 1866, JAMF-LAC.
40  J.H. Gray (NB) to Macdonald, March 18, 1865, JAMF-LAC, Confederation Correspondence, file 6, 68, cited in Bailey, "Basis and Persistence," 382.
41  Anglin to Gillmour, February 9, 1866, cited in Baker, *Timothy Warren Anglin*, 101.
42  New Brunswick Legislative Assembly Debates, April 6, 1866, cited in Baker, *Timothy Warren Anglin*, 103.
43  Argyle, *Turning Points*, 45–46.
44  Wallace, "Sir Leonard Tilley," 239–40.
45  Reproduced in the much more influential *Morning Telegraph*, June 16, 1866. See Wallace, "Sir Leonard Tilley," 242.
46  Richard Cartwright, *Reminiscences* (Toronto: William Briggs, 1912), 59.
47  Galt to Macdonald, August 31, 1866, in Wallace, "Sir Leonard Tilley," 251.
48  *Daily Evening Globe*, August 26, 1867, cited in Baker, *Timothy Warren Anglin*, 95.
49  Wallace, "Sir Leonard Tilley," 258.
50  *Morning Freeman*, August 27, 1867, 3.
51  "From the *Ch'town [Charlottetown] Patriot*," *Eastern Chronicle*, August 31, 1867, 2.
52  Tilley to Macdonald, May 6, 1867, cited in Wallace, "Sir Leonard Tilley," 262.
53  Brown to Holton, July 5, 1867, in Alexander Mackenzie, ed., *The Life and Speeches of Hon. George Brown* (Toronto: Globe Printing Company, 1882), 211–12.
54  *Morning Freeman*, August 11, 1867, 3.
55  *Morning Freeman*, July 23, 1867, 2.
56  *Morning Freeman*, August 13, 1867, 3.
57  *Morning Freeman*, July 16, 1867, 2.
58  James Hannay, *History of New Brunswick* (Saint John: John A. Bowes, 1909), 233.
59  *Morning Freeman*, August 8, 1867, 3.
60  *Morning Freeman*, July 16, 1867, 2.
61  *Morning Freeman*, July 2, 1867, 2.

254  *Notes to pages 96–104*

62  Baker, *Timothy Warren Anglin*, 97.
63  *Morning Freeman*, July 11, 1867, 3.
64  *Morning Freeman*, July 12, 1867, 3.
65  *Morning Freeman*, August 3, 1867, 3.
66  *Morning Freeman*, August 6, 1867, 3; see also *Morning Freeman*, August 27, 1867, 3.
67  *Morning Freeman*, July 23, 1867, 2.
68  *Morning Freeman*, July 6, 1867, 1.
69  *Morning Freeman*, July 23, 1867, 2.
70  Henry Olivier Lacroix, *The Present and Future of Canada* (Montreal: John Lovell, 1867), 17–18.
71  *Morning Freeman*, July 11, 1867, 3.
72  *Morning Freeman*, August 2, 1867, 1.
73  *Morning Freeman*, July 9, 1867, 4.
74  Argyle, *Turning Points*, 52.
75  *Morning Freeman*, September 3, 1867, 3.
76  *Morning Freeman*, September 3, 1867, 3.

### Chapter 3: A Proper Scottish *Square Go* in Ontario

1  Donald Creighton, *John A. Macdonald*, vol. 1, *The Young Politician* (Toronto: University of Toronto Press, 1998), 476–78.
2  Marvin L. Simner, "How London, Ontario, Celebrated the Birth of Confederation from 1867 to 1907," *The London and Middlesex Historian* 26 (2017): 6–20.
3  Macdonald to ?, August 13, 1867, Library and Archives Canada, John A. Macdonald Fonds (JAMF-LAC), document 873.
4  Macdonald to Alexander Drew, August 2, 1867, JAMF-LAC. See also Macdonald to Clarke (Guelph, Ontario), August 7, 1867, and Macdonald to Drew, August 9, 1867, where the prime minister reports that he had taken "steps to endeavour to secure the Catholic vote for you – whether I shall be successful or not remains to be seen." Drew was the grandfather of George Drew, premier of Ontario from 1943 to 1948 and leader of the Progressive Conservative Party from 1949 to 1956. The teasing is puzzling in that Drew, born and raised in Cornwall, Ontario, did his legal training with Sandfield Macdonald, a Catholic.
5  Macdonald to Alex Vidal, July 9, 1867, JAMF-LAC.
6  Macdonald to "My Dear Cotton," August 9, 1867, JAMF-LAC.
7  Macdonald to Geo. T. Denison, July 5, 1867, JAMF-LAC.

*Notes to pages 105–11*  255

8 Macdonald to Geo. T. Denison, July 6, 1867, JAMF-LAC.

9 Macdonald to Howland (?), [early July 1867], JAMF-LAC, document 659-62.

10 Macdonald to Howland (?), [early July 1867], JAMF-LAC, document 659-62.

11 Luther Holton to George Brown, July 16, 1867, Library and Archives Canada, George Brown Fonds (GBF-LAC).

12 Agnes Macdonald Diary, July 9, 1867, Library and Archives Canada (LAC) (online).

13 Agnes Macdonald Diary, July 9, 1867, LAC.

14 Agnes Macdonald Diary, July 10, 1867, LAC.

15 Agnes Macdonald Diary, July 13, 1867, LAC.

16 Agnes Macdonald Diary, July 14, 1867, LAC.

17 "Political Retrospect," *Globe,* August 3, 1867.

18 *Ottawa Times,* August 28, 1867.

19 "Special Telegrams," *Globe,* September 12, 1867.

20 Editorial, *Globe,* August 29, 1867, 2; see also "Sir John A. Macdonald on the Stump," *Globe,* September 2, 1867, 2. The issue of the Clergy Reserves would persist in Canada for a long time. Essentially, about 15 percent of Crown land had been set aside for use by the Church of England by the Constitutional Act of 1791. That was challenged in the mid-1820s by a wide assortment of church and community groups. The issue was essentially resolved in the 1850s but still lingered in the minds of those who were not satisfied by the outcome.

21 "Very Small," *Globe,* August 5, 1867, 2.

22 See *Montreal Herald,* August 6, 1867, 2.

23 "Corruptionist Jubilee," *Globe,* August 28, 1867.

24 Ged Martin, *Favourite Son? John A. Macdonald and the Voters of Kingston, 1841–1981* (Kingston: Kingston Historical Society, 2010), 89.

25 See William J. Smyth, *Toronto, the Belfast of Canada: The Orange Order and the Shaping of Municipal Culture* (Toronto: University of Toronto Press, 2015).

26 Macdonald to Lynch, July 3, 1867, JAMF-LAC, C25, document 637–646.

27 Reprinted in the *Morning Telegraph,* July 23, 1867, 3.

28 John A. Macdonald to Michael Hayes (?), July 9, 1867, JAMF-LAC.

29 John A. Macdonald to Francis Clarke, August 2, 1867, JAMF-LAC.

30 Macdonald to "My dear Lord" [John Farrell, Bishop of Hamilton], August 9, 1867, JAMF-LAC.

256  *Notes to pages 111–19*

31  Macdonald to "Very Reverend & Dear Sir" (Sandwich, Ontario), August 13, 1867, JAMF-LAC.

32  *Ottawa Times,* September 9, 1867.

33  *Ottawa Times,* September 6, 1867.

34  Brown to Luther Holton, January 17, 1867, cited in J.M.S. Careless, *Brown of the Globe,* vol. 2, *Statesman of Confederation, 1860–1880* (Toronto: Macmillan of Canada, 1963), 239.

35  Brown to Holton, May 13, 1867, in *The Life and Speeches of Hon. George Brown,* edited by Alexander Mackenzie (Toronto: Globe Printing Company, 1882), 211.

36  Mackenzie, *The Life and Speeches of Hon. George Brown,* 115.

37  Holton to Brown, May 31, 1867, cited in Careless, *Statesman of Confederation,* 245.

38  Cited in Mackenzie, *The Life and Speeches of Hon. George Brown,* 249–50.

39  Dale Thomson, *Alexander Mackenzie: Clear Grit* (Toronto: Macmillan of Canada, 1960), 104.

40  Luther Holton to George Brown, June 21, 1867, GBF-LAC (emphasis in original).

41  A very useful summary of the convention, with speech excerpts from Brown, is provided in the *Montreal Herald,* July 2, 1867.

42  John Blinnie (?) [the signature is undecipherable] to George Brown, June 25, 1867, GBF-LAC.

43  John Blinnie (?) [the signature is undecipherable] to George Brown, June 25, 1867, GBF-LAC.

44  Luther Holton to George Brown, July 2, 1867, GBF-LAC.

45  Luther Holton to George Brown, July 2, 1867, GBF-LAC (emphasis in original).

46  John A. Macdonald to Thomas Gibbs, July 11, 1867, JAMF-LAC.

47  *Ottawa Times,* September 4, 1867.

48  John A. Macdonald to (?) Davis (Delaware, Ontario), July 11, 1867, JAMF-LAC.

49  *Montreal Herald,* September 18, 1867, 1.

50  Brown to Holton, July 5, 1867, cited in Mackenzie, *The Life and Speeches of Hon. George Brown,* 211–12.

51  Macdonald to "Very Reverend & Dear Sir" (Sandwich, Ontario), August 13, 1867, JAMF-LAC.

52  John A. Macdonald to William Wilson, July 11, 1867, JAMF-LAC.

53  "Latest from Ottawa," *Globe,* August 7, 1867.

*Notes to pages 119–29* 257

54 "The Danger of the Hour," *Globe,* August 10, 1867.
55 "The Black Record against John A. Macdonald & Co.," *Globe,* August 3, 1867.
56 "Path Strewn with Dead Men's Bones," *Globe,* August 3, 1867; "The Coalition Party," *Globe,* August 13, 1867.
57 "The Danger of the Hour," *Globe,* August 10, 1867.
58 "The Question of Policy," *Globe,* August 7, 1867.
59 "Which Will You Support?" *Globe,* August 6, 1867.
60 Agnes Macdonald Diary, July 9, 1867.
61 Brown to Mackenzie, March 17, 1867, cited in Careless, *Statesman of Confederation,* 240.
62 Brown to Mackenzie, March 17, 1867, 103.
63 Thomson, *Alexander Mackenzie,* 104.
64 Joseph Schull, *Edward Blake: The Man of the Other Way, 1833–1881* (Toronto: Macmillan of Canada, 1975), 33.
65 "Why We Oppose the Two Coalitions," *Sarnia Observer,* August 23, 1867.
66 "The Intercolonial Railway," *Erie News,* August 29, 1867, 2.
67 *Sarnia Observer,* September 6, 1867.
68 George Brown to Anne Brown, July 25, 1867, GBF-LAC.
69 "The Elections," Quebec *Gazette,* August 19, 1867, 2.
70 Macdonald to Alexander Morris, July 1, 1867, cited in Sir Joseph Pope, *Correspondence of Sir John A. Macdonald* (Toronto, 1921), 46–47.
71 John A. Macdonald to John A. Donaldson, July 11, 1867, JAMF-LAC. O'Donoghue was eventually elected to the Ontario legislature as an independent but really made his mark as a leader of the Knights of Labour in the province.
72 Thomson, *Alexander Mackenzie,* 100.
73 Thomson, *Alexander Mackenzie,* 101.
74 Thomson, *Alexander Mackenzie,* 99.
75 See "South Ontario Monster Meeting at Whitby," *Ottawa Times,* August 23, 1867.
76 George Brown to Anne Brown, July 25, 1867, GBF-LAC.
77 *Erie News,* September 12, 1867, 1.
78 John Squair, *The History of the Townships of Darlington and Clarke* (Toronto: University of Toronto Press, 1927), cited in Schull, *Edward Blake,* 36.
79 "The South Ontario Election, Jubilation in Toronto," *Ottawa Citizen,* September 6, 1867, 1.

258   *Notes to pages 130–35*

80   "The South Ontario Election, Jubilation in Toronto," *Ottawa Citizen.*
81   "The South Ontario Election, Jubilation in Toronto," *Ottawa Citizen.*
82   "Mr. Lyon's Election; To the Editor of 'The Ottawa Citizen,'" *Ottawa Citizen,* August 30, 1867.
83   "The Elections – Toronto," Quebec *Gazette,* September 4, 1867, 2.
84   *Ottawa Times,* August 28, 1867.
85   Cited in Mackenzie, *The Life and Speeches of Hon. George Brown,* 118.
86   Holton to Brown, August 28, 1867, GBF-LAC.

### Chapter 4: Quebec's Contest of Nationalisms

1   "The Review and Proclamation of the Dominion," *Montreal Herald,* July 2, 1867, 3.
2   "The Dominion Day," *Montreal Herald,* July 2, 1867, 2. For background on the place of lacrosse in the culture of the time, see Gillian Poulter, *Become Native in a Foreign Land: Sport, Visual Culture and Identity in Montreal, 1840–85* (Vancouver: UBC Press, 2009), 126–29; photographs of the two teams appear on pages 126–27.
3   "The Dominion Day," *Montreal Herald,* July 2, 1867, 2.
4   "The Dominion Day," *Montreal Herald,* July 2, 1867, 2.
5   Dawson to Howe, November 15, 1866, cited in P.B. Waite, *The Life and Times of Confederation (1864–1867): Politics, Newspapers and the Union of British North America* (Toronto: University of Toronto Press, 1962), 135.
6   See *Proceedings of the Annual Convocation of the McGill University, 1867.* Dawson's speech starts at page 15; see 18.
7   See Macdonald to Sidney Bellingham, August 9, 1867, Library and Archives Canada, John A. Macdonald Fonds. Macdonald tells his correspondent that Cartier is handling affairs in Quebec. Bellingham had long held the seat of Argenteuil in the Legislative Assembly of the United Province of Canada and had won the election of 1858. John Abbott contested the result, arguing that over two hundred votes had been fraudulent, and won. See John C. Abbott, *The Argenteuil Case* (Montreal, 1860). Cartier, ably supported by Hector Langevin, initiated work as soon as they returned from London. See H. Langevin to A.T. Galt, March 29, 1867, cited in Andrée Désilets, *Hector-Louis Langevin: Un père de la confédération Canadienne* (Quebec: Presses de l'Université Laval, 1969).
8   *Le Journal des Trois-Rivières,* June 21, 1867, cited in Désilets, *Hector-Louis Langevin,* 185.
9   *La Minerve,* July 2, 1867, 2.

Notes to pages 135–40    259

10 Cited in Ramsay Cook, *Watching Quebec: Selected Essays* (Montreal and Kingston: McGill-Queen's University Press, 2005), 175.

11 *Le Courrier de Saint-Hyacinthe,* August 1, 1867, cited in Jean-Charles Bonenfant, *Les Canadiens français et la naissance de la confédération* (n.p.: Société d'Histoire du Canada, 1966), 12.

12 Éric Bedard, "Avoiding the 'Iniquitous Pit of Liberty': The Centralizing Federalism of Joseph-Édouard Cauchon," in *The Quebec Conference of 1864: Understanding the Emergence of the Canadian Federation,* edited by Eugénie Brouillet, Alain-G. Gagnon, and Guy Laforest (Montreal and Kingston: McGill-Queen's University Press, 2018), 103–16.

13 See Stéphane Kelly, "The Economic Arguments of the Quebec Opponents of Confederation," in Brouillet, Gagnon, and Laforest, *The Quebec Conference of 1864,* 238.

14 *Histoire de la Province de Québec,* vol. 1, *Georges*[sic]-*Étienne Cartier* (Montreal: Éditions Bernard Valiquette, 1940), 28.

15 Letter from Laflèche to Boucher de Niverville, March 2, 1864, cited in Walter Ullman, "The Quebec Bishops and Confederation," *Canadian Historical Review* 46, 3 (1963): 218.

16 Jean-Charles Bonenfant, *Les Canadiens français et la naissance de la confédération* (n.p.: Société d'histoire du Canada, 1966), 14.

17 Letters from Bourget from February 8 to November 4, 1867, cited in Marcel Bellavance, *Le Québec et la confédération: un choix libre? Le clergé et la constitution de 1867* (Quebec: Septentrion, 1992), 128.

18 "Mandement du 13 juin de l'évêque de Rimouski," *La Minerve,* June 24, 1867.

19 Robert Rumilly, *Histoire de la Province de Québec,* vol. 1, *Georges*[sic]-*Étienne Cartier* (Montreal: Éditions Bernard Valiquette, 1940), 99.

20 See Ullman, "The Quebec Bishops and Confederation," 213–34.

21 See Normand Séguin, "L'opposition canadienne-française aux élections de 1867 dans la grande région de Montréal" (MA thesis, University of Ottawa, 1968), 109–10. Séguin cites letters found in the Hector Langevin archives at Library and Archives Canada.

22 *La Minerve,* August 21, 1865, cited in Bellavance, *Le Québec et la confédération,* 104.

23 Cited in Rumilly, *Histoire de la Province de Québec,* vol. 1, 98.

24 Gil Remillard, "Les intentions des Pères de la Confédération," *Les Cahiers de droit* 20, 4 (1979): 828.

25 Bellavance, *Le Québec et la confédération,* 128.

260   *Notes to pages 140–45*

26  Pastoral letter of June 18, 1867, cited in Bonenfant, *Les Canadiens français et la naissance de la confédération,* 15.

27  *Le Courrier de Saint-Hyacinthe,* September 5, 1867, cited in Bellavance, *Le Québec et la confédération,* 141.

28  *La Minerve,* August 7, 1867, cited in Bellavance, *Le Québec et la confédération,* 141.

29  Bellavance, *Le Québec et la confédération,* 121. See also Jean-Paul Bernard, *Les Rouges: Libéralisme, nationalisme et anticléricalisme au milieu de XIXe siècle* (Montreal: Les Presses de l'Université du Québec, 1971), 415–18, for an inventory of abuses collected in the various *Rouge* newspapers following the election. See also Philippe Sylvain, "Libéralisme et Ultramontanisme au Canada français: affrontement idéologique et doctrinal (1840–1865)," in *The Shield of Achilles: Aspects of Canada in the Victorian Age,* edited by W.L. Morton (Toronto: McClelland and Stewart, 1968), pt. 1, 111–38; pt. 2, 220–55.

30  Benjamin Sulte, *Histoire des Canadiens-Français* (Montreal, 1892), 146, cited in Bellavance, *Le Québec et la confédération,* 167.

31  It is worth noting that Papineau, the *Patriote* leader, followed this line of thinking. He did not participate in the debates around the 1864 resolutions or in 1867. See Yvan Lamonde, "Papineau and the Refusal of Arrangements (1854–67)," in Brouillet, Gagnon, and Laforest, *The Quebec Conference of 1864,* 252–62.

32  Bernard, *Les Rouges.* Bernard devotes an entire chapter to the newspapers, in a study examining the *Rouges* through their published voices.

33  See Yvan Lamonde, *Louis-Antoine Dessaulles (1818–1895): un seigneur liberal et anticlérical* (Montreal: Fides, 1994).

34  Holton to Brown, October 14, 1859, Library and Archives Canada, George Brown Fonds (GBF-LAC), cited in Bernard, *Les Rouges,* 239.

35  Yvan Lamonde, "Breaches in Radical Liberalism, 1852–1867," in *Roads to Confederation: The Making of Canada, 1867,* vol. 1, edited by Jacqueline D. Krikorian, David R. Cameron, Marcel Martel, Andrew W. McDougall, and Robert Vipond (Toronto: University of Toronto Press, 2017), 195.

36  *Le Défricheur,* January 25, 1865.

37  Rumilly, *Histoire de la Province de Québec,* vol. 1, 22.

38  Rumilly, *Histoire de la Province de Québec,* vol. 1, 100.

39  *Représentation de la minorité parlementaire du Bas-Canada à Lord Carnarvon* (Montreal: Le Pays, 1866), 3.

40 *La Confédération: couronnement de dix années de mauvaise administration* (Montreal: Le Pays, 1867). Louis-Georges Harvey provides an excellent review of the *Rouge* arguments against Confederation in "Confederation and Corruption: The Republican Critique of the Quebec Resolutions," in Brouillet, Gagnon, and Laforest, *The Quebec Conference of 1864*, 220–32.

41 Rumilly, *Histoire de la Province de Québec*, vol. 1, 22.

42 See J.I. Little, "Watching the Frontier Disappear," *Journal of Canadian Studies* 15, 4 (1980–81): 102.

43 My translation. See citation in Rumilly, *Histoire de la Province de Québec*, vol. 1, 20. On Clerk, see Bruno Clerk, "Le Journal *True Witness and Catholic Chronicle* et la pensée politique de George Edward Clerk (1850–75)" (MA thesis, Université de Montreal, 1996).

44 *Le Pays*, June 1, 1867.

45 Rumilly, *Histoire de la Province de Québec*, vol. 1, 95.

46 See *Le Pays*, July 24, 1867, cited in Marie-Marthe Filion-Montpetit, "Médéric Lanctôt, journaliste engagé (1838–1877): Une biographie intellectuelle" (PhD diss., University of Ottawa, 2003), 310.

47 *Réponses aux censeurs de la confédération* (St. Hyacinthe: Imprimerie du Courrier de St. Hyacinthe, 1867), https://www.collectionscanada.gc.ca/obj/023012/f2/amicus-5755597.pdf.

48 This change of view was likely prompted by Archbishop Bourget. See Ullman, "The Quebec Bishops and Confederation," 213–34, 229.

49 See J.I. Little, *Patrician Liberal: The Public and Private Life of Sir Henri-Gustave Joly de Lotbinière, 1829–1908* (Toronto: University of Toronto Press, 2013), 103.

50 See Arthur Buies, "Troisième lettre," in *Lettres sur le Canada : Étude sociale* (La Bibliothèque électronique du Québec, n.d.). See section III, 78, https://beq.ebooksgratuits.com/pdf/Buies-Canada.pdf.

51 Buies, "Troisième lettre," 92.

52 Buies, "Troisième lettre," 96–97.

53 Buies, "Troisième lettre," 95n.

54 Filion-Montpetit, "Médéric Lanctôt," 70. The series of articles was published in the *Courrier de Saint-Hyacinthe*.

55 Yvan Lamonde, *Gens de Parole* (Montreal: Boréal, 1990), 104; see also Filion-Montpetit, "Médéric Lanctôt," 39–40.

56 This view was widely shared among the *Rouges*. See Kelly, "The Economic Arguments of the Quebec Opponents of Confederation," 241–42.

262  Notes to pages 150–61

57  *La Presse*, June 20, 1864, cited in Filion-Montpetit, "Médéric Lanctôt," 138.

58  "Cette Lettre," *L'Union Nationale*, November 10, 1864, 2, cited in Filion-Montpetit, "Médéric Lanctôt," 180 (my translation).

59  Filion-Montpetit, "Médéric Lanctôt," 76.

60  These details are drawn from Filion-Montpetit, "Médéric Lanctôt," 173–75.

61  Filion-Montpetit, "Médéric Lanctôt," 229.

62  See *L'indépendance pacifique du Canada* (n.p., 1867), 35.

63  See Filion-Montpetit, "Médéric Lanctôt," 274.

64  See Margaret Heap, "La grève des charretiers de Montréal," in *Le mouvement ouvrier au Québec*, edited by Fernand Harvey (Montreal: Boréal Express, 1980), 49–67.

65  *Montreal Herald*, September 19, 1867, 1.

66  Filion-Montpetit, "Médéric Lanctôt," 183.

67  Filion-Montpetit, "Médéric Lanctôt," 299.

68  Rumilly, *Histoire de la Province de Québec*, vol. 1, 103.

69  Cited in Filion-Montpetit, "Médéric Lanctôt," 312.

70  "La situation," *L'Union Nationale*, August 2, 1865, 2, cited in Filion-Montpetit, "Médéric Lanctôt," 192.

71  L.O. David, *Mes Contemporains* (Montreal, 1894), originally published in *L'Opinion Publique*, August 23, 1877, 1–2.

72  Jean Hamelin, "LANCTÔT, MÉDÉRIC," in *Dictionary of Canadian Biography*, vol. 10 (Toronto/Quebec: University of Toronto/Université Laval, 2003), http://www.biographi.ca/en/bio/Lanctôt_mederic_10E.html.

73  Rumilly, *Histoire de la Province de Québec*, vol. 1, 100.

74  This threat was referenced in a letter from McGee to W. McNaughton, the chair of McGee's organizing committee, was published in the *St. Catharines Constitutional*, August 15, 1867, 2.

75  See David A. Wilson, *Thomas D'Arcy McGee*, vol. 2, *The Extreme Moderate, 1857–1858* (Montreal and Kingston: McGill-Queen's University Press, 2011), 310–22.

76  *L'Union Nationale*, July 18, 1867.

77  *L'Union Nationale*, 314.

78  "Montreal West – Meeting of Mr. McGee's Supporters," *Quebec Gazette*, August 5, 1867, 1.

79  "Mr. McGee's Election Meeting," *Quebec Gazette*, August 7, 1867, 2.

80  See *Morning Freeman* (Saint John, NB), August 27, 1867.

Notes to pages 162–67    263

81 It is worth noting that McGee hedged his bets by running in the Glengarry riding of Ontario (he withdrew his candidacy after his victory in Montreal). See Wilson, *Thomas D'Arcy McGee*, vol. 2, 308.

82 "Banquet to the Hon. John A. Macdonald at the Burnett House," *Kingston Whig-Standard*, September 7, 1867, 1.

83 Wilson, *Thomas D'Arcy McGee*, vol. 2, 324.

84 "The Elections – Montreal," *Ottawa Times*, September 3, 1867.

85 Bellavance, *Le Québec et la confédération*, 125.

86 *Quebec Gazette*, September 4, 1867, 2.

87 Rumilly, *Histoire de la Province de Québec*, vol. 1, 101–2.

88 Lionel Groulx, *Les Canadiens français et la Confédération canadienne* (Montreal: Bibliothèque de l'Action française, 1927), 1–21.

## Chapter 5: The Clash of Imperialisms in Nova Scotia

1 *Morning Chronicle*, July 1, 1867.

2 Andrew Elliott, "Highlights from the Sir Sandford Fleming Diaries," Library and Archives Canada Blog, October 5, 2017, https://thediscover blog.com/tag/diaries/. Elliott refers to Fleming's diary of July 1, 1867.

3 Macdonald to Fleming, July 1, 1867, Library and Archives Canada, John A. Macdonald Fonds (JAMF-LAC).

4 *Weekly Citizen* (Halifax), August 20, 1867.

5 See Ged Martin, "The Case against Canadian Confederation," in *The Causes of Canadian Confederation*, edited by Ged Martin (Fredericton: Acadiensis Press, 1990), 40.

6 Martin, "The Case," 41.

7 Quoting the *Journal* in Summerside, Prince Edward Island. See *Eastern Chronicle*, August 31, 1867, 2.

8 D.A. Muise, "Parties and Constituencies: Federal Elections in Nova Scotia, 1867–1896," *Historical Papers/Communications historiques* 6, 1 (1971): 187.

9 See John Garner, *The Franchise and Politics in British North America, 1755–1867* (Toronto: University of Toronto Press, 1969), 33–37.

10 Kenneth G. Pryke, *Nova Scotia and Confederation, 1864–1974* (Toronto: University of Toronto Press, 1979), 26–27.

11 S.A. Saunders, "The Maritime Provinces and the Reciprocity Treaty," *Dalhousie Review* 14 (1934): 359.

12 Andrew Smith, *British Businessmen and Canadian Confederation: Constitution Making in an Era of Anglo-Globalization* (Montreal and Kingston: McGill-Queen's University Press, 2008), 109.

## 264  Notes to pages 168–75

13 A. Cosmopolitan, *Has the Country Been Sold? A Letter to the Electors of Nova Scotia, by a Cosmopolitan* (Halifax, July 1867).

14 *Has the Country Been Sold?,* 13.

15 *Eastern Chronicle,* September 4, 1867, 2.

16 *Eastern Chronicle,* September 4, 1867, 2.

17 "Candidates of the Nova Scotia Party in the County of Pictou," *Eastern Chronicle,* August 7, 1867, 2.

18 *Halifax Chronicle,* reprinted in *Montreal Herald,* September 25, 1867, 3.

19 Charles Tupper, *Recollections of Sixty Years in Canada* (London: Cassell and Company, 1914), 55.

20 See David Sutherland, "Joseph Howe and the Boosting of Halifax," in *The Proceedings of the Joseph Howe Symposium,* edited by Wayne A. Hunt (Sackville, NB: Centre for Canadian Studies, Mount Allison University, 1984), 71–86.

21 See J. Murray Beck, *Joseph Howe,* vol. 1, *Conservative Reformer, 1804–1848* (Montreal and Kingston: McGill-Queen's University Press, 1982).

22 See M.G. Parks, "The Editor Speaks: Joseph Howe as Exemplar, Promoter and Critic of Provincial Culture," in Hunt, *Proceedings of the Joseph Howe Symposium,* 87–102, as well as George L. Parker, "To Foster and Extend Our Provincial Literature: Joseph Howe and the Market for Books in Nova Scotia, 1828–1841," in Hunt, *Proceedings of the Joseph Howe Symposium,* 103–15; Paul Keen, "Radical Atlantic: Joseph Howe and the Culture of Reform," *Journal of Canadian Studies* 48, 3 (2014): 30–48.

23 See William B. Hamilton, "Joseph Howe and Education: An Overview," in Hunt, *Proceedings of the Joseph Howe Symposium,* 29–51.

24 J. Murray Beck, *Joseph Howe,* vol. 2, *The Briton Becomes Canadian, 1848–1873* (Montreal and Kingston: McGill-Queen's University Press, 1983), 182.

25 See Joseph Howe, *Confederation Considered in Relation to the Interests of the Empire* (London: Edward Stanford, 1866).

26 Cited in D.A. Muise, "The Federal Election of 1867 in Nova Scotia," *Collections of the Nova Scotia Historical Society* 36 (1968): 334.

27 See J. Murray Beck, "Joseph Howe: A Liberal, but with Qualifications," in Hunt, *Proceedings of the Joseph Howe Symposium,* 5–28.

28 J. Murray Beck, *Joseph Howe,* vol. 2, *The Briton Becomes Canadian, 1848–1873* (Montreal and Kingston: McGill-Queen's University Press, 1983), 220.

29 Beck, *Joseph Howe,* vol. 2, 220.

Notes to pages 175–81    265

30 Cited in James L. Sturgis, "The Opposition to Confederation in Nova Scotia, 1864–1868," in *The Causes of Canadian Confederation,* edited by Ged Martin (Fredericton: Acadiensis Press, 1990), 221.
31 Sturgis, "Opposition to Confederation in Nova Scotia," 222.
32 *Halifax Chronicle,* reproduced in *Yarmouth Herald,* August 15, 1867, 2.
33 *Weekly Citizen* (Halifax), August 24, 1867.
34 *Halifax Chronicle,* reproduced in *Yarmouth Herald,* August 15, 1867, 2.
35 *Weekly Citizen* (Halifax), August 20, 1867, 1.
36 Cited in Stanley B. Ryerson, *Unequal Union: Confederation and the Roots of Conflict in Canada* (Toronto: Progress Books, 1973), 352.
37 *Weekly Citizen* (Halifax), August 20, 1867.
38 "Open Letter to Mr. Townsend, Provincial Secretary's Office," *Eastern Chronicle,* August 7, 1867, 2.
39 Cited in Ryerson, *Unequal Union,* 352.
40 *Morning Chronicle,* reprinted in *Montreal Herald,* September 25, 1867, 3.
41 *Weekly Citizen* (Halifax), August 20, 1867.
42 "Our Judges and Confederation," *Eastern Chronicle,* August 24, 1867, 2.
43 *Weekly Citizen* (Halifax), August 20, 1867.
44 *Eastern Chronicle,* August 28, 1867, 2.
45 "To the Electors of the County of Pictou," *Eastern Chronicle,* August 28, 1867, 2.
46 "To the Electors of the County of Pictou."
47 Ryerson, *Unequal Union,* 351.
48 *Charlottetown Examiner,* August 6, 1867.
49 *Charlottetown Examiner,* August 6, 1867.
50 *Morning Chronicle,* September 17, 1868, cited in Muise, "The Federal Election of 1867 in Nova Scotia," 340.
51 Tupper, *Recollections of Sixty Years in Canada,* 55.
52 H. Moody, "Political Experiences in Nova Scotia, 1867–1869," *Dalhousie Review* 14, 1 (1934): 67.
53 Moody, "Political Experiences," 6.
54 "From the *Ch'town [Charlottetown] Patriot,*" *Eastern Chronicle,* August 31, 1867, 2.
55 *Globe,* August 13, 1867, reprinted in *Sun and Advertiser,* August 21, 1867.
56 *Sun and Advertiser,* August 28, 1867.
57 "Open Letter to Mr. Townsend, Provincial Secretary's Office," *Eastern Chronicle,* August 7, 1867, 2.

266 *Notes to pages 181–90*

58 "The Victory," *Sun and Advertiser,* September 20, 1867.
59 See *Eastern Chronicle,* August 14, 1867, 2.
60 *Eastern Chronicle,* August 14, 1867, 2.

## Chapter 6: The Outcome

1 This analysis is based on the official results provided by the Parliament of Canada at "General Election (1867-08-07 – 1867-09-20)," https://lop.parl.ca/sites/ParlInfo/default/en_CA/ElectionsRidings/Elections/Profile?election=1867-08-07. For the original report, see *Return of the First General Election for the House of Commons of Canada,* Sessional Paper 41, vol. 8, 31 Victoria 1868. There is one error in this report: Alfred Gilpin Jones, one of the two winners in the riding of Halifax, is listed as representing Labour. There is no evidence that this is true: he was a businessman and ran on an anti-Confederation platform.
2 *Morning Chronicle,* September 25, 1867, 1.
3 Cited in J. Murray Beck, *Joseph Howe,* vol. 2, *The Briton Becomes Canadian, 1848–1873* (Montreal and Kingston: McGill-Queen's University Press, 1983), 223.
4 See Kenneth Pryke, *Nova Scotia and Confederation, 1864–1874* (Toronto: University of Toronto Press, 1979), 60–80.
5 *Morning Freeman,* August 1, 1867, 2.
6 See *Morning Freeman,* August 27, 1867, 3.
7 See Gaetan Migneault, "French Canada and Confederation: The Acadians of New Brunswick," in *Roads to Confederation: The Making of Canada, 1867,* edited by Jacqueline D. Krikorian, David R. Cameron, Marcel Martel, Andrew W. McDougall, and Robert C. Vipond (Toronto: University of Toronto Press, 2017), 105.
8 *Globe,* "Statesman or Jobber?," cited in *Montreal Herald,* September 19, 1867, 4.
9 See Normand Séguin, "L'opposition canadienne-française aux élections de 1867 dans la grande région de Montréal" (MA thesis, University of Ottawa, 1968), 72–73.
10 Séguin considers him a Conservative. See Séguin, "L'opposition canadienne-française."
11 J. Murray Beck, *Pendulum of Power: Canada's Federal Elections* (Scarborough, ON: Prentice-Hall of Canada, 1968), 12.

Notes to pages 191–200 267

12 Jean-Paul Bernard's results charts, which include provincial results, include detailed results for "violets" and "unclassified" independents. It is a remarkable essay, but regrettably unconvincing.

13 Jean-Paul Bernard, *Les Rouges: Libéralisme, nationalisme et anticléricalisme au milieu de XIXe siècle* (Montreal: Les Presses de l'Université du Québec, 1971), 295–311. By Bernard's count, the Liberals were wiped out in the broad Montreal region, barely securing 18 percent of the vote, almost half the support they had secured in 1863. He calculated that in Montreal the Liberal vote dropped from 42 percent to 8 percent. The only area that supported the *Rouges* was Saint-Hyacinthe, where they received 41 percent of the vote.

14 "The Representation in Quebec," *Quebec Gazette,* September 2, 1867, 3.

15 See François Hudon, "Perrault, Joseph-Xavier," in *Dictionary of Canadian Biography,* vol. 13 (Toronto/Quebec: University of Toronto/Université Laval, 2003), http://www.biographi.ca/en/bio/perrault_joseph_xavier_13E.html.

16 *Ottawa Times,* September 9, 1867, 1.

17 "The Self-Condemned," *Expositor,* July 26, 1867, 2.

18 Pryke, *Nova Scotia and Confederation, 1864–1874,* 55.

19 D.A. Muise, "Parties and Constituencies: Federal Elections in Nova Scotia, 1867–1896," *Historical Papers/Communications historiques* 6, 1 (1971): 188.

20 *Halifax Chronicle,* reprinted in *Montreal Herald,* September 25, 1867, 3.

21 *Sun and Advertiser,* September 20, 1867.

22 D.A. Muise, "The Federal Election of 1867 in Nova Scotia: An Economic Interpretation," *Collections of the Nova Scotia Historical Society* 36 (1968): 342.

23 See Philip A. Buckner, "The Maritimes and Confederation: A Reassessment," in *The Causes of Canadian Confederation,* edited by Ged Martin (Fredericton: Acadiensis Press, 1990), 39, 95–96; see also Eric W. Sager and Gerry Panting, "Staple Economics and the Rise and Decline of the Shipping Industry in Atlantic Canada," in *Change and Adaptation in Maritime History: The North Atlantic Fleets in the Nineteenth Century,* edited by Lewis R. Fischer and Gerald Panting (St. John's: Memorial University of Newfoundland, 1985).

24 *Morning Freeman,* September 24, 1867, 3.

25 Muise, "The Federal Election of 1867 in Nova Scotia," 343.

268  *Notes to pages 201–8*

## Conclusion

1 Interview with Friedrich Meyer von Waldeck in the *St. Petersburgische Zeitung: Aus den Erinnerungen eines russischen Publicisten*, 2.

2 Agnes Macdonald Diary, September 29, 1867, Library and Archives Canada (online).

3 Agnes Macdonald Diary, November 17, 1867.

4 Macdonald to Mr. Eaton, Corresponding Secretary, July 28, 1867, Library and Archives Canada, John A. Macdonald Fonds (JAMF-LAC).

5 "What the Americans Think of Him," *Kingston Whig-Standard,* September 21, 1867, 2. It is not clear whether the *Republican* referred to in this article was the one from Winona (Minnesota), Baltimore (Maryland), or Springfield (Massachusetts).

6 Richard Cartwright, *Reminiscences* (Toronto: William Briggs, 1912), 62.

7 See Patrice Dutil, *Prime Ministerial Power in Canada: Its Origins under Macdonald, Laurier, and Borden* (Vancouver: UBC Press, 2017), 225–27.

8 Macdonald to P.C. Hill, October 7, 1867, JAMF-LAC.

9 See Frank Underhill, "Canada's Relations with the Empire as seen by the Toronto *Globe,* 1857–1867," *Canadian Historical Review* 10, 2 (1929): 127–28; J.M.S. Careless, *Brown of the Globe,* vol. 2, *Statesman of Confederation, 1860–1880* (Toronto: Macmillan of Canada, 1963), 25–26; Frank Underhill, "Some Aspects of Upper Canadian Radical Opinion in the Decade before Confederation," *Report of the Canadian Historical Association* (1927): 51–54; Frank Underhill, "Political Ideas of the Upper Canadian Reformers, 1867–78," *Canadian Historical Association Report* (1942): 109.

10 Andrew Smith, *British Businessmen and Canadian Confederation: Constitution Making in an Era of Anglo-Globalization* (Montreal and Kingston: McGill-Queen's University Press, 2008), 94.

11 A view notably supported by Harold Innis, *An Economic History of Canada* (Toronto: Ryerson Press, 1935).

12 Both needed to cross a river, but the scorpion, being unable to swim, asked the tortoise to carry him to the other shore. The tortoise agreed, but was stung by the scorpion as he swam to the other shore. Incredulous, the tortoise asked the scorpion why he would risk his own life, and the scorpion responded that "it was in his nature."

13 "The Banquet at Kingston Last Night," *Ottawa Citizen,* September 7, 1867, 2.

14 H. Moody, "Political Experiences in Nova Scotia, 1867–1869," *Dalhousie Review* 14, 1 (1934): 69.

Notes to pages 208–16    269

15  Martin I. Wilkins, *Confederation Examined in the Light of Reason and Common Sense and the British N.A. Act Shewn to be Unconstitutional* (Halifax: Z.S. Hall, 1867), 4.
16  Wilkins, *Confederation Examined.*
17  Wilkins, *Confederation Examined.*
18  Macdonald to P.C. Hill, October 7, 1867, JAMF-LAC.
19  "Nova Scotia Elections," *Globe,* September 19, 1867.
20  *Montreal Herald,* September 27, 1867, 1.
21  Charles Tupper, *Recollections of Sixty Years in Canada* (London: Cassell and Company, 1914), 58.
22  J. Murray Beck, *Joseph Howe,* vol. 2; *The Briton Becomes Canadian, 1848–1873* (Montreal and Kingston: McGill-Queen's University Press, 1983), 226.
23  Reported in *Morning Freeman,* August 11, 1868, 1.
24  Kenneth Pryke devotes a compelling chapter on Joseph Howe's experience in the Macdonald government in his *Nova Scotia and Confederation, 1864–1974* (Toronto: University of Toronto Press, 1979), 80–91.
25  Cited in J. Murray Beck, "Joseph Howe: A Liberal, but with Qualifications," in *Proceedings of the Joseph Howe Symposium,* edited by Wayne A. Hunt (Sackville, NB: Centre for Canadian Studies, Mount Allison University, 1984), 10.
26  Beck, "Joseph Howe," 17.
27  *Montreal Herald,* September 21, 1867, 1.
28  *Montreal Herald,* September 21, 1867, 1.
29  Careless, *Brown of the Globe,* vol. 2, 258.
30  Editorial, "Le Canada," *Le journal de Québec,* July 8, 1867, 2.
31  See Jean-Paul Bernard, *Les Rouges: Libéralisme, nationalisme et anti-cléricalisme au milieu de XIXe siècle* (Montreal: Les Presses de l'Université du Québec, 1971), 417–18.
32  Henry Olivier Lacroix, *The Present and Future of Canada* (Montreal: John Lovell, 1867), 10.
33  "Ignorant Voters," *St. Catharines Constitutional,* August 8, 1867, 4.
34  *Ottawa Times,* August 8, 1867.
35  "The Opposition in Nova Scotia," *Quebec Gazette,* August 5, 1867, 1.
36  *Sarnia Observer,* September 6, 1867, 1.
37  *Morning Freeman,* September 5, 1867, 3.
38  The *Headquarters* piece is reproduced as "Political Affiliates," *St. Catharines Constitutional,* August 15, 1867, 2.

270  *Notes to pages 216–23*

39 "The Result of the Contest," *Globe*, September 21, 1867.

40 *Montreal Herald*, September 23, 1867, 1.

41 *Le Pays*, September 26, 1867, gives a rundown of the corruption. *L'Ordre*, September 30, 1867, cited in Marcel Bellavance, *Le Québec et la confédération: un choix libre? Le clergé et la constitution de 1867* (Québec: Septentrion, 1992), 151.

42 *Canadian Champion*, September 12, 1867, 2.

43 *Canadian Champion*, September 12, 1867, 2.

44 "An Ottawa Rumour," reprinted in the *Globe*, September 21, 1867.

45 "The Brown Coalition," *Ottawa Times*, August 20, 1867.

46 Lacroix, *The Present and Future of Canada*, 6.

47 On Norris, see Peter Price, *Questions of Order: Confederation and the Making of Modern Canada* (Toronto: University of Toronto Press, 2022). On Ewart, see Peter Price, "Fashioning a Constitutional Narrative: John S. Ewart and the Development of a 'Canadian Constitution,'" *Canadian Historical Review* 93, 3 (2012): 359–81.

48 Lacroix, *The Present and Future of Canada*, 23.

49 *Kingston Herald*, cited in *Montreal Herald*, September 20, 1867, 1.

50 Narcisse Belleau to Macdonald, September 24, 1867, in Sir Joseph Pope, *Correspondence of Sir John A. Macdonald* (Toronto, 1921), 49.

51 House of Commons *Debates*, Speech from the Throne, November 7, 1867, 5.

52 House of Commons *Debates*, November 8, 1867, 15.

53 *Montreal Herald*, September 27, 1867, 1.

54 Agnes Macdonald Diary, cited in Richard Gwyn, *The Life and Times of John A. Macdonald*, vol. 2, *Nation Maker; Sir John A. Macdonald: His Life, Our Times* (Toronto: Random House Canada, 2011), 23.

55 See Patrice Dutil, "Sir John A. Macdonald and His 'Ottawa Men,'" in *Sir John A. Macdonald at 200: New Perspectives and Legacies*, edited by Patrice Dutil and Roger Hall (Toronto: Dundurn Press, 2014), 282–310.

56 James Williamson to Sir John Macdonald, December 31, 1867, in Pope, *Correspondence of Sir John A. Macdonald*, 63–64.

57 See R.S. Longley, "Cartier and McDougall: Canadian Emissaries to London, 1868–69," *Canadian Historical Review* 26, 1 (1945): 25–41.

58 Charles Ritchie, *The Siren Years; A Diplomat Abroad, 1937–1945* (Toronto: Macmillan of Canada, 1974), 6. Robert MacNeil, a Nova Scotian who eventually made his fame as a journalist in the United States, recalled his family's strong cultural and emotional attachment to all things British in

the 1930s and 1940s. See his *Looking for My Country: Finding Myself in America* (New York: Random House, 2002).

59 Marcel Martel makes the point that parliamentarians in the Province of Canada referred to world affairs constantly in their debates over the Quebec scheme. Certainly, the newspapers consulted for this study confirmed that awareness. See Marcel Martel, "La clé interprétative des débats parlementaires de 1865 sur la confédération: L'équation identitaire d'Yvan Lamonde," in *Autour de l'œuvre d'Yvan Lamonde: Colonialisme et modernité au Canada depuis 1867,* edited by Claude Couture, Srilata Ravi, and François Pageau (Quebec: Presses de l'Université Laval, 2019), 29–50.

# Suggestions
# for Further Reading

This is the first book on the first test of the "mystery" of the 1867 election, surely one of the most important elections in the history of Canada. While many historians have mentioned the first Canadian election, there have been no dissertations focused on the topic. Two young historians were inspired to do some research on the topic as Canada approached its centennial. D.A. Muise's "The Federal Election of 1867 in Nova Scotia," *Collections of the Nova Scotia Historical Society* 36 (1968), was an astute look at the election in Nova Scotia, and Normand Séguin's "L'opposition canadienne-française aux élections de 1867 dans la grande région de Montréal" (MA thesis, University of Ottawa, 1968), was a perceptive thesis on the Montreal campaign. Donald Kerr covered the very technical aspects of the election in Ontario in "The 1867 Elections in Ontario: The Rules of the Game," *Canadian Historical Review* 51, 4 (1970): 369–85. Ray Argyle did not cover it in his smart survey of key elections in Canadian history, *Turning Points: The Campaigns That Changed Canada* (Toronto: White Knight Books, 2004) but cleverly included a discussion of the very important New Brunswick election of 1866. John Duffy, a public relations specialist like Argyle, wrote in his bestselling book, *Fights of Our Lives: Elections, Leadership, and the Making of Canada* (Toronto: HarperCollins, 2002), that the 1867 election was "at best a ratification of a fait accompli, if not an outright rubber stamp" of the negotiations that had taken place in Charlottetown and Quebec in 1864 and in London in 1866. In light of what Henry Olivier Lacroix wrote in that hot summer of 1867, Duffy exhibited a classic case of reading history backwards. Canada may seem like a "fait accompli" today, but it certainly was not the case in 1867. J. Murray Beck, the always insightful Nova Scotia historian, was closer to the mark in his *Pendulum of Power: Canada's Federal Elections* (Scarborough, ON: Prentice-Hall of Canada, 1968), the first comprehensive treatment of Canada's elections by a scholar. He called the election of 1867 a "victory with a question mark."

Readers may want to consult the many works I referenced in the endnotes. The *Dictionary of Canadian Biography,* available online free of charge, makes it an essential reference for anyone interested in this subject. In this section, I restrict myself to a brief discussion of the key books that are essential to a further understanding of the election of 1867.

### The Context of 1867

With the exception of Marcel Bellavance's *Le Québec et la confédération: Un choix libre?* (Quebec: Septentrion, 1992), there is precious little to read on the 1867 election. Good places to start are works that examine the act of Confederation, starting with the conference at Charlottetown in September 1864, such as Donald Creighton's *The Road to Confederation: The Emergence of Canada, 1863–1867* (Toronto: Macmillan of Canada, 1964). W.L. Morton's *The Critical Years: The Union of British North America, 1857–1873* (Toronto: McClelland and Stewart, 1964), one of the first volumes published in the Centennial Series, remains after sixty years an excellent discussion of the era. It must be read alongside P.B. Waite's *The Life and Times of Confederation (1864–1867): Politics, Newspapers and the Union of British North America* (Toronto: University of Toronto Press, 1962) and Ged Martin's *Britain and the Origins of Canadian Confederation (1837–67)* (Vancouver: UBC Press, 1995), which provides rich insights on the thinking of British politicians. Christopher Moore's *Three Weeks in Quebec City: The Meeting That Made Canada* (Toronto: Allen Lane, 2015) and *1867: How the Fathers Made a Deal* (Toronto: McClelland and Stewart, 1997) features delightfully insightful portraits of the men who negotiated the critical arrangements and the politics that carried them. For readers looking for a handy packet of scholarship on the period, the two volumes of *Roads to Confederation: The Making of Canada, 1867,* edited by Jacqueline D. Krikorian, David R. Cameron, Marcel Martel, Andrew W. McDougall, and Robert C. Vipond (Toronto: University of Toronto Press, 2017), is an invaluable resource that brings together articles written on the period over the past sixty years but published only in scholarly journals. In 2014, a small group of scholars in Quebec City organized a conference to commemorate the 1864 Quebec Agreement. They produced an exceptional

274  *Suggestions for Further Reading*

volume of essays: *The Quebec Conference of 1864: Understanding the Emergence of the Canadian Federation,* edited by Eugénie Brouillet, Alain-G. Gagnon, and Guy Laforest (Montreal and Kingston: McGill-Queen's University Press, 2018). To understand the thinking in Upper Canada, Douglas Owram's *Promise of Eden: The Canadian Expansionist Movement and the Idea of the West, 1856–1900* (Toronto: University of Toronto Press, 1980) is invaluable.

### Key Conservatives

History is about people! There are no memoirs of the period save for Charles Tupper's *Recollections of Sixty Years in Canada* (London: Cassell and Company, 1914), but it is fairly mediocre, mostly citing his own speeches with precious little context or explanation. So we must turn to biography. Creighton's more focused examination of John A. Macdonald's politics in this era remains compelling, though he manages to entirely avoid the first election. Volume 1 of his *John A. Macdonald,* titled *The Young Politician,* takes the story to July 1, 1867. Volume 2 (*The Old Chieftain*) resumes the story with the problem of cementing Nova Scotia in Confederation. Nevertheless, Creighton provides such a uniquely compelling interpretation of what was going on in Macdonald's mind that it seems all other historians fell silent on the matter. The one stellar exception was J.K. Johnson's chapter on Macdonald in J.M.S. Careless's collection *The Pre-Confederation Premiers: Ontario Government Leaders, 1841–1867* (Toronto: University of Toronto Press, 1985). Another thirty years later, Richard Gwyn produced a more Liberal version of a two-volume biography of Macdonald. It is less researched than Creighton's treatment but brings to the story an experienced modern reporter's flair for political analysis. The first volume, *John A: The Man Who Made Us* (Toronto: Random House Canada, 2007), takes the story to the final negotiations of Confederation. Volume 2, *Nation Maker; Sir John A. Macdonald: His Life, Our Times* (Toronto: Random House Canada, 2011), devotes one page to the 1867 election. For newer takes on Macdonald, I also recommend *Sir John A. Macdonald at 200: New Reflections and Legacies,* edited by Patrice Dutil and Roger Hall (Toronto: Dundurn Press, 2014). The genial Ged Martin has written about Macdonald in many places, including a very accessible short study of his career in *John A. Macdonald: Canada's First Prime Minister* (Toronto: Dundurn Press, 2013) and *Favourite Son? John A. Macdonald and the Voters of Kingston* (Kingston, ON: Kingston Historical Society, 2010). Alastair Sweeny's *George-Étienne Cartier: A Biography* (Toronto: McClelland and Stewart, 1976) captures the politics of this utterly fascinating man admirably. Brian Young's *George-Étienne Cartier: Montreal*

*Bourgeois* (Montreal and Kingston: McGill-Queen's University Press, 1981) situates him in his socio-economic milieu. David A. Wilson's *Thomas D'Arcy McGee: The Extreme Moderate, 1857–1868* (Montreal and Kingston: McGill-Queen's University Press, 2011) sheds light on how this liberal became a conservative and got involved in the 1867 election, among hundreds of other things. Andrée Désilets's *Hector-Louis Langevin: Un père de la confédération Canadienne* (Quebec: Presses de l'Université Laval, 1969) is equally rich in detail, without peer in terms of its close attention to the details of one of the most important men of the period, even if entirely forgotten today. I made use of Agnes Macdonald's diary in this book. Readers who want to know more about this intriguing woman will benefit greatly by consulting Louise Reynolds's *Agnes: The Biography of Lady Macdonald* (Montreal and Kingston: McGill-Queen's University Press, 1990).

## Key Liberals

The second volume of J.M.S. Careless's biography of George Brown, *Brown of the Globe: Statesman of Confederation, 1860–1880* (Toronto: Macmillan of Canada, 1963), provides insights of all sorts on its subject, but quickly dispatches the election. Among the Liberals, Dale Thomson's *Alexander Mackenzie: Clear Grit* (Toronto: Macmillan of Canada, 1960) captures the thinking of the Reformers of Canada West. Joseph Schull's *Laurier: The First Canadian* (Toronto: Macmillan of Canada, 1965) remains the best, most detailed treatment of the life of a young politician in 1867 who would eventually have an outsized impact on the history of his country. William M. Baker's *Timothy Warren Anglin: Irish Catholic Canadian* (Toronto: University of Toronto Press, 1977) is an excellent study of the situation in New Brunswick in this period. J. Murray Beck's two-volume biography of Joseph Howe, notably the second volume, *Joseph Howe: The Briton Becomes Canadian (1848–1873)*, is essential. J.I. Little's *Patrician Liberal: The Public and Private Life of Sir Henri-Gustave Joly de Lotbinière, 1829–1908* (Toronto: University of Toronto Press, 2013) situates the first leader of the Liberal Party of Quebec in his context. There is regrettably no biography of William McDougall, but Daniel Livermore concocted a somewhat fictionalized "memoir" that is rewarding. See his *Wandering Willie: The Memoirs of William McDougall, 1822–1905* (Burnstown, ON: Burnstown Publishing, 2020).

There is still no biography of Antoine-Aimé Dorion. For a better understanding of what was going on in the minds of the *Rouges*, Jean-Paul Bernard's *Les Rouges: Libéralisme, nationalisme et anticléricalisme au milieu*

276  *Suggestions for Further Reading*

*du XIXe siècle* (Montreal: Les Presses de l'Université du Québec, 1971) remains the best, most sweeping treatment. Yvan Lamonde's vast output is always to be consulted and the footnotes to this book are peppered with his work. His *The Social History of Ideas in Quebec* (Montreal and Kingston: McGill-Queen's University Press, 2013) and *Louis-Antoine Dessaulles (1818–1895): Un seigneur liberal et anticlérical* (Montreal: Fides, 1994) are rich in detail and shed light on the politics of the Confederation moment. Robert Rumilly's *Histoire de la province de Québec*, Volume 1, *Georges*[sic]-*Étienne Cartier* (Montreal: Éditions Bernard Valiquette, 1940), always provides unexpected details. A.I. Silver's *The French Canadian Idea of Confederation, 1864–1900* (Toronto: University of Toronto Press, 1982) is very useful.

# Index

*Note:* Page numbers with (t) refer to tables; pages with (f) refer to figures.

Acadians, 23, 55, 71, 89, 98–99, 187, 188

*Advertiser and Eastern Townships Sentinel,* 24–25

Aesop, *The Fly on the Axle,* 53

agriculture. *See* farmers

Anglin, Timothy Warren
  about, 15, 93–100, 93(f), 224
  Acadian relations, 98, 99
  anti-Confederationist, xiv, 15, 64, 77–83, 85, 87, 92–93, 97–100, 186, 224
  Dominion Day, 77–78
  election results, 184, 186, 200
  elections (1861, 1882), 94, 224
  elections (1865, 1866), 82–83, 85, 87–90, 98, 224
  election (1867), 15, 92–100, 187, 224
  Intercolonial Railway, 96–98
  Irish Catholic, 82, 93–98
  key player in New Brunswick, 224
  Liberal MP, 97–98, 215–16, 224
  *Morning Freeman* editor, xiv, 17–18, 77–80, 92–96, 224
  New Brunswick legislature, 94, 98, 224
  personal qualities, 93–96
  political labels, 98–99, 189, 215–16
  press coverage, 92–97
  Speaker of the House (1874-78), 224
  suggestions for reading, 275

Annand, William
  about, 180, 224–25
  anti-Confederationist, 170, 180, 198–200
  election (1867), 180, 182, 198–200
  *Halifax Chronicle,* 170
  key player in Nova Scotia, 200, 224–25

278    *Index*

London lobbying on Confederation, 68–69

annexationists
about, 10, 179, 213
Dorion's views, 142, 214, 248n45
Galt's views, 177
Irish Canadians, 159
McGee's views, 61–62, 159
New Brunswick's election, 81
Nova Scotia's election, 131, 176, 179
Quebec's election, 142, 147

Anti-Confederation Party. *See* Nova Scotia political parties, Anti-Confederation Party

Archibald, Adams
Charlottetown meeting (1864), 50
Confederationist, 169, 175
election (1867), 185, 197, 199
Liberal opposition, 50
Macdonald's cabinet, 73–74, 199, 205, 211

Argyle, Ray, 272

Bachand, Pierre, 140
Baier, Gerald, vii–xi
Baker, William M., 275
Beck, J. Murray, 185, 190, 194, 273, 275
Bellavance, Marcel, 22, 140–41, 244n37, 273
Belleau, Narcisse, 112, 135, 220
belonging. *See* identity
Bernard, Agnes. *See* Macdonald, Agnes Bernard (John's wife)
Bernard, Hewitt (Agnes's brother), 55, 66, 67, 230

Bernard, Jean-Paul, 190–91, 260n29, 260n32, 267nn12–13, 275–76
Blair, Adam Fergusson, 72–73, 115, 117–18, 205, 214
Blake, Edward
about, 120–21, 225
elections (1867, 1871), 120–21, 184, 197, 225
key player in Ontario, 225
Reform Party, 115, 120–21
Blanchard, Hiram, 170, 200, 206
*Bleus,* as label, 14
BNA Act. *See* British North America Act (1867)
border defence. *See* defence
*Botheration Letters* (Howe), 59, 174, 236
Bourget, Ignace, 138, 261n48
Bowmanville (ON), Brown-Macdonald showdown, 128–31
Britain. *See* United Kingdom
*British Chronicle* (newspaper), 41–42
British Columbia
annexation fears, 69–70, 237
Confederation vision to include, 48, 58, 69–70, 127, 206, 237
joins Confederation (July 1871), 239
lack of interest in Confederation, 34
British North America Act (1867)
Catholic education, 111
Quebec Resolutions as basis, 237
railway (s. 145), 66, 81–82, 91
royal assent (March 1867), 70, 237
Brouillet, Eugénie, 273–74
Brown, George
about, 41–42, 41(f), 212–17, 225

anti-Catholicism, 34, 42, 109, 110, 119, 120, 139, 145, 213
career overview, 42, 225
coalition of Liberals/*Rouges*/anti-Confederationists, 5–7, 102, 183
Francophobic rhetoric, 34, 120
key player in Ontario, 225
Lanctôt on, 150, 157
personal qualities, 42, 112–14, 118, 120, 129–31, 212, 213–14
post-election politics, 212–17, 225
suggestions for reading, 275
views on Macdonald, 68, 114–15, 117, 119–20
views on Nova Scotia's secessionism, 209–10
*See also* Toronto (ON), *Globe* (newspaper)
Brown, George, Confederation (1864–67)
Charlottetown meeting (1864), 112
London meetings (1865, 1867), 68, 83, 112
pre-Confederation support for federalism, 33–34, 112
Quebec Conference (1864) and aftermath, 55–56, 59–60
*See also* Ontario, Confederation (1864–67)
Brown, George, election (1867)
about, xiv, 5–7, 15–16, 112–31, 184
anti-Confederationist, 122, 212
bribery and intimidation, 20–21
candidate, 118–20, 128–31, 184, 194, 205, 215, 216
Catholic voters, 119–20, 139
defeat, 184, 194, 205, 212, 215

his coalition of Liberals/*Rouges*/anti-Confederationists, 5–7, 102, 183
Liberal/Reform Party, 115, 117–18, 124–25, 212–17
Liberals, as label, 13–14
McDougall's attacks on, 123–28
platform, 119–22, 127–28
predictions, 120
press coverage, 118–19, 121–22, 130–31
railways, 81, 119–20
rationale for not running for office earlier, 113–14, 117–18
Reform Party founder (1867), 113–17, 225, 238
rivalry with Liberals, 113, 119–20
rivalry with Macdonald, 128–31
*See also* Ontario, election (1867); Ontario, election (1867), results; Ontario political parties, Liberal/Reform Party
Brown, John Young, 195
Brown, Peter (George's father), 41–42
Buies, Arthur, 148–49

Caisse, François-Xavier, 140
Cameron, David R., 273
Campbell, Alexander, 72–73
Campion, Augustin-Siméon, 140
Canada, Province of. *See* United Province (1841–67)
*Canada Farmer* (weekly paper), 123
Canada Party. *See* Nova Scotia political parties, Canada Party/Unionists
Cardwell, Edward, 64, 84
Careless, J.M.S., 114, 274, 275

280  *Index*

Carnarvon, Lord, 66, 69, 249*n*51
Carter, Frederic Bowker T., 247*n*29
Cartier, George-Étienne
  about, 42–44, 43(f), 134–37,
    225–26
  Companion of the Order of the
    Bath, 70–71
  Grand Trunk Railway lawyer, 134
  key player in Quebec, 225–26
  *La Minerve* (newspaper), 17–18,
    135, 153, 157
  Macdonald's coalition, 72, 106
  personal qualities, 42–44, 134
  political career, 42–44, 226, 258*n*7
  rebellions (1837–38), 43
  Rupert's Land acquisition, 222
  secessionism, 210–11
  suggestions for reading, 274–75
Cartier, George-Étienne, Confederation (1864–67)
  Charlottetown meeting (1864), 51
  London Conference (1866–67),
    67, 68, 83
  Quebec Conference (1864), 55–56
  views on Confederation, 33, 42–
    43, 62–63
Cartier, George-Étienne, election
  (1867)
  about, xiv, 15, 134–37, 164
  Catholic voters, 138, 139
  cost, 244*n*32
  debate with Lanctôt, 157–58
  intimidation and bribery, 21, 139,
    141, 158
  press coverage, 189
  results, 205
Cartwright, Richard, 60, 90, 204
Carty, R. Kenneth, vii–xi

Catholics
  about, 137–41, 145, 200
  Acadians, 23, 55, 71, 89, 98–99,
    187, 188
  *Bleus* and *Rouges,* 14, 141
  Brown's anti-Catholicism, 34,
    42, 109, 110, 119, 120, 139,
    145, 213
  Confederation support, 96–97,
    137–41, 145–46, 148, 157
  demographics (1860s), 29
  election results, 200
  identity and belonging, 11–12
  intimidation and bribery, 21, 22,
    138–41, 216–17
  Irish Catholics, 93–98
  Macdonald's relations, 105–6, 109–
    12, 119, 139
  marriage issues, 139
  oaths of allegiance, 23, 89, 245*n*41
  press coverage, 140–41
  school systems, 111, 136, 139
  ultra-montanism, xvi, 7
Cauchon, Joseph-Édouard, 22,
  135–37
Chapais, Jean-Charles, 55, 72, 74,
  139, 163–64
Chapleau, Adolphe, 158, 161
Charlottetown Conference (1864)
  about, 49–52, 235
  aftermath talks, 52–54
  delegations, 50–51, 55, 235
  historical locations, 8
  political issues, 51–52
  press coverage, 50
  *Queen Victoria* (ship), 8, 50, 51
  railroads issue, 49–50, 52
  suggestions for reading, 273

wheels, flies, and flywheels, 53, 58, 74–75

*Charlottetown Examiner,* 50, 179

Chauveau, Pierre J.O.
about, 136–37, 226
election (1867, 1871), 162, 191, 193
key player in Quebec, 226
Macdonald's coalition, 208
Quebec premier, 147, 162, 193

Christianity. *See* Catholics; Protestants

Clarke, Macneil, 16–17

Clear Grits movement. *See* Ontario political parties, Grits and Clear Grits movement

Clerk, George-Edward, 145–46, 157

communications
about, 25, 30–31
few photos, 7
telegraphs, xiii, 30
*See also* newspapers

Confederate, as term, 243n18

Confederation
about, xiv, 26
British ancestry, 28–29
Catholic support, 96–97, 137–41, 145–46, 148, 157
demographics (1860s), 28–29
Dominion Day celebrations, 70–75
economy, 12, 26, 29–31
as an election issue, 168
historical context in provinces, 35–49, 59
historical locations, 8–9, 9(f), 11(f)
key players list, 224–34
lack of participation by Newfoundland and PEI, 26, 50, 63, 66, 127

motivations of founders, 12, 26, 206
national vision, 3–4, 6, 12, 67, 206, 222–23
nationalists vs provincialists, 9–12
political stability, 12, 27–28
power of an idea, 12, 218, 219, 223
timeline of events, 235–39
United Province overview, 31–35
wheels, flies, and flywheels, 53, 58, 74–75
*See also* United Province (1841–67)

Confederation, first election. *See* election (1867); election (1867), United States and global influences

Confederation, first government. *See* Macdonald, John A., government coalition (Liberal-Conservative/Conservative/ *Bleus*)

Confederation, first Parliament. *See* Parliament, first (1867), House of Commons; Parliament, first (1867), Senate

Confederation, meetings. *See* Charlottetown Conference (1864); London Conference (1866–67); Quebec Conference (1864)

Confederation, provinces. *See* New Brunswick, Confederation (1864–67); Nova Scotia, Confederation (1864–67); Ontario, Confederation (1864–67); Quebec, Confederation (1864–67)

## Index

Connell, Charles, 187
Connolly, Thomas-Louis, 21, 175, 226
Conservatives
  diverging opinions, 14
  election results, 2(f), 5–6, 183, 240(t), 241(t)
  Macdonald's coalition (Liberal-Conservative/Conservative/*Bleus*), 5–7, 102, 183
  party labels as confusing, 185–86, 203–4
  Tory, as label, 14
Cooke, Thomas, 138–39
Coram, Joseph, 79
Costigan, John, 187, 188
Creighton, Donald, 273–74
Cudlip, J.W., 81
Currier, Joseph Merrill, 20, 196

Daoust, Charles, 150
David, Laurent-Olivier, 153, 158
Dawson, John William, 133–34
defence
  British report (1864), 54
  Fenian scare in New Brunswick and Nova Scotia, 86–90, 236
  identity and belonging, 12
  of Maritimes by British, 81, 84
  militias, 81, 86, 89
  railways for, 54
  St. Albans raiders (1864), 56–57, 59, 160, 235
  US Civil War impacts, 53–54, 56–57, 207
  *See also* Fenianism
Denison, George Taylor, 104
Désilet, Andrée, 275

Dessaulles, Louis-Antoine, 142–43, 276
Devlin, Bernard, 159–62
Dominion Day (July 1), celebrations, 7, 70–77, 100–2, 132–33, 165–66
Dorion, Antoine-Aimé
  about, 44–46, 45(f), 214–15, 226–27
  annexationist, 142, 214, 248n45
  Association de la réforme du Bas-Canada, 146
  candidate, 146, 184, 189, 205
  Confederation acceptance, 15, 144, 146, 148, 214–15, 216
  declined Confederation talks, 46, 144
  election (1867), xiv, 15, 145–49, 214–15
  key player in Quebec, 226–27
  *Le Pays* (newspaper), 17–18, 44–45, 142–43, 147
  personal qualities, 44–45, 150
  *Rouge* leader, 141–49, 189, 214–15
  suggestions for reading, 275–76
  views on politics, 15, 34, 44–45, 143–44
  views on Quebec City accord, 64
Doutre, Gonzalve, 150, 155
Doutre, Joseph, 146, 189
Dowd, Patrick, 24
Drew, Alexander and George, 103, 254n4
Drummond, Lewis, 34, 143
Duffy, John, 272
Durham, Lord, 32, 150, 153, 157
Dutil, Patrice, xii–xv, 274

*Eastern Chronicle* (newspaper),
168–70, 177, 181
economy
about, 29–31
Bank of Montreal as banker, 96,
119, 217
barriers to growth, 30–31
pre-Confederation, 31–35
railroads as foundation, 35, 206
shipbuilding, 30
*See also* railways
education
Catholic and Protestant systems,
111, 136, 139
provincial jurisdiction, 134
election (1867)
about, xv, 5–9, 15–18, 202–8,
217–22
aftermath, 217–23
anniversary celebrations, 8
Brown's coalition (Liberals/
*Rouges*/anti-Confederationists),
5–7, 183
elections before, 19–20
few photos of, 7
identity forces, xiv, 6–7, 9–16
Macdonald's coalition (Liberal-
Conservative/Conservative/
*Bleus*), 5–7, 102, 183
mystery of Canada as a nation,
3–4, 6, 223
newspapers overview, xiii, 17–
18, 25
political party labels, 13–16, 185–
86, 203
"politics of the possible," 204
as referendum on Confederation,
6–7, 102, 202–4

suggestions for further reading,
272–76
timeline of events, 235–39
turning point election, xv, 219
*See also* election (1867), United
States and global influences
election (1867), electoral system
about, 18–25, 219
announcements, 18–19, 183, 238
candidate in more than one
riding, 19
dual representation (provincial
and federal legislatures), 19,
193, 219
intimidation and bribery, 18–25
lack of records, 19–20
oaths of allegiance, 23, 89, 245n41
polling days and schedules, 18–
19, 25, 166, 219, 238
polling stations, 23
reforms (1874), 219
returning officers, 23
secret ballots, 18, 90, 100, 219,
243n25
voter qualifications, 21
election (1867), results
about, 5–7, 183–86, 203–4
acclamations, 183–84
aftermath, 217–23
announcements, 18–19, 183, 238
Brown's coalition (Liberals/*Rouges*/
anti-Confederationists), 5–7,
183
Liberals, as label, 13–14
Liberals as opposition, 185–86
Macdonald's coalition (Liberal-
Conservative/Conservative/
*Bleus*), 5–7, 183, 185–86, 203–4

284 *Index*

official report excludes party affiliation, 185

by party, 2(f), 240(t), 241(t)

party labels as confusing, 185–86, 203–4

percent of seats, 240(t)

popular vote, 241(t)

by province, 240(t), 241(t)

as referendum on Confederation, 202–4

seat count, 183, 240(t)

turnout, 183, 241(t)

*See also* Macdonald, John A., government coalition (Liberal-Conservative/Conservative/*Bleus*)

election (1867), United States and global influences

Alaska purchase, 69–70

annexationists, 10, 59, 61–63, 65, 69–70, 207

border security, 54–55, 56–57, 59

Civil War, 4, 27–28, 53, 56–57, 59, 207, 243*n*18

Fenianism, 86–90, 159–62, 232, 236

Germany and Italy as new countries, 22, 206

immigration from United States, 27, 61

Loyalist ideology, 61, 169, 246*n*15

St. Albans Confederate raiders, 56–57, 59, 160, 235

UK-US reciprocity treaty, 59–60, 65, 207

US military strength, 207

US model for federalism, 32

election (1872), 212, 216, 217

election (1874), 219

electors. *See* voters

*Erie News* (newspaper), 122

Évanturel, François, 135

Ewart, John S., 219

fables, 53, 207

farmers

demographics (1860s), 29

MP professions, 184, 188, 193, 196, 199–200

newspapers, 123–24

Farrell, John, 111

Farris, John, 187

federalism

about, 31–35

local vs national issues, 15, 33

popular in Canada East, 32

pre-Confederation proposals, 31–35

US model, 32

Fenianism

habeas corpus, 159

Montreal politics, 160–61, 232

New Brunswick politics, 86–90, 236

as threat, 90

transnational belonging, 7

Filion-Montpetit, Marie-Marthe, 154, 261*n*54

Fisher, Charles, 84–85, 87, 187

Fleming, Sandford, 165–66

*Flora Observer* (newspaper), 221

*The Fly on the Axle* (Aesop), 53

*Franco-Canadien* (newspaper), 212

Fredericton (NB), 9, 11(f), 76

*Fredericton Headquarter* (newspaper), 81, 215–16, 269*n*38

**Index** 285

Gagnon, Alain-G., 273–74
Galt, Alexander T.
  about, 51, 227
  annexationist, 177
  awards and honours, 70–71
  British ties, 83
  Charlottetown meeting (1864), 51
  election (1867), 119, 145
  key player in Quebec, 227
  London Conference (1866–67),
    66–67, 83
  Macdonald's cabinet, 72, 204, 205
  Protestant, 72
  Quebec Conference (1864), 55, 57
GAPOC (Grande association de
  protection des ouvriers du
  Canada), 154–57, 218, 229, 237
Garner, John, 245n41
Geoffrion, Félix, 190, 193
Gibbs, Thomas, 118, 126–27, 128–
  30, 194
Gladstone, William, 13, 54, 66, 70,
  209
global influences. *See* election
  (1867), United States and
  global influences
Gordon. *See* Hamilton-Gordon,
  Arthur
Gowan, James R., 57
Grand Trunk Railway. *See* railways,
  Grand Trunk Railway
Grande association de protection
  des ouvriers du Canada
  (GAPOC), 154–57, 218, 229,
  237
Gray, John Hamilton (NB), 50, 88,
  187
Gray, John Hamilton (PEI), 49, 52

Gray, John (on Prescott incident),
  16, 243n19
Grits and Clear Grits movement. *See*
  Ontario political parties, Grits
  and Clear Grits movement
Groulx, Lionel, 14, 164
Guy Fawkes Day, 58–59
Gwyn, Richard, 274

Halifax (NS)
  Charlottetown Conference after-
    math, 52–54
  Confederationists, 167–68
  economy, 49–50, 167
  election results, 199
  Province House, 8
  *Weekly Citizen,* 176, 177
  *See also* Nova Scotia
Halifax *Morning Chronicle*
  anti-Confederation views, 175–77,
    198
  *Botheration Letters,* 59, 174, 236
  Dominion Day, 165
  election results, 184–85, 198
Hall, Roger, 274
Hamilton-Gordon, Arthur
  about, 35–37, 36(f)
  dislike of petty politics, 35, 37,
    247n16
  Fenian scare (1866), 86–87
  Intercolonial Railway, 37, 52
  Lieutenant-Governor of New
    Brunswick, 35–36, 49–50,
    83–87, 236
  Maritime Union idea, 37, 84,
    247n16
Hannay, James, 95
Harvey, Louis-Georges, 261n40

286   *Index*

Hatheway, George L., 81, 82
HBC (Hudson's Bay Company), 59,
  64, 67, 127, 238
Hill, Philip Carteret, 206
historiography, 7–9, 272–76
Hogarth, William, *The Polling*
  (painting), 22, 23(f)
Holton, Luther
  about, 228
  anti-Confederationist, 145, 147
  Brown's contact for Quebec, 116–
    20, 131, 143, 147
  election, 184, 189
  key player in Quebec, 228
  leader of English wing of *Rouges*,
    143, 147
Horan, John, 111
House of Commons. *See* Parliament,
  first (1867), House of Commons
Howe, Joseph
  about, 169–75, 172(f), 227–28
  British ties, 169, 171–74, 227
  Catholic voters, 167, 171, 175
  election (1840, 1848, 1857, 1860),
    173
  election (1863), 167
  key player in Nova Scotia,
    227–28
  Liberal Reformers, 167
  Macdonald's cabinet, 182, 205,
    211–12, 269n24
  newspapers, 17–18, 171, 227
  party labels, 13
  personal qualities, 171, 211–12
  secessionism, 208–12
  suggestions for reading, 275
Howe, Joseph, Confederation
  (1864–67)

anti-Confederationist, 153, 167,
  173–74
*Botheration Letters*, 59, 174,
  236
lobbying in London, 68–69, 70,
  174
pre-Confederation proposal for
  federalism, 32
Howe, Joseph, election (1867)
  about, xiv–xv, 5–6, 15, 170–75,
    227–28
  aftermath, 218, 220
  Anti-Confederation Party, xiv–xv,
    5–6, 174–75
  anti-Confederationist, 15, 128,
    131, 166–67, 170–77, 214, 220
  bitter campaign, 179–82
  candidate, 180–82
  Nova Scotia Party, 174
  political views, 170–77
  predictions, 181–82
  results, 6, 184, 197–200, 204
Howland, William Pearce
  cabinet, 72–73, 205
  Companion of the Order of the
    Bath, 70–71
  Macdonald's coalition, 72–73,
    118, 124–25, 205, 214
  personal qualities, 73, 94
  Reform Party (ON), 115–16,
    117–18
Hoyles, Hugh W., 50
Hudson's Bay Company (HBC), 59,
  64, 67, 127, 238
*The Humours of an Election III: The
  Polling* (painting, Hogarth), 22,
  23(f)
Huntington, Lucius Seth, 145

## Index    287

identity
   about, xiv, 6–7, 9–16
   British ties, 7, 79, 83, 270n58
   francophones, 11–12
   internecine election contests,
      6–7, 223
   national unity, 10, 62–63, 166–67
   regional and provincial identity,
      xiv, 6–7
   religious identity, 7, 11–12
   transnational issues, 6–7, 10
   See also Fenianism
Indian Island (NB), 86, 236
Indigenous peoples
   federal jurisdiction in Constitu-
      tion, 56
   as voters, 21, 244n35
Institut Canadien
   about, 3–4
   Confederation views, 4, 61, 147,
      149, 155
   Lacroix as member, 3–4, 61, 228,
      242n3
   Lanctôt as member, 149, 154–55,
      228, 229, 242n3
intimidation and bribery of voters,
      19–25, 129, 140–41, 158, 161–
      64, 181
Irish Canadians
   annexationists, 159
   Fenianism, 7, 86–90, 160–61, 232
   New Era, 159
   transnational belonging, 7
   See also Fenianism
Iroquois of Kahnawake, 132–33

Jervois, William, 54
Johnson, J.K., 274

Joly de Lotbinière, Henri-Gustave,
      147–48, 193, 229, 275
Jones, Alfred Gilpin, 198, 199,
      266n1

Kamouraska (QC), 162–64, 185
Kenny, Edward, 71–73, 106, 110,
      160, 197, 210–11
key players list, 224–34
Kierzkowski, Alexandre-Édouard,
      140
Kingston (ON), 102
Krikorian, Jacqueline D., 273

La Fontaine, Louis-Hippolyte, 43,
      136, 226
La Minerve (newspaper), 61, 75,
      135, 150, 153, 157
La Presse (newspaper), 150–51,
      229
labour movement, 154–58, 218,
      229, 237
Lacroix, Henry Olivier
   about, 3–5, 228
   on Acadianism, 98
   Institut Canadien, 3–4, 61, 228,
      242n3
   key player in Quebec, 228
   mystery of Canada as a nation,
      3–4, 6, 223
   power of an idea, 4, 10, 12, 218,
      219, 223
   The Present and Future of
      Canada, 3–5, 12, 213, 242n3
Laflèche, Louis-François, 138
Laforest, Guy, 273–74
Laframboise, Maurice, 140, 146
Lamonde, Yvan, 276

288 *Index*

Lanctôt, Médéric
about, 149–58, 155(f), 218, 229
Association de la réforme du
Bas-Canada, 146
British ties, 154
city council (1866–67), 152–54,
156, 157
education, 150, 229
GAPOC labour organization,
154–58, 218, 229, 237
Institut Canadien, 149, 154–55,
229
key player in Quebec, 229
*L'indépendance pacifique du
Canada,* 154
marriage and family, 150
nationalists, 150–52, 157
newspaper editor (*La Presse* and
*Le Pays*), 149–51, 229
newspaper editor (*L'Union
Nationale*), 17–18, 146, 151,
152–54, 156, 212–13, 229
personal qualities, 149, 153, 158
post-election decline, 212–13, 229
pre-Confederation support for
federalism, 33, 150
*Rouge,* 15, 146, 151–52, 212–13
views on Brown, 34, 150, 157
views on Confederation, 150–54,
157, 229
Lanctôt, Médéric, election (1867)
about, 15, 149–58, 155(f)
activism, 152, 154–58, 218
candidate, 152–54, 156–58, 189
Catholic influence, 140
Confederation views, 15, 149–56
defeat, 189
radical Liberal, 146, 151–52

Langevin, Edmond, 138–39
Langevin, Hector-Louis
Confederationist, 138
London Conference (1866–67),
66–67, 258n7
Macdonald's cabinet, 72–74
Quebec Conference (1864), 55
suggestions for reading, 275
Langevin, Jean, 138–39
Larocque, Charles, 139–40
Laurier, Wilfrid, 148, 152–53, 191,
275
*Le Canadien* (newspaper), 135
*Le Courrier de Saint-Hyacinthe*
(newspaper), 34, 135, 145, 147,
149, 150, 261n54
*Le Défricheur* (newspaper), 145,
191
*Le Franco-Canadien* (newspaper),
147
*Le Journal de Québec* (newspaper),
135
*Le Moniteur Acadien,* 98
*Le Pays. See* Montreal (QC), news-
papers, *Le Pays*
League of the Maritime Provinces
(NS), 236
Letellier de Saint-Just, Luc, 163
Liberal-Conservative
election results, 2(f), 5–6, 183,
240(t), 241(t)
Macdonald's coalition (Liberal-
Conservative/Conservative/
*Bleus*), 5–7, 102, 183
party labels as confusing, 185–86,
203–4
United Province, use of coalition
label, 14

*See also* Macdonald, John A.,
government coalition (Liberal-
Conservative/Conservative/
*Bleus*)
Liberals
about, 13–14, 116, 184–86
acclamation, 184
British historical ties, 13
Clear Grit movement, 116
diverging opinions, 14, 115
election aftermath, 217–23
election results, 2(f), 5–6, 183,
240(t), 241(t)
as official opposition, 6
as party label, 13–14
party labels as confusing, 185–86,
203–4
provincial rights rhetoric, 217
relationships with French Canadians, 116
relationships with Reformers, 116
suggestions for reading, 275–76
Little, J.I, 275
Livermore, Daniel, 275
London (ON), 102
London, British government. *See*
United Kingdom
London Conference (1866–67)
about, 64–70, 69(f), 237
acquisition of Rupert's Land and
NWT, 64, 67
annexation fears, 67
British ties, 83
Canada as name, 237
defence cost-sharing agreement,
64
delegations, 64, 66, 83, 112, 236,
237

Intercolonial Railway, 66, 91
Macdonald's central role, 66
national vision, 67
Quebec Resolutions as basis for
BNA Act, 66–70, 237
timeline, 236–38
US-UK reciprocity treaty cancel-
lation, 64, 65, 207
*L'Ordre* (newspaper), 146, 147, 157
*L'Union Nationale. See* Montreal
(QC), newspapers, *L'Union
Nationale*
Lusignan, Alfred, 146
Lynch, John Joseph, 109–11, 229–30

Macdonald, Agnes Bernard (John's
wife)
about, 67–68, 230
brother (Hewitt), 67–68
diary entries, 103–8, 120, 201–2,
221
key player in Ontario, 230
personal qualities, 104
suggestions for reading, 275
Macdonald, John A.
about, 39–40, 40(f), 204–8, 230
key player in Ontario, 230
knighthood, 70–71
marriage to Agnes, 67–68
newspaper, 17–18
personal qualities, 39–40, 103–5,
120, 204–5, 210, 211–12, 220
political career, 39–40, 40(f), 230
Protestants, 72, 105
railway scandal, 216
rebellions (1837–38), 41
reconciliation of Catholics and
Protestants, 111–12

290   *Index*

Scottish, 39, 105
suggestions for reading, 274
United Province co-premier
(1858–62), 33, 39, 226
*See also* Macdonald, Agnes
Bernard (John's wife); Macdonald, John A., government
coalition (Liberal-Conservative/
Conservative/*Bleus*)
Macdonald, John A., Confederation
(1864–67)
broadening of support, 64, 84–85
Charlottetown meeting (1864), 51
London Conference (1866–67),
66–70, 83
post-Charlottetown talks, 52
post–Quebec City talks, 61
views on annexation threat, 63
views on Intercolonial Railway,
54, 58, 66
views on new nation, 52–55, 65
wheels, flies, and flywheels, 53,
58, 74–75
Macdonald, John A., election (1867)
about, xiv, 5–7, 15–16, 102–3,
128–31, 201–2
aftermath, 217–23
"big tent" party, 109–10, 205
Catholics, 109–12, 119, 139
coalition (Liberal-Conservative/
Conservative/*Bleus*), 5–7, 102,
183
criticisms of coalitions, 121–22
electoral system preparations, 103
funds for candidates, 216
influence on candidates, 103–4,
254n4
lack of personal records, 201–2

predictions, 75
as referendum on Confederation,
108–9, 202–4
rivalry with Brown, 109, 120,
128–31
travels, 108–9
Macdonald, John A., election (1867),
results
about, 5–7, 184–86, 202–8
acclamations, 184
aftermath, 217–23
coalition (Liberal-Conservative/
Conservative/*Bleus*), 5–7, 102,
183
party labels as confusing, 185–86,
203–4
as referendum on Confederation,
202–4
results by province, 2(f), 5–6, 183,
240(t), 241(t)
wins, 196
Macdonald, John A., government
coalition (Liberal-Conservative/
Conservative/*Bleus*)
about, 5–7, 105–9, 204–5
cabinet of rivals, 71–75, 204–5
Catholics and Protestants, 71–73
coalition government, 5–7, 10,
14, 71–75
election (1872) and after, 212,
217–23
first session, 220–23, 222(f)
Liberals, as label, 13–14
Nova Scotia's secessionism,
210–12
political parties and labels, 14
as prime minister, 204
senators, 73

Speech from the Throne, 220

Macdonald, Sandfield
about, 106–7, 230–31
Catholic, 107, 230
Confederationist, 107, 210
co-premier of United Province (1862–64), 34, 107, 226, 230
election (1867) for dual representation, 109, 123, 231
key player in Ontario, 230–31
Macdonald's coalition, 107, 109, 208, 231
personal qualities, 102, 107
premier of Ontario, 107, 197, 230–31
press coverage, 119, 197
rivalry with Brown, 107, 123

MacDonnell, Richard Graves, 49, 86

Mackenzie, Alexander
about, 231
attacks on opponents, 17, 124–25
elections (1862, 1867, 1874), 125–26, 184, 231
key player in Ontario, 231
Liberals, as label, 13
McDougall's attacks on, 125–26
newspaper editor, 231
personal qualities, 126
prime minister, 216, 231
Reform Party (ON), 115, 117–18, 231
suggestions for reading, 275

MacNab, Allan, 34

MacNeil, Robert, 270n58

*Manifeste des 20,* 144

Manitoba
joins Confederation (July 1870), 239

Maritimes
border security, 61, 81, 84, 89, 145–46
industrial associations, 60
Loyalist ideology, 61, 169, 246n15
Maritime Rights movement, 218
Maritime union idea, 37, 65–66, 79, 83–84, 88, 235
shipbuilding, 30
tariff protections, 60
*See also* New Brunswick; Newfoundland; Nova Scotia; Prince Edward Island

Martel, Joseph, 163

Martel, Marcel, 271n59, 273

Martin, Ged, 26, 274

Massue, Gaspard-Aimé, 190

McCarthy, John, 16–17

McDougall, Andrew W., 273

McDougall, William
about, 16, 73, 123–28, 125(f), 231–32
anti-Brown campaign, 16, 123–28, 231
Clear Grit movement, 106, 116, 123–25, 231
Companion of the Order of the Bath, 70–71
Confederation conferences, 67, 124, 231
election (1867), 16, 121, 123–28, 131
key player in Ontario, 231–32
Macdonald's cabinet, 16, 72–73, 106, 231
Macdonald's coalition, 16, 106, 118, 124–25, 214
personal qualities, 102, 123, 124

292   *Index*

Reform Party, 116, 117–18, 126–27
Rupert's Land Lieutenant-
  Governor, 222–23, 231
suggestions for reading, 275
McGee, Thomas D'Arcy
  about, 159–62, 214, 232
  annexationist, 61–62, 159
  bribery of voters, 21
  Confederation conferences, 51,
    160, 232
  Confederation views, 61, 143
  election (1867), 74, 159–62, 189,
    232, 263n81
  Irish Catholic, 51, 94, 97, 159–62,
    177, 232
  key player in Quebec, 232
  Macdonald's cabinet, 74, 160, 214
  personal qualities, 159–60, 162,
    232
  press coverage, 97, 161–62
  suggestions for reading, 275
McGill University, 133–34
McGillivray, Edward, 20
McLelan, A.W., 199
McMaster, William, 115
Methodists, 19, 29, 72
military defence. *See* defence
Mitchell, Peter
  about, 87
  Confederationist, 74, 87–89
  elections (1865, 1866, 1867),
    87–90
  Macdonald's cabinet, 72, 74, 189,
    214
  personal qualities, 87, 89
  premier of New Brunswick
    (1866–67), 87, 91, 236
  secessionism, 210–11

senator (1867), 91, 189, 210
Monck, Lord, Governor General,
  70–71, 85, 220, 232
Montreal (QC)
  demographics, 132
  Dominion Day celebrations,
    132–33
  election (1867), 159–62, 193
  Fenianism, 7, 160–61, 232
  GAPOC labour organization,
    154–58, 218, 229, 237
  industrial associations, 60
  Irish Catholics, 159–62
  labour activism, 154–56
  McGee-Devlin contest, 159–62
  McGill University, 133–34
  poverty, 149
  regional results, 193
  *Rouge* party decline, 143–44
  *See also* Institut Canadien
Montreal (QC), newspapers
  about, 17–18, 147
  *La Minerve (Bleus)*, 61, 75, 135,
    150, 153, 157
  *La Presse* (newspaper), 150–51,
    229
  *La Vérité (Bleus)*, 157
  *L'Ordre (Rouge)*, 146, 147, 157
  *Montreal Herald* (Liberal, Grit),
    145, 147, 155, 211, 220–21
  *Quebec Gazette* (English), 20, 123,
    130, 135, 191, 214
  *True Witness* (English Catholic),
    145, 147, 157
  *Witness* (Protestant), 147
Montreal (QC), newspapers, *Le Pays*
  Catholic influence, 140–41,
    216–17

Confederationists, 146–47
Dorion as founder, 44–45, 142,
  149–50
editors, 146, 149–50, 229
federalism, 33, 143
post-election decline, 212
*Rouge* party organ, 33, 142–43,
  212
Montreal (QC), newspapers, *L'Union
  Nationale*
anti-Confederationist, 146–47,
  151, 152–54, 229
labour movement, 154–56
McGee-Devlin fight, 161
post-election decline, 212–13
Moore, Christopher, 273
*Morning Freeman* (newspaper), xiv,
  75, 77, 92–97, 99, 224
Morton, W.L., 273
Mousseau, Joseph-Alfred, 134–35
Muise, D.A., 199–200, 272

New Brunswick
Acadians, 23, 55, 71, 89, 98–99,
  187, 188
by-election (1865), 84–85
Catholics, 77, 89–90, 96–99, 111,
  200
*Daily Evening Globe,* 90–91, 93, 95
demographics, 76
Dominion Day celebrations, 76
economy, 29–31, 96, 99–100
election (1870, 1872), 189, 212,
  217
Fenianism, 7, 86–90, 236
francophones, 11–12, 98–99
Hamilton-Gordon as Lt.-Gov,
  35–36, 36(f), 80, 83–87

Intercolonial Railway, 37, 52, 79,
  81–82, 91, 95–98
Liberals, as label, 13–14
Lieutenant-Governors, 35, 49–50,
  71, 80, 84, 233
Maritime Union idea, 37
*Morning Freeman,* xiv, 75, 77, 92–
  97, 99, 224
nationalists vs provincialists, 9–10
newspapers overview, 17–18
party labels, 215–16
Province Hall building (1870),
  11(f)
regional newspapers, 50
timeline of events, 235–39
*See also* Fredericton (NB); St.
  John (NB)
New Brunswick, about key players
overview, xiv, 15, 224–34
Timothy Anglin, xiv, 93(f), 224
Albert Smith, xiv, 232–33
Leonard Tilley, xiv, 38(f), 233
*See also* Anglin, Timothy Warren;
  Smith, Albert James; Tilley,
  Leonard
New Brunswick, Confederation
  (1864–67)
about, 35–39, 63
Charlottetown meeting (1864),
  49–52, 235
historical context (1864), 27–31
Liberal Party civil war, 78
London Conference (1866–67), 83
Quebec Conference (1864), 57,
  63, 235
Tilley's pro-Confederation
  government, 37–39, 38(f), 63,
  236

294   *Index*

New Brunswick, elections (1865
    and 1866)
  about, 78–90
  annexationists, 81
  anti-Catholic sentiment, 82, 85, 89
  anti-Confederationists, 78–80,
    82–85
  by-election (1865), 84–85, 87
  Catholics, 82, 85, 89–90, 200
  Confederation issues, 78–85
  election (1865), 78–79, 80–83,
    100, 186
  election (1866) and after, 78, 86–
    90, 100, 237
  Fenianism, 7, 86–90, 236
  Smith's government (1865–66),
    84–86
New Brunswick, election (1867)
  about, xiv, 5–7, 15, 90–100,
    187–89
  Acadians, 89, 98–99, 187, 188
  aftermath, 217–23
  anti-Confederationists, 15, 91–
    92, 95–96, 99–100, 186, 237
  Brown's coalition (Liberals/
    *Rouges*/anti-Confederationists),
    5–7, 183
  campaign issues, 96–98, 99–100
  Catholics, 96–97, 111
  Confederationists, xiv, 15, 91–93,
    187
  Intercolonial Railway, 96–98
  intimidation and bribery, 19–25
  Liberals, xiv, 13–14, 15, 78, 187,
    212–17
  Macdonald's coalition (Liberal-
    Conservative/Conservative/
    *Bleus*), 5–7

  party labels, 13–14, 99, 188–89
  predictions, 75, 187
  press coverage, 92–96, 98–99
  as referendum on Confederation,
    100, 202–4
  Reformers, 114
New Brunswick, election (1867),
    results
  about, 5–7, 186–89, 203–4
  acclamations, 184, 187
  aftermath, 217–23
  anti-Confederationists, 5, 186
  Brown's coalition, 5–7
  by-elections after, 90
  Conservatives, 186–88
  four-way races, 188
  independent/unidentified, 187–88
  Liberal-Conservatives, 186–87,
    212
  Liberals, 5, 186–88, 203–4, 223
  Macdonald's coalition, 5–7, 185,
    187, 214
  MP professions, 188
  overview, 2(f), 240(t), 241(t)
  by party, 2(f), 240(t), 241(t)
  party labels as confusing, 185–86,
    203–4
  popular vote, 186–88, 241(t)
  post-election "provincial rights"
    rhetoric, 217
  by province, 2(f), 240(t), 241(t)
  as referendum on Confederation,
    202–4
  seats, 2(f), 186–87, 240(t)
  turnout, 187, 241(t)
New Brunswick, electoral system
  about, 18–25
  announcements, 18–19, 183, 238

*Index*  295

candidate in more than one
  riding, 19
dual representation (provincial
  and federal legislatures), 19, 90,
  219
oaths of allegiance, 23, 89, 245n41
polling days and schedules, 18–
  19, 25, 90, 100, 166, 186, 238
secret ballots, 18, 90, 100, 243n25
voter qualifications, 21, 98
*New York Herald,* 59, 134, 217–18
Newfoundland
  Confederation vision to include,
    58, 127, 206
  lack of interest in Confederation,
    26, 50, 63, 66, 127
  liberalism, 116
  Quebec City resolution on seat
    count, 57, 127
  Quebec Conference observers, 55
newspapers
  about, xiii, 17–18, 25
  campaign communications, xiii,
    17–18, 25
  few photos, 7
  statistics, 17
  suggestions for reading, 272
  US coverage of Canada, 17–18,
    22, 59, 134, 217–18
  world affairs, 271n59
  *See also* Toronto (ON), *Globe*
    (newspaper)
newspapers, Quebec. *See* Montreal
  (QC), newspapers; Montreal
  (QC), newspapers, *Le Pays*;
  Montreal (QC), newspapers,
  *L'Union Nationale*; Quebec,
  newspapers

Norris, William, 218–19
*North American* (newspaper), 116
North-West Territories, 58, 239
Nova Scotia
  British ties, 53
  demographics, 175
  Dominion Day celebrations, 77,
    165–66
  economy, 29–31, 60, 167–68, 178,
    199
  election (1863), 167
  election (1872), 212, 217
  Fenianism, 7, 86–90
  history of coalition governments,
    173, 177
  Lieutenant-Governors, 49, 71, 84,
    170, 211, 228
  local vs national issues, 15
  Loyalist ideology, 61, 169, 246n15
  Maritime Rights movement, 218
  Maritime union idea, 37
  nationalists vs provincialists,
    9–11
  newspapers overview, 17–18
  railways, 167, 173, 178
  secessionism, 208–12
  taxation, 178–79
  timeline of events, 235–39
  *See also* Fenianism; Halifax (NS)
Nova Scotia, about key players
  overview, xiv–xv, 15, 224–34
  William Annand, 224–25
  Joseph Howe, xiv–xv, 172(f),
    209–12
  Charles Tupper, xiv–xv, 47(f),
    233–34
  *See also* Annand, William; Howe,
    Joseph; Tupper, Charles

## 296 Index

Nova Scotia, Confederation
(1864–67)
about, 46–49, 63–64, 166–67
Charlottetown meeting (1864),
49–52, 235
historical context (1864), 27–31
legislative approval (1866), 236
Maritime Union idea, 83–84, 235
as a new "nationality," 166–67
pre-Confederation proposal for
federalism (1854), 32
Quebec Conference (1864), 57,
63–64, 235, 236
secessionism delegation to United
Kingdom (1868), 208–10
senate representation, 51, 176
Tupper's role, 46–49, 47(f), 63–64,
236
Nova Scotia, election (1867)
about, xiv–v, 5–7, 15, 166–67,
175–82, 197–200
aftermath, 217–23
annexationists, 131, 176, 179
anti-coalition arguments, 176–78,
180–81
anti-Confederationists, 166–69,
175–82, 220
bitter contest, 166, 179–82
bribery and intimidation, 19–25,
181
Brown's coalition (Liberals/
Rouges/anti-Confederationists),
5–7, 183
campaign, 179–82
Catholics, 110–11, 165, 175, 200
Confederationists, 166–67,
179–82
Liberals, as label, 13–14

Macdonald's coalition (Liberal-
Conservative/Conservative/
Bleus), 5–7
party labels, 168–69
predictions, 75, 181–82, 197
press coverage, 175–77, 179–81,
198
as referendum on Confederation,
202–4
Reformers, as label, 13–14
suggestions for reading, 272
Nova Scotia, election (1867), results
about, 5–7, 184–86, 197–200,
208–12
acclamations, 184, 197
aftermath, 217–23
Anti-Confederationist Party,
197–200
Brown's coalition (Liberals/
Rouges/anti-Confederationists),
5–7, 183
historical analyses, 199–200
Howe's Liberals/Conservative/
anti-Confederationists, 5–6
independents and unknowns, 5,
198
Macdonald government, 211–12
Macdonald's coalition (Liberal-
Conservative/Conservative/
Bleus), 5–7, 185, 203, 206, 208,
220–21
MP professions, 199–200
overview, 2(f), 240(t), 241(t)
by party, 2(f), 181, 184, 198–200,
240(t), 241(t)
party labels as confusing, 185–86,
203–4
popular vote, 200, 241(t)

by province, 2(f), 200, 240(t)
as referendum on Confederation, 202–4, 220–21
seats, 2(f), 240(t)
secessionism, 208–12
tight races, 199
Tupper's win, 197, 198–99, 220–21, 240(t), 241(t)
turnout, 197, 198–99, 241(t)
Nova Scotia, electoral system
about, 18–25
announcements, 18–19, 183, 238
candidate in more than one riding, 19
dual representation (provincial and federal legislatures), 19, 166, 219
polling days and schedules, 18–19, 25, 166, 238
secret ballot, 18, 243n25
voter qualifications, 21, 171
Nova Scotia political parties, Anti-Confederation Party
about, 15, 208–12, 216
Brown's coalition (Liberals/Rouges/anti-Confederationists), 5–7, 183
decline in Liberal reformism, 216
Eastern Chronicle (newspaper), 168–70, 177, 181
election results, 2(f), 5–6, 183, 240(t), 241(t)
Howe's Liberals/Conservative/anti-Confederationists, xiv–xv, 5–6, 167–68, 174, 209–12, 216, 236, 238
identity issues, 168
newspapers, xv, 181

Nova Scotia Party label, 15, 181, 198
post-election decline, 216
secessionism, 208–12
Nova Scotia political parties, Canada Party/Unionists
Canada Party and Unionists, 174, 180–82, 238
Confederationists, 15, 174
identity issues, 168
results, 197–98
Tupper as key player, 15, 167–69, 174, 198–99, 209–10

O'Donoghue, Daniel, 125, 257n71
O'Hanley, J.L., 194
Ontario
Dominion Day celebrations, 102
economy, 29–31
election (1872), 212, 216
harsh political culture, 16–18
Lieutenant-Governors, 71, 84
newspapers overview, 17–18
provincial election (1867), 166, 197
provincial government after Confederation, 106–7
timeline of events, 235–39
See also Ottawa (ON); Toronto (ON); Toronto (ON), Globe (newspaper); United Province (1841–67)
Ontario, about key players
overview, xiv, 15–16, 224–34
Edward Blake, 225
George Brown, xiv, 41(f), 225
Agnes Macdonald, 230

John A. Macdonald, xiv, 40(f), 230
Sandfield Macdonald, 230–31
Alexander Mackenzie, 231
William McDougall, 125(f), 231–32
*See also individual main entries*
Ontario, Confederation (1864–67)
about, 39–42, 61–64
Brown's role, 41–42, 41(f)
historical context (1864), 27–31
Macdonald's role, 39–40, 40(f)
Quebec City accord, 57, 61–64
Ontario, election (1867)
about, xiv, 5–7, 15–16, 102–3
aftermath, 217–23
anti-coalition arguments, 121–22
anti-Confederation arguments, 122
Brown's coalition (Liberals/ *Rouges*/anti-Confederationists), 5–7, 102, 183
Catholics, 109–11, 200
intimidation and bribery, 16–17, 19–25, 126, 129, 243n19
Liberals, as label, 13–14
Macdonald's coalition (Liberal-Conservative/Conservative/ *Bleus*), 5–7, 102, 183
nationalists vs provincialists, 9–10
predictions, 75
press coverage, 121–22, 130–31
as referendum on Confederation, 202–4
Ontario, election (1867), results
about, 5–7, 184–86, 193–97
acclamations, 184, 194

aftermath, 217–23
Brown's coalition (Liberals/ *Rouges*/anti-Confederationists), 5–7, 102, 183
Catholics, 200
close races, 194–96
Conservatives, 193–95
historical analyses, 194
independents and unknowns, 109, 194
Liberals, 193–95, 212–17
Macdonald's coalition (Liberal-Conservative/Conservative/ *Bleus*), 5–7, 102, 185, 193–95, 206
MP professions, 196
overview, 2(f), 240(t), 241(t)
by party, 2(f), 240(t), 241(t)
party labels as confusing, 185–86, 194, 203–4
by province, 2(f), 240(t), 241(t)
regional results, 193–94
seats, 2(f), 193, 240(t)
three-way races, 195
turnout, 195–96, 241(t)
Ontario, electoral system
about, 18–25
announcements, 18–19, 183, 238
candidate in more than one riding, 19
dual representation (provincial and federal legislatures), 19, 121, 219
polling days and schedules, 18–19, 25, 102, 166, 238
secret ballots, 18
voter qualifications, 21, 196

*Index* 299

Ontario political parties, Grits and
 Clear Grits movement
 Brown followers, 42
 label for rebels, 14, 42
 Macdonald's appeal to, 205
 McDougall's leadership, 123–24,
  231
 newspapers, 116, 145
 policies, 42, 73, 116, 123–24, 213
Ontario political parties, Liberal/
 Reform Party
 about, 13–14, 113–17, 212–17
 anti-Confederation arguments,
  122, 212
 attack on coalitions, 121–22
 attacks on opponents, 124–25
 Brown's coalition (Liberals/
  *Rouges*/anti-Confederationists),
  5–7, 183
 Brown's defeat, 184, 194, 212, 215
 convention in Toronto (June
  1867), 116–18, 124–25, 238,
  256n41
 election (1872), 216, 217
 election results, 185, 193–95
 founding (April 1867), 115–16,
  146, 225, 238
 Liberals, as label, 13–14
 local culture, 116–17
 platform (1867), 119–22
 post-election decline, 212–17
 post-election "provincial rights"
  rhetoric, 217
 press coverage, 121–22
 railways, 119–20, 122
 Reformers, as label, 13–14
 Toronto branch, 115, 117

 *See also* Ontario political parties,
  Grits and Clear Grits movement
Ontario political parties,
 Macdonald's coalition (Liberal-
 Conservative/Conservative/
 *Bleus*). *See* Macdonald, John
 A.; Macdonald, John A.,
 election (1867); Macdonald,
 John A., government coalition
 (Liberal-Conservative/
 Conservative/*Bleus*)
Orangemen, 79, 80, 94, 103
Ottawa (ON)
 bribery and intimidation, 19–20
 Dominion Day celebrations, 70–
  75, 101
 historical locations, xiii(f), 8,
  9–10
 newspapers, 20, 135
 Parliament Hill, xiii(f), 8, 56, 70
 turnout, 196
*Ottawa Times,* 10, 21, 112, 131, 194,
 214
Owram, Douglas, 274

papers. *See* newspapers
Papineau, Denis-Émery, 34
Papineau, Louis-Joseph, 32, 43, 137,
 142, 143, 260n31
Parliament, first (1867), House of
 Commons
 about, 5–7, 184–86, 204–5, 220–
  23, 222(f)
 acclamations, 184
 aftermath, 217–23
 Liberals, as label, 13–14
 Liberals, as opposition, 6, 185–86

300 *Index*

Macdonald's government, 185–86, 204–5

MP professions, 184, 188, 193, 196, 199–200

official report, 185–86

overview of results, 2(f), 5–6, 183, 240(t), 241(t)

Parliament Hill, xiii(f), 8, 56, 222(f)

by party, 2(f), 240(t), 241(t)

party labels as confusing, 185–86, 203–4

as referendum on Confederation, 202–4

seats (181), 6

*See also* Macdonald, John A., government coalition (Liberal-Conservative/Conservative/*Bleus*)

Parliament, first (1867), Senate

Catholic representation, 97, 110, 136–37

Cauchon as first speaker, 137

Macdonald's cabinet, 72–73, 74

seat count by province, 57

*Patriote* movement (1830s), 14, 32, 43, 137, 142, 226, 229, 260n31

Pelletier, Pantaléon, 163–64

Pilon, Dennis, 245n41

Plinguet, J.A., 146

political parties

about, 13–16

candidates without party labels, 6

civic education needed, 13

diverging opinions, 14

election as referendum on Confederation, 202–4

election results overview, 2(f), 5–6, 183, 240(t), 241(t)

local vs national issues, 15

loose discipline, 186

newspapers for communications, xiii, 17–18, 25

origins, 243n17

party labels, 13–16, 185–86, 203

party labels as confusing, 185–86, 203–4

reformist roots in local cultures, 116

*See also specific provinces*

*The Polling* (painting, Hogarth), 22, 23(f)

Pope, William Henry, 49–50

Prescott (ON), 16–17, 243n19

press. *See* newspapers

Prince Edward Island

Confederation vision to include, 127, 206

demographics, 28–29

joins Confederation (1873), 8, 239

lack of interest in Confederation (1864–67), 26, 63, 66, 127

location of Charlottetown meeting (1864), 8, 49–51, 235

Maritime Union idea, 37

Quebec City resolution on seat count, 57

shipbuilding, 30

*See also* Charlottetown Conference (1864)

Protestants

*Christian Guardian,* 19

Clergy Reserves for Anglicans, 109, 123

Index 301

demographics (1860s), 29
identity and belonging, 11–12
Province of Canada. *See* United
Province (1841–67)
Pryke, Kenneth, 269n24

Quebec
about, xiv
assimilationists, 153
Cauchon as premier, 135–37
Confederation acceptance, 214–
15, 216
Dominion Day celebrations,
132–33
economy, 29–31
elections (1863, 1872), 191, 212
lacrosse, 132–33, 258n2
Lieutenant-Governors, 71, 84,
135, 220
nationalists, 10, 150–52, 157,
223
newspapers overview, 17–18
Parliament building (1880), 9(f)
*Patriote* movement (1830s), 14,
32, 43, 137, 142, 226, 229,
260n31
post-election "provincial rights"
rhetoric, 217
Protestant education issue, 136
provincial election (1867), 166
rebellions (1837–38), 14, 41, 43,
123, 145, 229
timeline of events, 235–39
Union Nationale party, 218
*See also* Montreal (QC); Montreal
(QC), newspapers; United
Province (1841–67)

Quebec, about key players
overview, xiv, 15, 224–34
George-Étienne Cartier, xiv,
225–26
Pierre Chauveau, 226
Antoine-Aimé Dorion, xiv, 48(f),
226–27
Alexander Galt, 227
Luther Holton, 228
Henry Lacroix, 228
Médéric Lanctôt, xiv, 155(f), 229
Thomas McGee, 232
*See also individual main entries*
Quebec, Confederation (1864–67)
about, 42–46, 61–64
anglophone apathy, 133–34
anti-Confederation sentiment, 61
assimilation fears, 63
Cartier's role, 42–44, 43(f)
Catholic views, 61, 65, 110–11,
134, 137–41
Charlottetown meeting (1864), 51
Dorion's role, 42–46, 45(f)
francophones, 11–12, 65
historical context (1864), 27–31
Quebec Conference (1864), 57,
61–64
report on federalism (1859), 33
Quebec, election (1867)
about, xiv, 5–7, 15, 145–49, 164
aftermath, 217–23
annexation fears, 134
Brown's coalition (Liberals/
*Rouges*/anti-Confederationists),
xiv, 5–7, 183
Cartier as key player, 134–37,
225–26

302  *Index*

Catholics, 22, 110–11, 134, 137–41, 145, 146, 159–62, 191, 200
Church as pro-Confederation, 137–41, 145–46
critique of Confederation, 148–49
Dorion as key player, 141–49
intimidation and bribery, 19–25, 138–41, 158, 161–64
Irish Catholics, 159–62, 191
Kamouraska fiasco, 162–64, 185
Liberals, as label, 13–14
Macdonald's coalition (Liberal-Conservative/Conservative/*Bleus*), 5–7, 185
McGee-Devlin contest, 159–62
"peaceful revolution," 134
predictions, 75
press coverage, 135, 140–41, 145
Protestants, 191
railways, 135
as referendum on Confederation, 145, 202–4
Reformers, as label, 13–14
Quebec, election (1867), results
about, 5–7, 164, 184–86, 189–93
acclamations, 141, 164, 183–84, 190, 193, 244*n*37
aftermath, 217–23
Brown's coalition (Liberals/*Rouges*/anti-Confederationists), 5–7, 183
Catholics, 23–24, 191–92, 200
historical analyses, 190–91
independents, 192
Liberals, as label, 13–14
Macdonald's coalition (Liberal-Conservative/Conservative/

*Bleus*), 5–7, 185, 189, 190, 203, 206
MP professions, 193
overview, 2(f), 240(t), 241(t)
by party, 2(f), 240(t), 241(t)
party labels as confusing, 185–86, 190–91, 203–4
popular vote, 190, 241(t)
Protestants, 191–92
by province, 2(f), 240(t), 241(t)
as referendum on Confederation, 202–4
regional results, 193
*Rouges*/Liberals, 185–86, 189, 190, 203–4, 212–13
seats, 2(f), 189, 240(t)
three-way races, 192–93
tight races, 192–93
turnout, 189–90, 241(t)
Quebec, electoral system
about, 18–25
announcements, 18–19, 183, 238
candidate in more than one riding, 19
dual representation (provincial and federal legislatures), 19, 193, 219
polling days and schedules, 18–19, 25, 161–62, 166, 238
secret ballot, 18, 243*n*25
voter qualifications, 21
Quebec, newspapers
about, 17–18, 147
*La Minerve (Bleus)*, 61, 75, 135, 150, 153, 157
*La Vérité (Bleus)*, 157
*L'Ordre (Rouge)*, 146, 147, 157

*Quebec Gazette* (English), 20, 123, 130, 135, 191, 214
*True Witness* (English Catholic), 145, 147, 157
*Witness* (Protestant), 147
*See also* Montreal (QC), newspapers; Montreal (QC), newspapers, *Le Pays;* Montreal (QC), newspapers, *L'Union Nationale*
Quebec City
election results, 193
historical locations, 8–9, 9(f)
*Quebec Chronicle,* 135
Quebec Conference (1864)
about, 55–66
*Botheration Letters,* 59, 174, 236
delegations, 55–56, 235
Lanctôt's criticisms, 152
legislative votes on Resolutions, 80
Macdonald's central role, 57
"new nationality" vision, 62–63, 166
Nova Scotia's anti-Confederation stance, 59, 78–79, 236
provincial responses, 58–66, 80
Resolutions, 57, 66, 70, 80, 236
suggestions for reading, 272–73
UK government support, 60–61
wheels, flies, and flywheels, 53, 58, 74–75
Quebec Conference (1864), issues
about, 56–66
basis for BNA Act, 237
British ties, 56–57, 79
federal government, 55–58
foreign affairs, 56–57
joining of other colonies, 58

official languages, 55–56
Ottawa as capital, 56–57
Parliament, 55–57
provincial government, 55–58, 79
railways, 79, 81
religious rights, 57
taxation and tariffs, 55, 60, 81
transportation, 56
US annexation fears, 61–63
Quebec political parties, *Bleus/* Conservative coalition
about, 5–7, 14, 134–37, 203
*Bleus,* as label, 14
Cartier as key player, 134–37
Catholics, 137–41, 191
Cauchon's publications, 135–36
Chauveau as key player, 136–37
Confederationists, 135–37
Conservative, as label, 14
election results, 2(f), 190, 240(t), 241(t)
historical roots, 14, 145
Macdonald as key player, 134, 135–36
Macdonald's coalition (Liberal-Conservative/Conservative/ *Bleus*), 5–7, 185, 189, 190, 203, 205–6
newspapers, 135, 157
party labels as confusing, 185–86, 203–4
"peaceful revolution," 134
political views, 14, 135–37
Quebec City resolutions, 63
Quebec political parties, *Rouges/* Liberals/Reformers
about, 5–7, 14–15, 141–42, 191, 212–17

304  *Index*

annexationists, 142, 147
anti-Confederationists, 5, 128, 141–42, 148, 203, 261n40
Brown's coalition (Liberals/ *Rouges*/anti-Confederationists), 5–7, 183
Buies's critique of Confederation, 148–49
Cartier as key player, 15, 141–42
Catholics, 159–62, 191
Confederation acceptance, 5, 14, 15, 145–48, 214–15, 216
divisions within, 14, 141–42, 146–47
Dorion as key player, 141–49, 214
Holton as anglophone leader, 143, 147
Lanctôt as key player, 15–16, 149–58, 155(f), 229
Liberals, as label, 13–14
newspapers, 145, 260n29
party labels, 13–14, 142
*Patriote* roots, 5, 14, 32
policies, 14, 128, 142
post-election decline, 212–17
"provincial rights" rhetoric, 217
Quebec City resolutions, 63
Reformers, as label, 13–14
*Rouges*, as term, 14
suggestions for reading, 275–76
*See also* Montreal (QC), newspapers, *Le Pays*

railways
British support, 85
Confederation issue, 35, 37, 49–52, 54, 58, 79, 178
defence benefits, 54
economic benefits, 30, 35, 49–50, 54
election issue (1867), 120, 122
incomplete and unreliable, 12, 25
national vision, 206
railways, Grand Trunk Railway
about, 30
Brown's platform, 120, 122
Cartier as lawyer, 134
Holton's construction, 228
joining with Intercolonial, 143, 178
Liberal decline, 217
*Rouge* forces against, 150
scandal (Macdonald-Cartier), 34–35, 122, 216
railways, Intercolonial Railway
about, 37
British North America Act (s. 145), 66, 81–82, 91, 210
Brown's platform, 119–20, 122
construction and costs, 85, 122
Fleming's career, 165–66
joining with Grand Trunk, 143, 178
Maritime support, 37, 48, 49–50, 52, 58, 81–82, 85, 95
in Quebec, 135
reading suggestions, 272–76
Rebellions of 1837–38, 14, 41, 43, 123, 145, 229
Reform Association of Upper Canada. *See* Ontario political parties, Liberal/Reform Party
Reformers, as label, 13–14
Reynolds, Louise, 275
Ritchie, Charles, 223
Roche, E.P., 16

Rohmer, Richard, 249*n*51
Roman Catholics. *See* Catholics
Rose, John, 204–5
*Rouges. See* Quebec political parties, *Rouges*/Liberals/Reformers
Rumilly, Robert, 145–46, 156, 246*n*7, 276
Rupert's Land
  Confederation vision to include, 48, 127, 206
  HBC ownership and surrender, 59, 64, 67, 222, 238–39
Ryerson, Egerton, 13, 19

Saint-Hyacinthe (QC), 139–40, 142, 144, 191, 267*n*13
*Sarnia Observer,* 20, 122, 215
Schull, Joseph, 39, 275
scorpion and tortoise fable, 207, 268*n*12
Séguin, Normand, 190–91, 259*n*21, 266*n*10, 272
Senate. *See* Parliament, first (1867), Senate
Seward, William, 27, 69
Sewell, Jonathan, 32
Shanly, Walter, 16
Shea, Ambrose, 247*n*29
shipbuilding, 30
Sicotte, Louis-Victor, 143
Silver, A.I., 276
Simard, Georges Honoré, 192–93
Smith, Albert James
  about, 15, 232–33
  anti-Confederationist, xiv, 78–82, 88, 99, 186, 251*n*17
  election (1867), 99, 186, 188, 233

elections (1852, 1865, 1866), 78–80, 82–83, 88–90, 232–33, 237
  key player in New Brunswick, 232–33
  Liberal, 92–93, 215
  premier of New Brunswick (1865–66), 15, 84–87, 90, 95, 236
St. Albans, Vermont, Confederate raiders (1864), 56–57, 59, 160, 235
*St. Catharines Constitutional* (newspaper), 10, 213–14, 262*n*74
St. John (NB)
  demographics, 76–77, 93
  Dominion Day celebrations, 76–77
  elections (1866, 1867), 88, 186–87
  Irish Catholics, 93–94
  *Morning Freeman* (newspaper), xiv, 17–18, 75, 77–80, 92–97, 99–100, 224
  newspapers, 50, 93
  riots, 88, 94
Stacey, C.P., 58
Stanley, Lord, 186
Starnes, Henry, 132
Stewart, W.J., 109
Street, Thomas, 111
suggestions for further reading, 272–76
Sulte, Benjamin, 141
*Sun and Advertiser* (newspaper), xv, 181
Sweeny, Alastair, 274
Sweeny, John, 89

## 306 Index

Taché, Étienne-Paschal, 10, 34, 51, 55, 112, 151, 152
Taché, Joseph-Charles, 32–33, 246n12
taxation, 4–5, 6–7, 153, 178–79
telegraphs, xiii, 30
Thomson, Dale, 275
Tilley, Leonard
  about, 37–39, 38(f), 78–100, 188–89, 233
  anti-Catholic sentiment, 80, 82–83, 89, 95, 97
  awards and honours, 71
  Confederationist, xiv, 15, 74, 78–84, 86, 88, 90–92, 95–96, 114, 203–4
  election (1867), 15, 90–92, 186, 188–89
  elections (1854, 1861, 1865, 1866), 38, 63, 78–90, 91, 236
  Intercolonial Railway, 58, 66, 74, 79, 81–82, 85, 91
  key player in New Brunswick, 233
  Liberal party label, 13, 79, 203–4
  Liberal-Conservative, 99, 186
  Macdonald's cabinet, 72, 74, 91, 99, 203–4, 214
  newspaper, 17–18
  party labels, 13
  personal qualities, 38–39, 79, 86, 90, 94, 188
  political career in New Brunswick, 37–39, 38(f), 82
  press coverage, 90–91, 93, 95, 99
  prime minister of New Brunswick, 37, 78–79, 236
  temperance movement, 38, 82–83, 95

Tilley, Leonard, Confederation (1864–67)
  Charlottetown meeting (1864), 50
  Confederationist, 78–79, 236
  London Conference (1866–67), 66, 90, 91
  Maritime Union idea, 38, 79, 83–84
  Quebec Conference (1864), 55–56, 63, 78–79
Toronto (ON)
  Catholics, 109–11, 119
  Dominion Day celebrations, 101–2
  election (1867), 109–11, 115, 117–18, 119
  Guy Fawkes Day (Nov 5), 58–59
  historical locations, 9
  industrial associations, 60
  Lynch as archbishop, 109–11, 229–30
  population, 76
  Reform Association branch, 115, 117–18
  *Toronto Leader* (newspaper), 29, 108, 121, 130
Toronto (ON), *Globe* (newspaper)
  about, 17–18, 42
  on Anglin, 93, 95
  Brown as key player in Ontario, 225
  Brown's election loss, 131, 216
  Brown's paper, 42, 60, 97–98, 101, 113, 117, 124, 131, 147, 157, 209–10, 215
  cultural context, 17–18
  on Dominion Day, 101
  reformist ideals, 42

on secessionism in Nova Scotia,
209–10
on Tilley, 90–91
tortoise and scorpion fable, 207,
268n12
Tory, as label, 14
*See also* Conservatives
trade
about, 29–30
Brown's views, 119
railroads as foundation, 35
US-UK reciprocity treaty cancel-
lation, 59–60, 65, 207
*True Witness* (newspaper), 145–46,
147, 157
Tupper, Charles
about, 46–49, 47(f), 169–71,
233–34
British ties, 169–70, 233–34
Canada Party founding (April
1867), 165, 174, 238
candidate for Liberal-
Conservative coalition, 6,
74, 180–82
*Colonist* (newspaper), 66
Companion of the Order of the
Bath, 70–71
Confederationist, 15, 130, 165–
66, 169–71, 220–21
election (1867), xv, 6, 15, 179–82,
198–99, 233–34
election results, 6, 198–99, 209,
220–21
elections (1855, 1863, 1887, 1900),
167, 233–34
key player in Nova Scotia, 233–34
lobbying of secessionists, 209
Macdonald's cabinet, 74, 160, 211

medical career, 46–49, 233
personal qualities, 46–47
premier of Nova Scotia (1864),
49, 167, 169–70, 233
press coverage, 170, 198
*Recollections,* 171
suggestions for reading, 274
Tupper, Charles, Confederation
(1864–67)
Charlottetown meeting (1864),
48–50, 52, 170
London Conference (1866–67),
66, 169–70
Quebec Conference (1864), 52,
55–56, 170, 236
Turgeon, Pierre-Flavien, 138
turning point elections, xv, 219

Uniacke, James Boyle, 173
United Kingdom
Fenianism, 7, 86–90, 160–61
Gladstone government, 54, 66,
70, 209
Liberals, as label, 13
middle class voting rights, 14
Nova Scotia delegation on seces-
sionism (1868), 208–10
secret ballot, 18, 243n25
suggestions for reading, 272–73
Tory, as label, 14
transnational belonging, 7
UK-US reciprocity treaty, 59–60,
65, 207
*See also* British North America
Act (1867); London Conference
(1866–67)
United Province (1841–67)
about, 31–35

Canada East vs West rivalries,
31–35

Catholic views on Confederation,
65

Charlottetown meeting (1864)
and aftermath, 51–52

coalition governments, 14, 34, 44

Confederation as fix for democratic flaws, 31–32, 205–6

demographics (1860s), 28–29

economy, 29–31

elections (1861, 1863), 31,
244n26

Great Coalition formed (June
1864), 235

Liberal-Conservative, as label, 14

Macdonald's coalition, 14, 112

Quebec Conference (1864) and
aftermath, 61–64

Reform Party, 16

votes for Confederation, 63, 236

United States

aftermath of election (1867),
217–18

Alaska purchase, 69–70

cabinet size, 99

demographics (1860s), 28

electorate, 22

expansionism, 27

fears of Canada's strength, 217–18

Fenianism, 7, 86–90, 236

secret ballot, 18, 243n25

See also Fenianism

United States, influences on election
(1867). See election (1867),

United States and global
influences

Upton, L.F.S., 246n15

Victoria, Queen
announcement of Dominion
Day, 70

royal assent to BNA Act (1867),
237

Vidal, Alexander, 103

violence and intimidation, 19–25,
129, 140–41, 158, 161–64, 181

Vipond, Robert C., 273

voters
about, 19–21, 183–84

Indigenous peoples, 21, 244n35

intimidation and bribery, 19–25,
129, 140–41, 158, 161–64, 181

Macdonald's promise on right to
vote, 220

qualifications, 21

statistics, 183–84

See also election (1867), electoral
system

Waite, P.B., 46–47, 79, 248n45, 273

Wallace, Carl, 251n17, 252n23

Wetmore, Andrew, 91

Whelan, Patrick James, 161

Wilkins, Martin, 208–9

Williams, William Fenwick, 170, 185

Wilson, David A., 275

Young, Brian, 21, 274–75

Young, William, 173

Printed and bound in Canada
Set in Zurich Condensed and Minion by Artegraphica Design Co.
Copyeditor: Francis Chow
Proofreader: Kristy Lynn Hankewitz
Indexer: Judy Dunlop
Cartographer: Eric Leinberger
Cover designer: Will Brown